Reframing
Human Resource
Management

Reframing Human Resource Management

Power, Ethics and the Subject at Work

BARBARA TOWNLEY

SAGE Publications
London • Thousand Oaks • New Delhi

SAGE Publications Ltd
6 Bonhill Street
London EC2A 4PU

SAGE Publications Inc
2455 Teller Road
Thousand Oaks, California 91320

SAGE Publications India Pvt Ltd
32, M–Block Market
Greater Kailash – I
New Delhi 110 048

British Library Cataloguing in Publication data

Townley, Barbara
  Reframing Human Resource Management:
  Power, Ethics and the Subject at Work
  I. Title
  658.3

  ISBN 0-8039-8493-6
  ISBN 0-8039-8496-0 pbk

Library of Congress catalog card number 94-66361

Typeset by M Rules
Printed in Great Britain by Biddles Ltd, Guildford

To Richard

Contents

Acknowledgements

The ideas formulated in this book have a long genesis and have been shaped by my experience of teaching personnel management and industrial relations over several years at the Universities of Lancaster, Warwick and Alberta. Three aspects of this experience have guided my approach in this book. The first has been students' reception of the way personnel management is traditionally presented. Often they are sceptical of the ability of textbooks and journals to illuminate their day-to-day experiences of work. The second has been my own experience of being a female academic in this area. When I first started teaching there was an implicit belief that personnel management was not quite a respectable or serious academic subject. It was disparaged within both management and academic circles as being the 'soft' end of management, in contrast to the 'hard' business of industrial relations. The third aspect has been the transmogrification of personnel into 'human resource management', reflected in changed textbook and journal titles, and departmental names. But the reluctant acceptance of the newly labelled human resource management has a cost. It has gained credibility through its association with strategic management and business policy. The administrative details of earlier personnel management courses, the 'how to' of personnel, has been relegated to the sidelines, stirring debate as to whether universities should be involved in skills training. This book, its focus and perspective, are in response to these experiences.

Since academic work is a social not an individual endeavour, any author has many debts. I first began teaching personnel management in the Department of Behaviour in Organizations at Lancaster University. I was fortunate in having a female head of department, Sylvia Shimmin, whom I thank for her help during that time. Her successor at Lancaster is Karen Legge. Karen's book, *Power, Innovation and Problem-solving in Personnel Management* (1978), had a powerful impact and convinced me that personnel could be an important and academically credible subject. Karen was kind enough to take time out of a very busy schedule to read an earlier draft of this book and offer very helpful suggestions. I would also like to thank other friends and colleagues at Lancaster, where I first encountered Foucault's work, in particular Steve Ackroyd, a non-Foucauldian, who insisted that I read Baldamus.

I also thank Gibson Burrell, formerly of Lancaster, now at Warwick

University, who encouraged my initial interest in the relationship between Foucault and personnel, and who read and commented on an earlier draft of this book. Also at Warwick, Richard Hyman's sceptical, but supportive, comments on my earlier work helped a lot. I thank also my students on the MA in Industrial Relations at Warwick who took a module in which I developed my initial thoughts on Foucault's relevance for HRM. I know they were confused at the time, but their responses were helpful in formulating the ideas expressed in this book. I am also very grateful to James Barrett, whose knowledge and skill introduced me to a different way of seeing. His stress on the importance of a theoretically informed analysis of practices has influenced my approach in this book.

At the University of Alberta, I should like to thank David Cooper, who in addition to being a friend and a stimulating colleague, introduced me to the critical accounting literature, which has been important in developing my Foucauldian analysis of HRM. My friends and colleagues, Leslie Oakes and Dallas Cullen, have increased my awareness of the feminist literature which has also been important to the development of my thoughts on HRM. I should like to thank them for providing helpful suggestions and references, particularly for Chapter 6, and for tolerating cancelled appointments. My thanks also to Deborah Neale, who undertook the laborious task of retrieving references and handling the bibliographic software package, with her usual diligence and thoroughness. The Pearson Fellowship, awarded by the Faculty of Business, released me from a full teaching load and gave me the time to write this book. I should also like to thank Sue Jones of Sage for encouraging me to develop some implicit themes of earlier drafts.

Finally, I should like to thank my partner, Richard Marsden, who teaches industrial relations at Athabasca University. In many ways my sternest critic, he provided detailed comments on earlier drafts, and gave support and encouragement when enthusiasm gave way to despondency. Most of all, I thank him for the love and the laughter.

1

A Foucauldian Analysis of
Human Resource Management

Any study of human resource management (HRM), or personnel management, faces two problems.[1] First, what subjects should be covered? Normally this issue is settled, by tradition and precedent, in favour of human resource planning, recruitment and selection, performance appraisal, compensation and 'reward' systems, training and development, collective employee relations, 'exiting', and so on. But, in deciding to consider these topics, the question remains: what gives the body of practices commonly understood as HRM their coherence? The second issue is how can the academic study of HRM help people at work? To do so, it must articulate their practical experience. Whether explicitly acknowledged, or not, the experience of work is located in, and constituted by, power relations. To be relevant, therefore, HRM must provide people with a framework for understanding power.

The thesis of this book is that the work of Michel Foucault can help us address these two issues. Foucault was Professor in the history of systems of thought at the Collège de France, until his death in 1984. His work covers a wide range of seemingly unrelated subjects – psychiatry (Foucault, 1973b), medicine (Foucault, 1973a), the human sciences (Foucault, 1970), the penal system (Foucault, 1977), and sexuality (Foucault, 1981a, 1988a, 1990). Three themes run throughout this work. The first is how we understand the unity of a discipline. What constitutes a body of knowledge and demarcates one subject from another? This issue is addressed primarily in his earlier work (Foucault, 1970, 1973a, 1973b). The second theme is the relationship between power and knowledge. This is the focus of the middle body of his work (Foucault, 1975, 1977, 1980a, 1980b). The third theme is the nature of the individual subject: how do we come to have knowledge of ourselves and how do we conduct our relationships with others? This was the concern of his final work, completed shortly before his death (Foucault, 1984a, 1984b, 1988a, 1988b, 1990, 1991c).

What can all this possibly have to do with HRM? I shall argue that it allows us to better understand seemingly disparate personnel techniques; the operation of power and the day-to-day practices which constitute people's experiences of work. I begin with a brief introduction to Foucault's work on the unity of discourse; the interrelationship between power and knowledge; and the individual subject. I then demonstrate its relevance for HRM.

An Introduction to Foucault

The Order of Things

Foucault's work deconstructs what we take for granted and regard as self-evident. It shows how objects of knowledge are not natural, but are ordered or constructed by 'discourse'[2] which determines what is the 'see-able and the sayable'. Foucault's early works, for example, illuminate the transformations which affect the 'seeable and the sayable' within psychiatry and medicine. *Madness and Civilization* (1973a) examines the conditions within which psychiatry and psychology developed as sciences. *The Birth of the Clinic* (1973b) is an account of the emergence of the medical conception of pathology. Both books re-examine how knowledge of these things is constructed. In *The Order of Things* (1970) Foucault traces how general grammar, analysis of wealth and natural history became, by the nineteenth century, the subjects of philology, political economy, and biology. In these analyses, Foucault indicates the importance of challenging 'knowledge' and its assumptions. He rejects a view of knowledge as a smooth, continuous development, reflecting the progression of reason and the findings of positivist science. For Foucault, science and the institutions which produce it need to be questioned. Indeed, the questioning of science and scientific concepts is a theme which 'haunts all of Foucault's books from the very beginning' (Eribon, 1991: 273).

His next work, *The Archaeology of Knowledge* (Foucault, 1972) is a more explicit outline of his method in these early histories. In this, Foucault examines the 'conditions of possibility' which come to sustain a certain way of thinking, and allow it to prevail throughout a certain period – how particular practices and concepts become accepted at certain historical periods as being natural, self-evident and indispensable. Discourse is a central concept of this text. It refers to the underlying rules, the *a priori*, assumed parts of knowledge which limit the forms of the 'sayable'. Discourse or discursive practices determine what is taken as known and how this is established. More colloquially, it refers to how objects become spoken of in a certain manner. The analysis of discourse involves tracing its conditions of existence and the factors which affect both what is known and what is done. Discursive analysis informs all Foucault's work. As Rajchman (1985: 52) notes: 'Foucault does not write a history of madness, sickness, crime or sex, but a history of how it ever came to be taken for granted.'

The first lesson to be drawn from Foucault's work is that areas of knowledge, the boundaries of a discipline, are not given: they are constructed. This raises several questions for the study of HRM. How is HRM constructed? What is the theoretical coherence which has defined or circumscribed the boundaries of HRM? What is the effect of constructing the subject in a particular way? To what has our attention been directed and from what has it been averted? What are the limits of the seeable and the sayable within the discourse of HRM?

One means of identifying these limits is to consult textbooks in the area, not necessarily for a cogent theoretical defence of a body of knowledge, but at least for a review of the subjects or topics which should be covered. A glimpse at personnel textbooks illustrates an evolution in the topics considered to be important to this area of study. An early text (Moxon, 1943), identifies six principal areas: employment; wages; negotiation and joint consultation; health and safety, welfare (employee services); and education and training.[3] By 1960 (Northcott, 1960), this had expanded to include: employment, supply and placement; employment, records, labour turnover and absenteeism; selection and training; wage administration; education; health, safety and working conditions; employee services and industrial relations.[4] More recent personnel textbooks now group topics under more generic headings. For example, Thomason (1981) considers personnel under the headings of: the employment function; contribution to the production function; and the organization's function.[5] In the US, Beer et al. (1984) identify four components of personnel practice: employee influence, human resource flow, reward systems and work systems.[6] In the UK, Sisson (1989) identifies: the design of organizations; employee resourcing; employee development; the wage–work bargain; and participation and involvement, as the principal areas for personnel.[7]

The evolution of these texts confirms an observation by Beer et al. (1985) that personnel is a series of seemingly disjointed activities. This echoes an earlier view of Baldamus (1961: 347) that what is encompassed by its subject matter is 'anything from supervision, incentives and profit sharing to machine-paced production, methods of training and employee selection'. The gradual accretion of functions within personnel has led one management writer (Drucker, 1961) to refer to personnel as a 'dustbin', or, more politely, a residual role in organizations. He writes, 'personnel administration . . . is largely a collection of incidental techniques without much internal cohesion . . . They are neither one function by kinship of skills required to carry out the activities nor are they one function by being united together in the work process' (Drucker, 1961: 243). Often this heterogeneity is excused in terms of the ad hoc and reactive nature of personnel's origins, and its historical conflict with line management (Jacoby, 1985; Niven, 1967; Ozanne, 1967). This discussion highlights the importance of discovering the organizing principle, as opposed to common sense description, that gives HRM its analytical focus. It stresses the importance of an order 'that turns a set of bits, which have limited significance on their own, into an intelligible whole' (Turner, 1983: 191). Certain areas appear to be of central concern – 'manpower' or human resource planning, recruitment and selection, performance appraisal, compensation and 'reward' systems, training and development, collective employee relations, and 'exiting'. Whilst there may be agreement that these lie within the province of HRM, the question remains: what is it that constitutes the unity of this discipline? What organizing principle or analytical focus, gives personnel practices a theoretical coherence, and makes them recognizably 'personnel'?

As a series of categories, manpower planning, recruitment and selection, performance appraisal, compensation, training and development have become so familiar that they are seen as 'an order which is in the phenomena' rather than as a 'way of ordering' (Turner, 1983: 192). These categories, however, reflect how personnel has understood the unity of its own discourse. The ordering of material necessarily operationalizes an underlying theoretical model, as statements are made as to what subject matter is important, if not why. Although rarely directly addressed, these topics, and the order in which they are usually considered, reflect an underlying functionalist or systems maintenance model derived from classical managerial concerns of organizational efficiency. Personnel is the 'black box' of production, where employees – organizational 'inputs' – are selected, appraised, trained, developed and remunerated to deliver the required output of labour. Personnel functions appear in successive order, from employee entrance to exit. HRM is the necessary set of tasks and roles for the efficient achievement of organizational objectives. It is a systematic characteristic of organizations functioning in a model of means–end rationality, an organizational mechanism through which goal achievement and survival may be promoted. From this perspective the aim of personnel is to make the organization more orderly and integrated; connotations of goal-directed activity, inputs and 'outputs', stability, adaptability and systems maintenance predominate.

Foucault's work shows that what counts as 'truth' depends on the conceptual system in operation, and that established ways of ordering material limit our analysis. He illustrates this at the beginning of one of his early works, *The Order of Things* (1970), where he quotes a passage from a short story by the Argentinian writer Jorge Luis Borges of a Chinese encyclopedia which classifies animals into the following categories: (a) belonging to the Emperor, (b) embalmed, (c) tame, (d) sucking pigs, (e) sirens, (f) fabulous, (g) stray dogs, (h) included in the present classification, (i) innumerable, (k) drawn with a fine camel hair brush, (l) et cetera, (m) having just broken the water pitcher, (n) that from a long way off look like flies (Foucault, 1970: xv). As Philp (1985: 70) notes, 'when we classify objects we operate within a system of possibility – and this system both enables us to do certain things, and limits us to this system and these things'. Applied to HRM, Foucault's work suggests that we question our taken-for-granted assumptions. From it we learn that self-evidencies 'are not a tranquil locus on the basis of which other questions may be posed, but . . . they themselves pose a whole cluster of questions' (Foucau~ 1972: 26). Analysis is a process of demolishing and reorganizing.

Power and Knowledge

A necessary step in disrupting the self-evident assumptions of HRM is to consider Foucault's understanding of the relationship between power and knowledge. These are usually understood as independent. Foucault shows them to be different sides of the same social relations, hence 'power/knowledge': 'the successful control of an object . . . requires a degree of understanding of its forces, its reactions, its strengths and weaknesses' (Garland, 1987: 853). Mechanisms of power are simultaneously instruments for the formation and accumulation of knowledge. 'The more it is known the more controllable it becomes' (Garland, 1987: 853).

The interrelationship between power and knowledge is illustrated in *I, Pierre Rivière* (Foucault, 1975), which documents the confession of a man who murdered his mother, sister and brother. Foucault contrasts this confession with other documents of local authorities, who include the doctor, police, and presiding judge, and their reports on whether Rivière is a criminal or insane. These later commentaries illustrate how the individual Rivière becomes constituted through the documentation which surrounds him, so that he becomes known in a particular way and, as a result, subject to actions by the authorities. A similar work of this period, *Herculine Barbin* (Foucault, 1980b), reports the case of an hermaphrodite, and how it was important for the governing authorities that the individual be designated as either a man or a woman.

Power/knowledge is examined in more depth in *Discipline and Punish* (1977), perhaps Foucault's most well known work. Subtitled *The Birth of the Prison*, it is concerned with the changes which took place in methods of punishment in Europe between the late eighteenth and early nineteenth century, from the end of public torture to the development of the prison system. This change of emphasis, from the crime to the the the criminal, has several effects. The first is that it requires knowledge of the criminal. Knowledge of the individual is necessary in order to have a degree of control over him or her in order to transform them. In contrast to conventional interpretations of the role of civilizing or humanitarian influences, Foucault develops an analysis in terms of 'disciplines', practices which operate to create both knowledge and power. Disciplines are techniques designed to observe, monitor, shape and control behaviour. Through constituting the individual – 'the criminal' – in a particular way, disciplines come to know individuals more precisely, and also act on them 'so that they operate as one wishes' (Foucault, 1977: 138). Knowing the individual in a particular way situates them in a possible range of practices and defines the type of intervention which results. Disciplines are not, however, identified with a particular institution (the prison), but are a type of power which may be identified in a number of different locations – monasteries, the military, schools, hospitals, factories. It is their ubiquity which leads to what Foucault terms 'the veritable technological take-off in the productivity of power' (1980a: 119).[8]

Foucault's conception of power/knowledge is embodied in 'governmentality', a neologism derived from a combination of 'government' and 'rationality'. 'Government' is understood, by Foucault, in a broad sense, as 'the conduct of conduct: a form of activity aiming to shape, guide or affect the conduct of some person or persons' (Foucault, 1979: 2).[9] Government is not just the operation of political institutions. 'Rationality' recognizes that before something can be governed or managed, it must first be known. Government is intrinsically dependent upon particular ways of knowing. Programmes of government require vocabularies, ways of representing that which is to be governed: ways of ordering populations, mechanisms for the supervision and administration of individuals and groups. They depend on specific knowledges and techniques to render something knowable. Governmentality, therefore, refers to those processes through which objects are rendered amenable to intervention and regulation by being formulated in a particular conceptual way. Ways of thinking about or perceiving a domain render it visible and through this visibility open to intervention.

Intervention is achieved through procedures for the formation and accumulation of knowledge: modes of representation which render into information the events and phenomena which are to be governed. Technologies, however, are not neutral instruments for the presentation of the real, they re-present 'pertinent features' of a realm. They are an example of disciplinary power, simultaneously constituting a way of knowing, a system of knowledge; and an order, a system of power. They act as grids for the perception and evaluation of things and include methods of recording and calculation; methods of observation; written inscriptions; ways of coding, etc. and operate, for example, in balance sheets, audits, populations tables and census. Once an arena is captured or inscribed, knowledge about it may then be translated to other decision-making bodies, often far removed from the original site of inscription. Governmentality relies on 'centres' being able to administer disparate entities through the knowledge it acquires of them. In pointing to the political dimensions of visibility, the crucial role of knowledge in rendering realms thinkable and calculable, Foucault offers a novel understanding of power. 'Power is exercised by virtue of things being known and people being seen' (Foucault, 1980a: 154). It is the 'will to knowledge' or the desire to know. To 'know' something is to create a new power relation.

Procedures for the formation and accumulation of knowledge, including investigation and research, are not natural instruments for accessing and presenting the 'real'. A classificatory table, for example, operates as a procedure of knowledge, and as a technique of power, making an arena 'known' in a particular way and thereby rendering it amenable to be acted upon. The processes involved in the construction of knowledge – processes of classification, codification, categorizing, precise calibration, tables and taxonomies – constitute an arena of knowledge, and, in constituting something as known, provides the basis for action and intervention – the operation of power.[10]

Foucault's conception of power/knowledge can be contrasted with traditional, 'economistic' concepts of power. In the latter, not only is power deduced from, and in the service of, the economy; more importantly, the metaphor for understanding its operation is that of the commodity. Power is something externally 'held' or possessed, embodied in a person, a group, an institution or a structure, to be used for individual, group, organizational or class purposes. It is something to be acquired or seized, 'a system of domination exerted by one group over another' (Foucault, 1981a: 92). As a commodity, power is portrayed in zero-sum or negative terms, commonly presented as 'power over': the traditional representation of As getting Bs to do something they would, or should, not otherwise do.

Conceiving power as a commodity, prompts the questions, 'who holds power?' or 'where does it reside?' It assumes a central organizing focus or source, the study of which involves examining how power percolates from a centre or organizational apex, that is, a 'descending' analysis of power. It involves a search for determinants in the conscious intentions or decisions of voluntaristic subjects or in the constraining institutional sources of power. Traditional concepts of power pose a dualism between agency and structure.

Foucault's understanding of power relations operates on a different set of assumptions from economistic models of power. He says, 'I hardly ever use the word "power" . . . [but] . . . relationships of power . . . when one speaks of "power", people think immediately of a political structure, a government, a dominant social class, the master facing the slave and so on. That is not at all what I think of when I speak of "relationships of power" ' (Foucault, 1991c: 11). For Foucault, the analysis of power relations within a society cannot be reduced to the study of a series of institutions, class or the state – not even those institutions which would merit the name 'political'. Foucault states, 'in analysing power relations from the standpoint of institutions one lays oneself open to seeking explanation and the origin of the former in the latter'. Power, in other words, is normally seen as emanating from and being in the service of institutions. He continues, 'one must analyse institutions from the standpoint of power relations – not vice versa' (Foucault, 1983: 222). To understand institutions, we have to understand the mechanics of power relations within them. For Foucault, therefore, power is associated with practices, techniques and procedures. Power is relational: it is not a possession. Power is not something 'that is acquired, seized or shared, something one holds on to or allows to slip away' (Foucault, 1981a: 94). It is exercised rather than held, a property of relations, manifest through practices. Finally, power does not have a necessary central point or locus. Rather it is employed at all levels, has many dimensions, and is evident in all social networks: 'in human relations, whatever they are – whether it be a question of communicating verbally . . . or a question of a love relationship, an institutional or economic relationship – power is always present' (Foucault, 1991c: 10). Power has to be analysed in all its diverse forms, in its exercise or practice, and not limited to centralized institutional locus.

Reconceptualizing power as a relational activity has several implications for the way it is studied. Power can no longer be portrayed as 'external', something which operates on something or someone. It is integral to that relation. It is also 'productive' in the sense that it *creates* 'objects'. Power is positive and creative, not just negative or repressive. As Foucault (1977: 194) writes: 'we must cease once and for all to describe the effects of power in negative terms: it "excludes", it "represses", it "censors", it "abstracts", it "masks", it "conceals". In fact, power produces; it produces reality; it produces domains of objects and rituals of truth.' This constitutive nature of power does not acknowledge a neutral concept of knowledge formation, as Foucault's play on the word discipline – at once a branch of knowledge and a system of correction and control – suggests. The dual nature of power – creative and repressive – also points to the ambiguity inherent in its operations. Relations of power are always contestable. They are, Foucault says, 'changeable, reversible and unstable' (Foucault, 1991c: 12). Power is ambiguous and plurivocal, a site of conflict and contestation.

Foucault's conception of the ubiquity of power relations, their diffuseness and heterogeneity, expands our understanding of the political. In ascribing a political element to all social and personal relationships, we must recognize that power operates in areas which may be obscured by traditional theories. As Fraser (1989: 26) states: 'It shows that power is as present in the most apparently trivial details and relations of everyday life as it is in corporate suites, industrial assembly lines, parliamentary chambers, and military installations.' The personal is political, as feminists have argued for years. Expanding conceptions of the operation of power increases an awareness of one's own existence and, in doing so, opens up the possibilities of countering and changing it. As Foucault (1991a) himself points out, the identification of the nature of power, how it operates as a 'microphysics', and how it is experienced in practice is the foundation of a political agenda which 'allows for the questioning of the mode of existence and the functioning of discourse in the name of political practice' (Foucault, 1991a: 68).[11]

Understanding power as a relational activity widens the scope of attention from the 'who' and the 'why' of power to the 'how'. If 'power is not a thing or the control of a set of institutions . . . then the task for the analyst is to identify how it operates' (Dreyfus and Rabinow, 1983: 185). From the more traditional 'who has power?' or 'where, or in what, does power reside?', questions focus on the 'how' of power, the practices, techniques and procedures by which it operates. For Foucault (1983), power exists with three distinct qualities – origins (why), nature (what) and manifestations (how). The implication of his work is that we broaden analysis from the 'what' and 'why' of power to the 'how':

> 'How', not in the sense of 'How does it manifest itself?' but 'By what means is it exercised?' and 'What happens when individuals exert (as they say) power over others' . . . If I grant a certain privileged position to the question of 'how' it is not because I would wish to eliminate the question of 'what' and 'why'. Rather it is that I wish to present these questions in a different way; better still to know if it is legitimate to imagine a power which unites in itself a what, a why and a how . . . The little question, 'What happens?' although flat and empirical, once it is scrutinized is seen to avoid accusing a metaphysics or an ontology of power. (Foucault, 1983: 217)

A Foucauldian analysis involves tracing knowledge production and its power effects, an analysis of webs of power rather than classes or groups (Silverman, 1985). Most importantly, it involves an 'ascending' analysis of power, the study of power 'at its extremities, in its ultimate destinations' (Foucault, 1980a). Starting from its 'infinitesimal mechanisms', an ascending analysis aims to delineate the way power is exercised, concretely and in detail. It is a study of how mechanisms of power affect everyday lives.

This aspect of Foucault's work is relevant to the question: How has HRM or personnel traditionally handled the issue of power? All too often there has been a reluctance to address the issue of power. Frequently prescriptive and technique orientated, HRM or personnel practices are usually presented as the tools or instruments designed to enable the effective attainment of goals. This presentation reflects a belief that these techniques could be made progressively more objective and more accurate. This normative, technicist, presentation of personnel has been ameliorated by recent analyses of personnel practices which provide a more analytical framework (see for example, Sisson, 1989). Where power has been explicitly addressed, its incorporation into an analysis of personnel has taken a number of forms. For example, Karen Legge's *Power, Innovation, and Problem Solving in Personnel Management* (1978) considers the issue of power in terms of the personnel function's relative lack of status in organizations *vis-à-vis* others. Defining power as influence, Legge discusses the extent to which the latter may be enhanced or diminished through the control of strategic contingencies. For Legge, the potential of the personnel function to enhance its power lay in its use of expert and non-substitutable knowledge, and in handling the uncertainties of increasing legislation in the personnel–IR field; the militancy of labour; the growth (as was then) of white collar and managerial staff and the introduction of organizational change. Having established power within a managerial hierarchy, personnel would then be in a position to propose personnel practices suited to organizational contingencies.

Studies of management in the 1980s were heavily influenced by the labour process debate and radical critiques of power (Lukes, 1974). Orthodox portrayals of management as the selection and achievement of goals and the direction and co-ordination of organizational activity were criticized for their failure adequately to confront the issue of power, their neglect of political economy and broader capitalist relations of production (Chua et al., 1989; Knights and Willmott, 1986; Machin and Lowe, 1983). Drawing on Marx's distinction between labour power, as the capacity to work, and labour, as the actual effort expended, the employment exchange was depicted in terms of the 'powerful' and 'powerless'.[12] The dominant motif of these analyses is that of control over the labour process. This emphasis on control focuses on motive, the 'who' and the 'why' of power. This approach tends to dismiss HRM as ideology.

Although they introduce different emphases and perspectives, both Legge's work and labour process analysis have certain similarities. They both operate with an economistic model of power, that is, they conceive of power as a commodity or possession. This model of power underlines the presentation of HRM. Paralleling the analysis of the state in political theory, HRM offers an analysis of management based on a centralized view of power: power has a source and emanates from a centre. Research focuses on the degree of integration between HR and business strategies; the position of the personnel function in the managerial hierarchies; the effects of decisions emanating from this site; how much power personnel has, or who within a corporate hierarchy is the more powerful;[13] managerial responses to HR strategies, the relative roles of line and personnel. The model of power informing a descending analysis describes only one form of power. It fails to capture the myriad of power relations at the micro-level of society, the mundane, taken for granted, day to day experiences which directly affect people at work.

The Subject

Foucault's conception of power sustains an alternative understanding of the individual or subject. Foucault states that his 'objective for more than twenty-five years has been to sketch out a history of the different ways in our culture that humans develop knowledge about themselves' (Foucault, 1983: 208). His early work, *The Order of Things* examines how the academic subjects of philology, political economy and biology come to focus on the figure of man 'who comes to reside in them as an object of knowledge: the man who speaks, the man who works, and the man who exists' (Foucault, quoted in Eribon, 1991: 158). His last works – *The History of Sexuality*, Volume 1: *The Will to Knowledge* (1981a), Volume 2: *The Use of Pleasure* (1988a), and Volume 3: *The Care of the Self* (1990) and a series of essays (Foucault, 1988b, 1989) – analyse the individual as subject, that is, how individuals come to see and understand themselves in a particular way and, through this, become tied to a particular conception of their identity or subjectivity. In this there is a logical conclusion to earlier themes of how individuals govern them-selves and others by the production of 'truth' (Foucault, 1979). In denying the existence of an 'essential' human subject, whose nature is to be discovered or uncovered, Foucault, as Eribon (1991: 148) notes, 'dynamited the serene unity of subjectivity'. This emphasis on the con-stituted nature of self is explicitly adopted in post-structuralist and feminist literature (Gilligan, 1982; Henriques et al., 1984; Keller, 1986), but has only recently been incorporated into psychology (Rose, 1990) and occupational psychology (Henriques et al., 1984; Hollway, 1991), and remains relatively rare in general studies of management (Calas and Smircich, 1990; Roberts, 1984, 1991). It is an approach, however, which has important implications for personnel.

Traditional approaches in personnel have taken the individual as a self-evident phenomenon – an observable reality, a unit continuous in time, possessing an essential personal identity – to be recruited, appraised, remunerated, etc. The individual is the 'given' which the (scientific) observer takes for granted. Foucault offers a relational and dynamic model of identity. The individual is continuously constituted and constructed through social relationships, discourses and practices. When Foucault writes that power produces reality, he concludes, 'the individual and the knowledge that may be gained of him belong to this production' (Foucault, 1977: 194). The individual is constituted through power/knowl-edge. 'Certain bodies, certain gestures, certain discourses, certain desires come to be constituted as individuals. The individual . . . is I believe one of [power's] prime effects' (Foucault, 1980a: 98). Individuals and their identity are the product of the social techniques of power. Rather than being reducible to an internal core of meaning, the individual is continu-ously being constituted and constructed, through discipline. As Rose (1990: 218) explains:

'The self' does not pre-exist the forms of its social recognition; it is a hetero-geneous and shifting resultant of the social expectations targeted upon it, the social duties accorded it, the norms according to which it is judged, the plea-sures and pains that entice and coerce it, the forms of self-inspection inculcated in it, the languages according to which it is spoken about and about which it learns to account for itself in thought and speech. Thus 'belief systems' con-cerning the self should not be construed as inhabiting a diffuse field of 'culture', but as embodied in institutional and technical practices . . . through which forms of individuality are specified and governed.

For Foucault, individuals are constructed and known through being made an 'object' of knowledge and a target of power. Or, they may be constituted as a subject, that is, tied to a particular concept of subjectivity, so that they come to see themselves, and be seen, in a particular way. It is to the ambiguity in the terms subject/object which Foucault (1982: 778) refers in claiming that the general theme of his research has been 'how human beings constitute themselves as subjects and how they treat one another as objects'; and 'to detail the modes of objectification which transform human beings into subjects'. Foucault's early work, for example, emphasizes how individuals are constituted both as objects of knowledge – the mad, the criminal, the insane; and as subjects of discourse – psychiatry, criminology, penology, medicine. These constructs – the mad, the criminal—influence the identity and subjectivity of the individual who is known in this way. Foucault refers to the processes through which individuals become the object of knowledge, as 'objectification'. This is brought about through the introduction of scientific enquiry, which constructs the individual as an object of knowledge. Through 'technologies of the self', individuals may also constitute themselves as subjects, that is, they situate and define themselves by becoming tied to an identity. In both processes, however, identity is viewed as contingent, provisional, achieved, always in process; rather than a given or essential component of the subject, fixed in its expression,

A Foucauldian analysis of the individual subject does not, therefore, assume an uncovering of a given essential identity of skills, abilities and personality traits. Rather, its focus is the processes involved in rendering the individual knowable. The emphasis is on the techniques through which human beings understand themselves and others. It asks: what are the processes by which the individual becomes known, how do these processes become established and used, and what are their effects? This approach emphasizes the importance of studying in detail the actual practices which enunciate individuals and render them visible: the mechanisms of inscription, recording and calculation which constitute the discursive practices which make knowledge of the individual possible. As Rose (1990) notes, it is a history of the self which should be written at the 'technological' level. This focus on how subjects are constituted by power relations stresses the importance of identity and identity-securing strategies in the reproduction of power relations (Knights and Willmott, 1985). Again, however, it is important to stress that, although the individual is situated in power relations, because relationships are often contradictory and unstable there is the possibility of challenge and redefinition. 'Individuals are both the site and subjects of discursive struggle for their identity. Yet the interpellation of individuals as subjects within particular discourses is never final' (Weedon, 1991: 97).

Foucault and HRM

Although Foucault never directly addresses production, he argues that the logic or rationality of power is transferable across different domains. To illustrate the relevance of his work for personnel, we must follow his recommendation to question the self-evident and return to the basic building block on which personnel practices are premised: the employment relationship. Central to this relationship is the indeterminacy of contract, the naturally occurring space between expectation and deliverance of work. The 'gap', or space, between what is promised and what is realized, inevitably exists in a transaction between the parties. In the employment relationship, this gap is between the capacity to work and its exercise. The employment relationship describes only in general terms services to be provided, allowing details to be elaborated later. As Baldamus writes:

> Though it [the employment contract] stipulates precise wage payments for the employer, nothing definite is ever said about effort or efficiency; nor anything about the components of effort, the acceptable intensity of impairment, the intolerable degree of tedium or weariness. Instead it merely mentions hours of work, type of job, occupational status and similar external conditions. At the most there are vague and concealed references to an implied level of effort . . . Thus the formal contract between employer and employee is incomplete in a very fundamental sense. (Baldamus, 1961: 2)

The significance of this basic unit of analysis – the exchange embodied in the employment relationship – has been blurred by the dominance of an economic paradigm and the reification of 'the market' and 'administration' (Townley, 1993b). The questions that this space or gap raises, however, are: How is this relational exchange organized? How is the indeterminacy of contract resolved, in particular, how is the analytical space between expectation and performance articulated?

Foucault provides the means of answering these questions. In the process, we can reconceptualize HRM. There are three principal areas of knowledge which the management of personnel requires: (a) knowledge of the workforce or 'population'; (b) knowledge of the activity or labour to be undertaken, that is, 'work'; and (c) knowledge of the individual, the 'worker'. All these dimensions or spaces must be known and articulated before they may be managed. Foucault's concept of power/knowledge, in which a system of knowledge operates as a modality of power, illustrates how personnel orders the exchange inherent in the employment contract.

A Foucauldian analysis of HRM construes it as a discourse and a set of practices which attempt to narrow the gap between the capacity to work and its exercise. It constructs and produces knowledge which renders visible the arena of work for the purposes of governance. It operates as the 'will to knowledge', which organizes the analytical space of the employment relationship, attempting to reduce the indeterminacy resulting from the unspecified nature of contract. Through its discourse and practices, personnel renders organizations and their participants calculable arenas. In a variety of technologies, personnel provides the means by which activities and individuals become knowable and governable. These personnel practices do not 'reflect' reality: they actively order and create it. They 'discipline' the interior of the organization, by organizing time, space and movement, and by categorizing and measuring tasks, behaviour and interactions. Personnel practices measure both the physical and subjective dimensions of labour, and offer a technology which aims to render individuals and their behaviour predictable and calculable. In so doing, personnel helps to bridge the gap between promise and performance, between labour power and labour, and organizes labour into a productive force or power.

This Foucauldian conception of HRM prompts questions related to the production of knowledge and its effects. It points to the crucial role of knowledge in rendering realms thinkable, calculable and manageable. A Foucauldian analysis highlights those mechanisms by which power is exercised through its intersection with knowledge. For example, methods of observation, techniques of registration – mechanisms for the supervision and administration of individuals and groups: 'The apparently humble and mundane mechanisms which . . . make it possible to govern' (Miller and Rose, 1990: 8). The focus becomes, in Foucault's term, 'governmentality' – the processes by which objects are rendered amenable to intervention and regulation by being formulated in a particular way. Such an approach emphasizes the mechanisms of inscription, recording and calculation which constitute the discursive practices which make government possible. Its focus is those regulatory mechanisms which make a domain or arena open to regulation, the mechanisms and processes through which aspects of life at work become governable.

For too long, the 'apparently insignificant tricks' (Foucault, 1977: 223) of HRM have been neglected in favour of larger political struggles. An emphasis has been on the 'what' or the 'why' of power, to the neglect of the 'how'. This has been exacerbated by recent attention focused on the phenomenon of 'human resource management'.[14] British academics have debated both the relevance and the distinction between HRM and personnel (Blyton and Turnbull, 1992; Legge, 1989). A primary distinction is the separation of planning or directive roles ('human resource management') from an essentially secondary information control function ('personnel management or administration'). The latter is regarded as an aid for management designed to enhance rational decision-making. HRM is promoted as a central organizational concern, associated with a long-term perspective, and strategic integration with business planning. Emphasis is placed on the role of employees as a valued resource, an ethos informing organizational culture and corporate goals. HRM stresses coherence in employee relations policies to ensure a strategic response for competitive advantage. Much more managerialist in focus, HRM is an area of senior management responsibility and line management implementation. HRM is now very closely tied with the strategic management and the leadership literature, and from this adopts the themes of the importance of planning and the imposition of control over change in an era of uncertainty. In this it reflects the broader reification of management which has been influential in determining business school curricula (Armstrong, 1987; Whitley, 1986). As policy formulation at the strategic level, HRM is demarcated from personnel management or administration, the secondary information control function, and the latter's association with marginality, ambiguity and lack of status.

This construction of HRM, and the research it informs, brings us to the gendered nature of personnel. Until quite recently, personnel management literature, textbooks in particular, have been gender blind, issuing descriptive and prescriptive statements concerning a seemingly homogeneous workforce, irrespective of issues of class, race or gender. The changing composition of the workforce, and concern with equal pay, discrimination and harassment, has stimulated interest in equal opportunities or employment equity. For some, this is the 'gender issue' sufficiently dealt with. A Foucauldian analysis, however, allows for the issue of gender to be more centrally placed in personnel management, above and beyond considerations of 'counting the number of women'.

The mutually constitutive nature of knowledge and power indicates that consideration of gender issues should not rest here. Feminist critiques have pointed to the gendered character of many disciplines and the importance of critiquing supposedly gender-neutral social theory (Alcoff and Potter, 1993; Fonow and Cook, 1991). Just as management is a heavily gender invested term (Calas and Smircich, 1990), it is important to recognize that the language of personnel management, the constructs it uses, and the questions it poses are also heavily gendered. These debates have never been neutral academic issues.

Gender is inherent, for example, in how personnel has been constituted as a subject for study. The history of the association of personnel managers in the UK, particularly in debates over its name and the image it wished to present, reflects gender issues. The association changed its name six times from its initial inscription as the Welfare Workers' Association in 1913, until finally deciding on its present title in 1946. Debates centred on the image projected – welfare was thought to reflect the feminine – with elements amongst the membership, conscious of employment prospects, wishing to insert more strenuous terms into the title. In 1924, the name changed to Industrial Welfare Workers, in 1931 to the Institute of Labour Management, only finally deciding on the Institute of Personnel Management, in 1946, when, for the first time, male membership of the Institute exceeded female membership (Niven, 1967). Gender was a dimension in the relative positions of industrial relations versus personnel management in the 1960s and 1970s. It was reflected not only in the relative employment opportunities in organizations, as senior IR negotiating positions went to men and administrative clerical positions or 'soft' areas such as training devolved to women (Legge, 1986; Long, 1984), but was also reflected in the relative status of the two as academic subjects. The present division between personnel and HRM in the 1980s and 1990s equally reflects the same gendered elements. Put bluntly, the focus of HRM – an agenda, in the main, prescribed by men – has been 'important' men in one field talking to, reflecting and reporting on 'important' men in another.

A Foucauldian analysis denies the premiss upon which the personnel management/HRM distinction is founded – the distinction between directive or 'managerial' roles and secondary information functions. The constitutive interdependence of power and knowledge means that knowledge is not secondary, detached and independent, a source of illumination, but is integral to the system of administration and governance which it helps establish. Knowledge is integral to the operation of power. Information systems are an active component of an organization's system of management, directly implicated in the forms of organizational segmentation, hierarchy and control which emerge. This emphasizes the importance of studying in detail the actual practices which introduce domains and individuals to enunciation and visibility – the mechanisms of inscription, recording and calculation which constitute the discursive practices which make knowledge of arenas and the individual possible. The focus becomes personnel management or as it was known earlier personnel administration – those day-to-day practices which affect individuals at work.

This focus highlights the main advantage of a Foucauldian analysis – its political potential. One of the main criticisms of HRM's emphasis on a descending and economistic view of power, and its search for a locus of power, is that it diminishes the possibility of political engagement. A Foucauldian examination of 'personnel management' introduces politics and a political agenda, in the sense of addressing issues of power, to its study, and in doing so opens up the possibility of political action.[15] A Foucauldian analysis focuses on those practices and discourses which establish domains and objects and the power relations which most directly affect people at work, those microphysics of power, which directly inform people's experiences. The emphasis is on what is involved in rendering an arena or an individual knowable: what are the processes by which they become known, how do these processes become established and used, and with what effects? It is a sufficiently detailed approach to allow for the micropolitics of power to be addressed but allows for highly individualized practices to be related to an intelligible whole. An emphasis on the minutiae of power also helps dispel the notion that these are in anyway normal, and, therefore, somehow irrevocable.

This focus on practices – the 'how' of power – has drawn criticism. To examine practices apart from intentions prompts resistance from a modernist perspective which demands to know the 'who' and the 'why' of power.[16] This is particularly the case in dealing with critiques of production, where both traditional and Marxist analyses centre on the presentation of management and labour as agents. The argument is made that to concentrate on 'how' as opposed to 'who' or 'why' denies the role of the subject and, in doing so, offers an inadequate politics. Not so. For Foucault, explication of 'how' is part of a political process. An analysis of the nature and limits of practices through which experience is constituted undermines their 'naturalness', and with this comes the possibility of imagining something different. Seeing normal practices in a Foucauldian way undermines their self-evident nature and opens up the possibilities of challenge. Recognizing the effects of power/knowledge is the basis for challenging the assumptions on which it is based. In this sense, as Sawicki (1991: 47) notes, Foucault's theories 'serve less to explain than to criticize and raise questions'. In critique, however, lies the basis for change. Foucault stresses its importance:

> A critique is not a matter of saying that things are not right as they are. It is a matter of pointing out what kinds of assumptions, what kinds of familiar, unchallenged, unconsidered modes of thought the practices we accept rest . . . criticism is a matter of flushing out that thought and trying to change it: to show that things are not as self-evident as one believed, to see that what is accepted as self-evident will no longer be accepted as such . . . criticism is absolutely indispensable for any transformation . . . as soon as one can no longer think things as one formerly thought them, transformation becomes both very urgent, very difficult and quite possible. (Foucault, in Kritzman, 1988: 154)

Foucault's work, therefore, is not a process which aims 'to fix the foundations for knowledge . . . but to occasion new ways of thinking' (Rajchman, 1985: 123). Critique is the constant questioning of the 'politics of truth',[17] the questioning of what enables knowledge to become an instrument of policies and practices, and forms the basis of a political position. The 'how' of power is an important dimension of Foucauldian politics and political action. It constitutes part of the disruption of self-evidencies, challenging technicist beliefs in the progressive development of practices through the application of reason. It also allows the recognition that techniques of power can be used for different ends. Practices and discourse may attach to different strategies. They are not essential. The focus on practices, however, offers an opportunity for challenge in the way that sovereign theories of power, with their debilitating focus on source, do not. 'Why' takes issues as being 'real' and seeks explanation. It defers action. 'How' takes things as being contingent and thus points to its change. It allows for the power effects of administration to be recognized and worked against. As such, it refocuses the locus of political action and in doing so gives everyone the opportunity to participate – in this sense it is very productive. It stimulates revolt and is deeply political, as will be argued in Chapter 6.

Studying HRM

A Foucauldian conception of HRM has major implications for how it is studied. Following Foucault, analyses does not begin with the intentions of individuals or an occupational group (e.g. managers, employees, work-groups), the role of institutions (management, the State), or with an identifiably coherent strategy on the part of a dominant class. Nor does it search for the origins of power. The focus is practices and their effects, not power and its source. Nor is analysis driven by considerations of 'what' (the market, or administration), or 'why' (efficiency, shirking, problems of trust, the rationale of control, etc.). The focus does not privilege either the (alienated) individual and the presence or absence of motivation; or man-agerial intentions and strategies of control. The focus of study is techniques rather than institutions, practices rather than intention, 'with the aim of grasping the conditions which make these acceptable at a given moment' (Foucault, 1991b: 5). A Foucauldian analysis stresses the impor-tance of practices of organizing, not organization: how individuals and their activities become organized and translated, and the mechanisms and the practices which have been developed for this. The emphasis is with issues of 'how': how the indeterminacy of contract is resolved, in partic-ular, how the 'analytical space' between expectation and deliverance of performance is articulated. The focus of analysis is how the relational nature of exchange and the inevitable indeterminacy of social relations are ordered.

   This entails a 'decentring' of the economic. The discourse and practices of HRM cannot be 'read off' from forms of technology, or economic development. In other words, the discourse which sustains a set of prac-tices is not a functional response to, or legitimation of, economic needs. Foucault (1983: 213) writes, 'it is certain that the mechanisms of subjec-tion cannot be studied outside their relation to the mechanisms of exploitation and domination. But they do not merely constitute the "ter-minal" or more fundamental mechanisms. They entertain complex and circular relations with other forms.' Whilst the economic has implications for the conditions of emergence of a discourse and its functioning, it does not produce the discourse per se.[18] Certainly, economic factors influence the perceived need for the disciplines and may influence the adoption of certain techniques at certain times. Equally, personnel practices may be introduced on the grounds of an economic rationale, the importance of controlling costs, the need to stress a performance-oriented culture, motivating individuals and groups to attain key strategic goals of the organization. But this is to confuse the take-up of practices with the nature of the practices themselves. It is not economic circumstances alone or even the usual variables which are tested such as size, unionization, gender, etc. which can account for the adoption of different types of personnel practices; for example, the adoption of point-factor job evaluation plans, semi-automatic pay progression to the range maximum, directly controlled performance measures or profit sharing, or their effects. There can be no assumption that discourse is an 'expression' of an economic situation or institutional developments. They may modify the rules of a discourse's formation but do not account for the objects of discourse (Foucault, 1991a: 68).[19] Economic factors may influence the former but the latter is the result of the intersection of many discourses, for example, educational, scientific, accounting and legal discourses.

This approach highlights the importance of examining other power/knowledge systems with the recognition that personnel is influenced by different discourses with unknown and unpredictable effects. It may be in opposition to or complementary with these. An examination of the development of personnel shows its intersection with a range of other discourses. Its history reflects the gradual accretion of areas of knowledge (Jacoby, 1985; Niven, 1967; Ozanne, 1967), for example its conjunction with the behavioural sciences in its attempt to gain legitimacy as an organizational diagnostician (Lupton, 1978; Rose, 1981). Military support for behavioural research has been particularly influential in extending areas of power/knowledge. The State has introduced, reinforced or challenged disciplinary practices, either through its role as employer or through direct government policies, or in its actions as the guarantor of a system of rights in court decisions. The State's role as guarantor of rights introduces the complex area of the relationship between disciplinary power and what Foucault terms the juridico-political structures of society.[20] The extent to which 'rights' are identified and fought for has an impact on the nature of disciplinary practices which might result. Nor should the role of organized labour in extending practices of power/knowledge be overlooked. Trade unions have also operated so as to intensify or perhaps mitigate certain aspects of discipline, acting in some cases as surrogate personnel managers in the control of labour (Batstone, 1984).[21] All have implications for the way in which personnel discourse has developed.

From a Foucauldian perspective, what is needed within personnel is a genealogy, a 'form of history which can account for the constitution of knowledges, discourses and domains of objects' (Foucault, 1980a: 117). Genealogical enquiries into the past aim to make intelligible the 'natural' or 'objective' nature of the present, including its unquestioned rationales. What is required, therefore, is an analysis of the rules of formation of a personnel discourse, tracing the conditions of its existence and those factors which affect both what is known and what is done. A discursive analysis would involve an investigation of the processes by which objects become known; how these processes become established and used and with what effects. This requires an analysis of HRM in terms of its correlations with other statements, and those statements it excludes. In addition, it involves the analysis of the situations which prompted the discourse of personnel; consequences to which it gives rise; the practical field in which it is deployed; who is accorded the right to speak; the institutional sites from which discourse derives its legitimation; the position in which it places its subjects; what is recognized as valid; the concepts or objects to which it gives rise, and who has access to the discourse (Foucault, 1991a). Only with studies of this nature would the discourse of personnel be constituted.

To conduct a genealogy of HRM would be the basis of a long-term research agenda. This book offers the basis for such an analysis through its examination of the operation of some personnel practices.[22] It gives a perspective on the present with the intention of disrupting self-evidencies, to see practices in a different light. In presenting the 'how' of personnel practices, illustrating the involvement of knowledge in the production process, the primary focus becomes the *order* these techniques create, not the 'accuracy' of their operation. The focus, therefore, is on how HRM practices operate to create order and knowledge, and through this produce a technology of power.

The Organization of the Book

As was stated earlier, there are three principal areas of knowledge which the management of personnel requires: knowledge of the 'body of labour' or the workforce; knowledge of the activity or labour to be undertaken; and knowledge of the individual worker. The framework of this book reflects this ordering. Chapter 2 analyses the practices available to gain knowledge of the population and how it becomes 'an ordered multiplicity', with the effect that both the population and the place of the individual within it become known. It explains how HRM accomplishes this via taxinomia and mathesis. Chapter 3 extends this analysis by concentrating on those practices which attempt to inscribe the nature of work activity, and then align it with time to specify effort. Chapters 4 and 5 illustrate those personnel activities which attempt to constitute individuals, making them 'known' in a particular way. These chapters introduce two further technologies upon which personnel relies – the examination and the confession. Chapter 4 analyses those processes which constitute the individual as an object of knowledge, whilst Chapter 5 analyses those practices which constitute the individual as a subject. Chapter 6 summarizes the argument of the book and addresses the question of how Foucault's work may be used to introduce change. It is informed by feminist critique and presents an examination of what might constitute alternative power/knowledge practices, and how these might form the basis of an emancipatory agenda for change.

Notes

1 For reasons explained later in this chapter, I use HRM and personnel (management) interchangeably.

2 'Discourse' was adopted primarily because 'other words were overladen with conditions and consequences' (Foucault, 1972: 48). It is a concept designed to capture 'ways of doing things', how certain acts become accepted at a certain historical period as being natural, self-evident and indispensable. Although discourse examines the existence of statements, it is not reducible to language and speech. It is not the analysis of signs, or linguistic analysis – the 'mere intersection of things and words, or a slender surface of contact between a reality and a language' (Foucault, 1972: 48). Discourse examines discursive rules and categories, the a priori, assumed constituent parts of a discourse (and therefore knowledge). Its focus is not that which was said or thought per se, that is, the consciousness of a speaking subject or the will of an author, but underlying rules which form what is possible and limit the forms of the sayable (Foucault, 1991a, 1991b).

3 Largely self-explanatory, these six areas had several sub-areas, thus employment involves personnel records including statistics, employee interviews, transfers, releases and dismissals. Welfare includes advice on individual problems, assisting employees in transport, housing, shopping and other problems. Training includes the encouragement of further education, suggestion schemes, and the works magazine.

4 All of this was proceeded by a section on the principles of personnel management, which included references to the role of incentives, an analysis of the working situation, and the psychology of the working group and the dynamics of industrial relations.

5 After considering the context of personnel, Thomason (1981) considers under these headings: the contract of employment, manpower planning, recruitment and selection; performance control, reward strategies, communications and training and development; collective labour relations, organizational and management development. Thomason also provides an analysis of other textbooks' coverage of personnel.

6 These include, respectively, industrial democracy, employee ownership and collective bargaining; recruitment, appraisal, career development and 'exiting'; remuneration systems; job content and QWL.

7 These include the principles and practice of work design; manpower planning, recruitment and selection, employee appraisal; training, supervision and development; remuneration, status divisions and discipline; communication, quality circles and joint consultation.

8 Because its emphasis is more explicitly on the role of 'disciplines', *Discipline and Punish* is sometimes perceived as a break in his work, but, as Eribon (1991: 226) notes, 'everything that would interest him during the 1970s was already simmering in *Madness and Civilization*'. Foucault's studies generally have been concerned with the way in which there

has been a gradual expansion of the discipline of populations. The same processes which for Foucault enabled the practices of clinical medicine, psychiatry and the human sciences, ensured the rationalization of labour. 'In a word the disciplines are an ensemble of minute technical inventions that made it possible to increase the useful size of multiplicities by decreasing the inconveniences of a power which must control them' (Foucault, 1977: 220).

9 Another concept Foucault uses in a particular way. Not only does it include 'legitimately constituted forms of political or economic subjugation, but also modes of action . . . which were destined to act upon the possibilities of action of other people. To govern, in this sense, is to structure the possible field of actions of others' (Foucault, 1983: 221). More broadly conceived than political structures or the management of states governance is 'the way in which the conduct of individuals or of groups might be directed' (Foucault, 1983: 221), be this in families, organizations, or communities, etc.

10 Foucault shows how discourses on 'sanity', 'health', 'knowledge' and 'punishment' have developed and the implications this has for the individual who becomes an 'object' of knowledge. He shows how 'madness' is not a pre-given entity, but something constituted historically as both an object of knowledge and a target of institutional practices. In other words, madness is not an object whose history must be 'discovered', but is the product of a discourse. Psychiatric knowledge, for example, invents, moulds and carves out its object – mental illness. It is this questioning of self-evidencies and ahistorical naturalness that leads to the transgression of disciplinary boundaries in his work thus making it difficult to define.

11 As Sawicki (1991: 10) notes: 'Its appreciation of the heterogeneity, complexity and discontinuity of power relations, was more successful than prevailing theories had been in accounting for the role of new social movements.' It also makes us more aware of political technologies which may be used in the name of political ideologies. In this sense Foucault's work offers a respite from the inhibiting and totalizing effects of total theories.

12 Managerial control strategies were related to the nature of capitalist development in terms of degree of competition in the product market, the degree of concentration of economic resources, and the scale of production. On these grounds, Edwards (1979) distinguishes between technical control and bureaucratic control. Friedman (1977) identified a dichotomy between direct control and responsible autonomy, types of control that have characterized management throughout capitalism, and might be found in the same company at the same time.

13 This rather phallocentric analysis of management, analysis in terms of power and size underlies a lot of management analyses (see Calas and Smircich, 1990).

14 Whether intentionally or not, academia, with its collective presentation as offering an unmediated access from university to the 'outside' world has been complicit in this shift of focus. Studies of HRM hide the myth of academics as neutral observers rather than participant constructors. Although HRM is identified as a means of legitimation in managerial hierarchies, its role as legitimation within academic hierarchies in the search for students and research funds in an era of restricted university funding is neglected. Those who have talked in terms of HRM are in danger of 'creating' it, then 'finding' it. The emergence of HRM lies at the confluence of a range of factors one of which, and rarely commented on, is the changing funding circumstances of universities. Factors associated with the identification of HRM are the changing sources of research funding with the change from SSRC to ESRC in the UK; the increased reliance on private sources of finance; the financial circumstances of the publishing houses with their influence on how things become marketed (Abercrombie, 1991); the rise of business schools in the UK, and the processes of mimetic isomorphism as the 'top' UK business schools try to emulate their US counterparts. These factors are mutually reinforcing of HRM. It is perhaps no coincidence that the evolution of HRM in US schools paralleled the decrease in state funding of Higher Education and the move to

increased private funding (Kerr, 1963; Kochan and Cappelli, 1984; Miles, 1965). This is not to deny that things have not been changing in the external studied environment, but that both the changes which are taking place and the processes which have generated HRM are part of the same phenomena, not that HRM has successfully captured what is taking place, but is part of it. HRM in this respect has operated as a process of materialization or objectivization – the constitution of something which then becomes taken as self-evident fact. This is not to deny that HRM exists as a discourse. The rethinking of courses, textbooks, academic departments, the designation of chairs and creation of journals would indicate that it does. A Foucauldian analysis would enquire how this discourse emerged and with what effects, rather than assume it to be reflective of some external facticity.

15 Again, the funding of universities has been important in this. As money became channelled from social sciences to their bastardized form in business schools, there was a corresponding shift in homes for a number of academics, many of whom were uncomfortable with teaching the specifics of personnel, accountancy, etc. and channelled their activities into a critical 'overview ' of the field.

16 Foucault offers a non-voluntaristic, nonhumanistic view of history, where change is not 'caused' by internal contradiction or external forces. It is non-deliberate and non-necessitated which particularly presents problems for traditional theorists. It is, however, important to make two points. A non-intentional view of history is not to argue that people, groups, do not benefit from the operation of practices and that others are disadvantaged by such practices. This is most obviously the case. Nor is it to claim that there are no interests in the operation of power, again this is obviously the case. The problem, for Foucault, lies in equating intention and interests with causality and the implications that this has for a view of political change. Interests, for Foucault, are not 'given' but open to change and contestation, and are dependent on one's place in a social field and time. They are not quasi-transcendental, and are therefore open to contestation and local response. The question as to whether the operation of power works in a particular way is the basis of empirical investigation.

17 For Bernauer (1990), Foucault's work is concerned with an incessant interrogation, and concludes that whilst he left no teaching 'he did engrave a manner of questioning' and sees his work as being concerned with three primary questions: 'how a field of learning is constituted (knowledge); what forces are operating in relation to that learning (knowledge/power); how self-formation is tied to both (knowledge/power/liberty)' (Bernauer, 1990: 4).

18 Foucault explains this point: 'Though membership of a social group can always explain why such and such a person chose one system of thought rather than another, the condition enabling that system to be thought never resides in the existence of the group. We must be careful to distinguish here between two forms and two levels of investigation. The first would be a study of opinions in order to discover who in the eighteenth century was a Physiocrat and who an Anti-physiocratic; what interests were at stake; what were the points and arguments of the polemic; how the struggle for power developed. The other, which takes no account of the persons involved, or their history consists in defining the conditions on the basis of which it was possible to conceive of both "physiocratic" and "utilitarian" knowledge in interlocking and simultaneous forms. The first analysis would be the province of a doxology. Archeology can recognize and practice only the second' (Foucault, 1970: 200).

19 For example, political practice affected the conditions of emergence, insertion and functioning of medical discourse but did not transform the meaning or form of medical discourse. It transformed the mode of medical discourse but not the specifics of its practices (Foucault, 1991a: 67).

20 Rights have to be supported by a system of non-egalitarian, asymmetrical micropowers, in other words the disciplines. The disciplines, for Foucault constitute the foundation of

formal, judicial liberties. He writes that 'the enlightenment which discovered the liberties, also invented the disciplines . . . in the space and during the time in which they exercise their control and bring into play the asymmetries of their power, they effect a suspension of the law that is never total, but is never annulled either . . . although the universal juridicism of modern society seems to fix limits on the exercise of power, its universally widespread panopticism enables it to operate on the underside of law' (Foucault, 1977: 223).

21 In some cases, a well established shop steward organization delaying the emergence of the personnel professional (Batstone, 1984).

22 The material presented is taken from both academic and practitioner journals as being indicative of best practice. Where possible I indicate the extent to which these practices are in operation.

2

Dividing Practices

The co-ordination of large numbers of people and the ability to differentiate between them is one of the major requirements of managing an organization. This chapter examines the methods available for knowing those within the organization, its population or workforce. The rational and efficient deployment of a workforce requires the development of techniques through which it becomes known and potentially manageable. The first stage in managing a population en masse is to develop an analytical framework by which it can be ordered. This requires the use of techniques through which the workforce may be classified, enumerated and ordered to 'eliminate imprecise distributions, uncontrolled disappearances . . . and [individuals'] diffuse circulation' (Foucault, 1977: 143). These techniques comprise an 'art of distribution' (Foucault, 1977). Their principal purpose is to 'establish presences and absences, to know where and how to locate individuals' (Foucault, 1977: 143). This 'art of distribution' consists of three techniques: *enclosure* – the creation of a space closed in upon itself; *partitioning* – the division of enclosed space; and *ranking* – the hierarchical ordering of individuals within these partitioned spaces. I examine them in turn and then demonstrate their role in constructing seemingly normal and innocuous personnel practices.

The 'Art of Distribution'

The Enclosure of Work

To 'enclose' is to create a 'place heterogeneous to all others and closed in on itself' (Foucault, 1977: 141). This practice is analysed in Foucault's work on the asylum (Foucault, 1973b), the clinic (Foucault, 1973a), and the prison (Foucault, 1977); and in studies of 'total organizations', such as monasteries, military barracks, fortresses and schools (Goffman, 1961; P. Johnson, 1992; Pierce, 1992). Work organizations are enclosures. Early work organizations were located in monasteries and, later, prisons and workhouses. Only later, with capital investment and mechanization was there the independent establishment of manufactories, which assimilated many of the disciplinary regimes of prisons and workhouses. The privatization of property reinforced this process of enclosure with the gradual dissolution of the contracting out system and its replacement with factory organization (Marglin, 1974). This privately owned, homogenous space also tended to be physically enclosed by high walls and fences.

Many of these physical enclosures have perished, but the conceptual enclosures they helped erect remain. This is evident in the parallel distinctions between work and non-work, paid and unpaid labour, the public and the private. Work occurs at a work-place and is paid for. It is demarcated from leisure, social or domestic lives. People are known and classified according to their location on either side of these conceptual dichotomies: unemployed, housewife, retired. Legal definitions of employees reinforce this enclosure by excluding certain forms of labour from statutory protection. In the UK, for example, the self-employed, trainees, and temporary employees are denied the legal protection accorded to those with the status of employees.

The enclosure of work is also gendered. With the development of capitalism, the enclosure of work excluded women. From the seventeenth century there was a decline in the number of trades and professions open to women. They were systematically denied access to training, apprenticeships and education, and skills; they were restricted from practising their traditional professions (Witz, 1986); and they were excluded from new crafts and trades (Baron, 1992; Schiebinger, 1992), which, with the exception perhaps of textiles, became monopolized by men. By the nineteenth century, domestic service was the main occupation for women (Walby, 1986). It is only in the twentieth century that female participation rates in the labour force have increased significantly.

The gendered division of labour is evident in the distinction between home, as primarily the place for 'personal feelings', associated with women, and work, as the place for 'economic production', associated with men. Men's labour is typically understood to be central to the creation of value, while women's work is considered peripheral, subordinate 'support' work, and marginalized.[1] These divisions constitute conceptions of skill, sexuality, identity and worth. Masculinity and skill are interdependently constructed in male dominated spheres of employment (Cockburn, 1983; Collinson, 1992; Knights and Collinson, 1987). The division between the private domain of the home and the public domain of work compounds the low status of 'natural' and 'unskilled' women's work. Certain types of labour, particularly emotional labour, nurturing, supporting and caring, is invisible in job descriptions and job analyses, nor is it reflected in levels of remuneration (Hochschild, 1983).

Partitioning the Work Organization

Whilst enclosure differentiates a population from the 'outside', the population within the enclosure remains undifferentiated until it is partitioned, both horizontally and vertically. Foucault (1977: 143) writes: 'the principle of "enclosure" is neither constant, nor indispensable, nor sufficient in disciplinary machinery. This disciplinary machinery works space in a much more flexible and detailed way. It does this first of all on the principle of elementary . . . partitioning.' Partitioning is the first stage of imposing an order, or a 'rational' classification, on the enclosed population. It is most evident in the physical layout of production: the ordering of space, the distribution of bodies and their integration with technology. In a description of early factories, Foucault explains how this integration operates:

> By walking up and down the central aisle of the workshop . . . it was possible to carry out a supervision that was both general and individual; to observe the worker's presence and application, and the quality of his work; to compare workers with one another, to classify them according to skill and speed; to follow the successive stages of the production process. *All these serializations formed a permanent grid: confusion was eliminated.* That is to say production was divided up and the labour process was articulated, on the one hand according to its stages or elementary operations, and on the other hand, according to individuals, the particular bodies, that carried it out: each variable of this force – strength, promptness, skill constancy – would be observed, and therefore characterized, assessed, computed and related to the individual who was its particular agent. Thus, spread out in a perfectly legible way over a whole series of individual bodies, the workforce may be analyzed in individual units. At the emergence of large-scale industry, one finds, beneath the division of the production process, the individualizing fragmentation of labour power; the distributions of the disciplinary space often assured both. (Foucault, 1977: 145, emphasis added)

Although reflected in the physical organization of machinery and activity, the principal importance of partitioning is as an analytical device. It provides a conceptual grid within which a workforce may become known, analysable, and manageable. It is reflected in simple partitions or classifications – for example, master/hands; manual/non-manual; blue-collar/white-collar; productive/non-productive; direct/indirect – which create the political ordering of a population. This is reinforced through recruitment patterns, the operation of internal labour markets, employment practices and union jurisdictions. Now associated with the flexible firm, the nature of employment subsystems brought about by organizational partitioning within organizations has undergone a degree of change. Reference is now made to core and periphery employees, rather than more traditional distinctions of blue-collar/white-collar.[2]

Partitioning within the workforce has been recognized in the analysis of labour markets, where divisions based on sex, race, class, age, union status and ethnic origin ensure differentiation in experiences between the groups. Early studies of partitioning are reflected in Kerr's (1977) analysis of labour markets structured through institutional rules.[3] Later studies differentiated between primary and secondary labour markets (Doeringer and Piore, 1971), in terms of stability, working conditions, compensation, skill levels, access to training, chances of advancement and due process. This dualism was later qualified in analyses of segmented labour markets to include greater partitioning, identifying secondary, subordinate primary and independent primary labour markets (Edwards, 1979; Gordon et al., 1984).[4] Further partitions are identified in labour market shelters as niches or areas of interest (Freedman, 1976).[5] Analyses consider mechanisms which reinforce these divisions, for example, the role played by technology and internal labour markets (Osterman, 1984; Wilkinson, 1981).

At a more disaggregate level, Hakim (1979) has identified partitioning in the form of horizontal and vertical occupational segregation which reinforce gendered division of labour. In horizontal segregation, men and women work in different types of occupation, whilst in vertical segregation men occupy higher grades than women in the same occupation. She argues that whilst horizontal segregation has declined, vertical segregation has increased. These gendered segregations also impact the type of employment practices which result. In their study of part-time employment, for example, Beechey and Perkins (1987) note how in the hospital sector, segregation between porters (all male) and manual work (all female) influenced the reorganization of work to introduce greater 'flexibility', whereby the former were granted a three-shift system whilst the later were employed on a part-time basis.

Partitioning is a basic device for organizing a population and rendering it intelligible. These divisions still leave a population distributed in groups and relatively undifferentiated. A more comprehensive and exhaustive distribution is provided through ranking.

Ranking the Partitions

Ranking is the third technique of the art of distribution. Whilst partitioning delineates horizontal divisions amongst the population, ranking is the mechanism whereby those divisions are further differentiated. Rank indicates a place in a classification, the point at which a line and column intersect (Foucault, 1977: 146). Ranking is exemplified in the classroom. The pupil is assigned to a place 'that corresponds to the function of each individual and to his value' (Foucault, 1977: 146). In other words, the physical distribution of individuals, through rows or ranks, reflects their educational order or 'merit', with each pupil occupying a rank, according to age, performance or behaviour. Foucault (1977: 147) cites an educational reformer of the eighteenth century whose dream was a classroom 'in which spatial distribution might provide a whole series of distinctions at once: progress, worth, character, application, cleanliness and parents fortune'. The classroom, in other words, is organized according to a classificatory 'table' 'with many different entries, under the scrupulously "classificatory" eye of the master' (Foucault, 1977: 147). Rank defines the place occupied in a series. This may reflect a hierarchy of knowledge or ability, or any other criteria used for designation. Foucault concludes: 'the organization of serial space was one of the great technical mutations of elementary education' (Foucault, 1977: 147). Ranking arranges individuals, or, more accurately, serially orders 'spaces', into which individuals may be hierarchized according to whatever criteria are stipulated. An important aspect of ranking is that although the place is fixed, the position of individuals is not. They are able to change places, be promoted or demoted, according to their meeting the accepted criteria.

Rank necessarily ensures hierarchy and pyramidal supervision, it provides the machinery for supervising and rewarding:

> in organizing cells, places and ranks, the disciplines create complex spaces that are at once architectural, functional and hierarchical. It is spaces that provide fixed positions and permit calculation; they carve out individual segments and establish operational links; they work places and indicate values; they guarantee the obedience of individuals . . . They are mixed spaces: real because they govern the disposition of buildings, rooms, furniture, but also ideal, because they are projected over this arrangement of characterizations, assessments and hierarchies. (Foucault, 1977: 148)

Ranking constitutes a *tableau vivant* (a living table) – a serial, or hierarchical, ordering among a population. It is a process through which 'confused, useless or dangerous multitudes' may be transformed into 'ordered multiplicities' (Foucault, 1977: 148).

Traditional analysis of the partitioning of the workforce has focused on the relative advantages and disadvantages for the employer and the employee. Internal labour markets, for example, are typically examined according to the advantages for employees in security of employment and privileged access to promotion; and whether or not they enhance collective bargaining power. For employers, reference is made to the advantages of securing a stable skilled workforce and easier on-the-job training; skill specificity and productivity maximization; or securing labour control, appropriation of skill and acquiring a return on investment. Debate centres around whether partitions reflect 'objective' labour market characteristics such as skill; the requirements of what might be termed 'hard technology' or the physical aspects of production; or whether the motivation is division and control of the workforce. Focus, in other words, has been on the 'why' of practices and posed in terms of the imperative of control or motivation through management, and concerns with efficiency or control. There has been a neglect, however, of the 'soft' technology of personnel. Where the latter has been considered it has been interpreted as the final registration, recording or enforcement of the outcomes of these divisions. In the remainder of this chapter, I consider the art of distribution as an analytical device, with definite material effects, for capturing a workforce within disciplinary systems. In doing so, I argue that personnel practices do not simply reflect self-evident analytical divisions within a workforce: they actively create them. They construct rational classifications and an ordered succession of individuals, which serve to make a population more known and manageable. To understand how this is achieved, it is necessary to examine two principal technologies: taxinomia and mathesis, which together provide the basis for producing a disciplinary matrix or grid by which a workforce is managed.

Taxinomia, Mathesis and Disciplinary Matrix

The terms taxinomia and mathesis, which I shall shortly explain, derive from one of Foucault's earlier works, *The Order of Things* (1970), which analyses how knowledge is constituted. Taxinomia and mathesis formed the foundation of knowledge of the classical episteme[6] in which there was a belief that knowledge about the 'nature' of things stemmed from means of comparison. This approach to knowledge attempted to provide an exhaustive census of all elements constituting the envisaged whole and was based on the techniques of classification and tabulation. The drawing up of tables was one of the great problems of scientific, political and economic technology of the eighteenth century. Foucault identifies their elaboration as a technique for ordering human multiplicities, allied to the population growth of the seventeenth and eighteenth centuries, which represented a change of a quantitative dimension in the scale of the population to be supervised. For example, problems were faced by the military in its composition of the register of the armed forces, and the hospitals with the distribution of patients as well as the classification of disease.[7] The purpose of this order is amplification. It is designed to increase the utility of individuals, to enhance production, be this of health through treated patients, skills through educated pupils, or economic production. It is achieved through organizing: clearing up confusion and establishing calculated distributions, and increasing the particular utility of each element of a multiplicity.

Classification and tabulation operate through the process of comparison. Generally there are two systems of comparison: the creation of an order through a taxonomy, a sequence of descriptive language (taxinomia); or the establishment of an order through measurement (mathesis). A mathesis is a numerical order, a quantitative taxinomia, where the relation between things is conceived of as one of order, or degree, and measurement. (The latter provides the basis for the mathematization of empirical knowledge.) Foucault (1977: 148) writes: 'It was a question of organizing the multiple, of providing oneself with an instrument to cover it and to master it; it was a question of imposing upon it an "order".' Taxinomia and mathesis are mechanisms for the arrangement and ordering of entities, including human beings. They are disciplinary technologies – at once both a technique of power and a procedure of knowledge – which provide an order that simultaneously circumscribes a whole, and specifies its component parts.

These mechanisms have interesting effects. Comparison requires that entities are analysed according to a common unit which provides the basis for equivalences to be identified. Through a common denominator, things are arranged serially, they appear in order. 'Comparison by means of order is a simple act which enables us to pass from one term to another, then to a third, etc. by means of an absolutely uninterrupted movement' (Foucault, 1970: 53). (Arithmetical values of a mathesis can always be arranged according to a series.) It opens the way to successive identities and differences. One entity is sufficiently like another to be compared to it, but sufficiently different to be placed in a category different from it: although similar it is not the same. In arranging an order there is simultaneously proximity and distance, adjacency and separateness. As Foucault notes, 'Taxinomia implies a continuum of things . . . and a certain power of the imagination that *renders apparent what is not*, but makes possible by this very fact, the revelation of that continuity' (1970: 72, emphasis added).

Classification through taxinomia and mathesis is also a process of standardization, that is, the imposition of a degree of homogenization for the purpose of 'taming the social meaning of categories' (Meyer, 1986: 347). A taxonomy, which has the function of characterizing and constituting classes, necessarily reduces individual differences. In doing so it delimits the totality of a field of knowledge. It arbitrarily ignores all differences and identities not related to the selected denominator. The selection of a common unit reduces a whole arena of that which is experienced or known to a system of variables, often but not always, restricted to dimensions of the apparent or visible. These variables are designated either in numerical terms or 'by a perfectly clear and always finite description' (Foucault, 1970: 136). The common unit is therefore dependent on the ease of re-presentation, of its being transcribed into language, or represented in numerical form. Appearances, or the visible, constitute a domain of knowledge. As an approach to knowledge 'it constitutes a whole domain of empiricity as at the same time describable and orderable' (Foucault, 1970: 158). The process of establishing a taxinomia or mathesis, creating an order, also works to deny any hidden or internal or organic relations between entities. The necessity of designation necessarily simplifies, indeed oversimplifies, and although subdivisions may be developed, this 'secondary' language is based upon the 'primary'. There is also a transmutation which often occurs in the imposition of order. 'A multiplicity of units can . . . be arranged according to an order such that the difficulty, which previously lay in the knowing of measurement, comes finally to depend solely on the consideration of order' (Foucault,

1970: 54). The practice and application of a mathesis of taxinomia, in other words, is often reduced to validity of the particular order which has been established, rather than the relevance or validity of its common denominator.

Both taxinomia and mathesis facilitate management or governance. They provide for the arrangement of identities and differences into ordered tables and create a grid, a configuration of knowledge, which may be placed over a domain. There is an analytical distribution of identities and differences which separate and unite things. They state the conditions under which it is possible to know things. Both procedures define a relation, stating what is to be associated with what. They allow things to be placed in relation to one another, establishing relations of equality and difference. They constitute systems of recording, classifying, and measuring, and in doing so they provide the basis for the operation of governmentality. Whilst Foucault elaborates on the nature of knowledge established through taxinomia and mathesis in *The Order of Things*, their significance as disciplinary mechanisms which provide the basis of governance awaits elaboration in his later work, most notably, *Discipline and Punish* and the essays on governmentality (Foucault, 1977, 1979). This work by Foucault examines the shift from knowledge based on 'order' and 'tabulation' to a disciplinary matrix which allows for the individual to be seen in relation to the whole.

There is necessarily an evaluative dimension to the table, a process of attribution and judgement, and it is this which provides the true disciplinary function. Evaluation results from measurement in relation to the denominator (less than, more than, etc.) and suggests the possibility of establishing a *progressive* series. The discipline of taxinomia and mathesis may be used to define hierarchical networks. It is the operation of the latter dimension which distinguishes a taxonomy from a disciplinary table, or matrix. Whilst the taxonomy provides a 'table of order', a disciplinary matrix is a hierarchical organization or an evaluative matrix which enables the individual entity to be linked to the whole. (In essence, it is the distinction to be drawn between nominal and ordinal scales.) Lists in themselves are an ordering, and a taxinomia states the assumed relationship between things; a disciplinary matrix or disciplinary function, however, is only achieved when the individual is linked to the population. The latter provides the means through which both the object or individual and its population may be assessed and directed. It facilitates the ordering of individuals:

> in the form of the disciplinary distribution . . . the table has the function of treating multiplicity itself, distributing it and deriving from it as many effects as possible. Whereas natural taxonomy is situated on the axis that links character and category, disciplinary tactics is situated on the axis that links the singular and the multiple. It allows both the characterization of the individual as

individual and the ordering of a given multiplicity. It is the first condition for the control and use of an ensemble of distinct elements: the base for a microphysics of what might be called a 'cellular' power. (Foucault, 1977: 149)

The role of taxinomia and mathesis and their conjunction in a disciplinary matrix or grid form the core of HRM, offering a comprehensive and exhaustive mechanism for the analytical ordering of a population and its direction or management.

Taxinomia and Mathesis in HRM

Several personnel techniques operate to classify and order individuals hierarchically: job classifications, job ladders, skills inventories, performance appraisal systems, assessments and evaluation methods. All are arrangements for ranking which facilitate an ordering of individuals on a scalar or serial grid. Classification schemes are often presented as techniques to analyse labour, reflective of a naturally occurring division or ordering of ability, skill, and aptitude, etc. Taxinomia and mathesis, however, are very much disciplinary techniques, power/knowledge practices which create divisions. They proceed primarily through enhancing the 'calculability' of individuals, as each classificatory or ranking system designates individuals to their own space, making it possible to establish their presence and absence. With the analytical organization of a workforce, it becomes possible to locate individuals more precisely in reference to the whole. It provides the basis for 'knowing' individuals.[8] Two procedures exemplify this process: job evaluation and performance appraisal.

Job Evaluation
Job evaluation attempts to establish systematically the relative importance or relative value of jobs within a specified group or organization. It is a process by which management identifies and categorizes positions, and ranks each job for salary administration purposes. Based on a study of job content (rather than performance of actual job incumbents), it determines the relative value of various forms of work. Job evaluation is based on the premiss of paying for the position, not the person. Whilst job evaluation estimates the relative value of jobs within an organization, performance appraisal focuses specifically on how an employee performs assigned job duties.

Job evaluation is usually discussed as a system of remuneration. I want to analyse it as an example of the practical application of a process of taxinomia and mathesis which forms a disciplinary matrix. Job evaluation helps order the workforce. It poses the basic question, what is the relationship of the individual positions to the multiplicity? What is the basis or common measure through which the equivalence of individual positions may be stated or decided? Job evaluation is an example of ranking, an extension of power/knowledge practices which have the effect of organizing a workforce in detail. Through a systematic ranking procedure, it provides the analytical organization of a workforce. A process of comparison and the development of taxinomia and mathesis creates a disciplinary matrix or grid which allows individual places to be linked to the whole. In addition to allowing for jobs to be compared within the organization to determine their relative worth, it also allows comparison outside an organization to determine their 'market value'. Thus not only is the individual position related to the population of positions within the organization, it may also be captured within a wider matrix of positions.

Although the overall aim of job evaluation is to establish a matrix of the value of jobs to the organization, it actually measures job content not job worth, that is, it provides a grading based on the 'size' of jobs not their financial equivalence. Only in its later stages does job evaluation attempt to define an overall job-worth hierarchy by relating job size to pay. The criteria to be used for movement within a job grade, however, whether further ranking is based on seniority or merit or performance criteria is dependent on the pay policy in operation. Pay strategies also influence the relative weights attached to market surveys versus job evaluation information in formulating estimates of 'worth'.

There are two basic job evaluation systems: non-analytic methods (ranking and classification); and analytic methods (factor comparison and points method). These systems vary according to whether the whole job or its specific components are to be evaluated; whether they are measured against a standard or against each other. Non-analytical job evaluation schemes compare whole jobs against each other to provide a hierarchy on some assessment of value or job content. Whole-job ranking ranks jobs from highest to lowest with respect to overall job value. Classification ranks according to levels of skill and responsibilities. These job evaluation systems are often referred to as qualitative job evaluation systems and have a number of limitations such as a lack of clearly defined and objective criteria for comparison of jobs, and an enormous amount of comparisons between jobs to be made. Analytic evaluation schemes subdivide, or further partition, 'jobs', using subfactors derived from job analysis (see Chapter 3) which are weighted on quantitative ratings. In factor comparison and points method, the content of jobs are broken into factors and jobs are evaluated according to the degree to which they possess each factor, with each job scored against a series of predetermined factors of job value, hence their being labelled quantitative job evaluation methods. In other words, their functioning depends on a taxonomy of job content, which is then translated into a numerical equivalent or mathesis. The final stage in this process lies in equating a mathesis with a financial equivalent determined through a salary scale.

The most common job evaluation system in both the US and UK is that of points rating. It is considered to be more objective than ranking or classification systems because of its identification of independent, measurable job requirements, despite groups using non-analytical methods showing a high degree of consistency in their rankings or classifications (Scheele et al., 1988). The point factor method involves several steps: a description of the job; choosing compensable factors; rating jobs on these factors; giving weights, or assigning proportional value to the factors to get the total points for each job; using points to set pay, which may be based on internal values or external survey data. In this sense, job evaluation epitomizes the development of a taxinomia and a mathesis, an example of how numerical value is placed on definitions.

The common denominators which form the basis of taxinomia formed by job evaluation are known as 'compensable factors'. These provide the expression of a value system against which jobs are to be assessed. Table 2.1 provides a list of potential compensable factors. Their choice is determined by organizational objectives, those factors the 'organization' values and wishes to reward. It should be noted, however, that these are usually all factors which delineate hierarchy, thereby faithfully reproducing hierarchical structures. There have been attempts to limit the number of compensable factors, as, for example, to reduce the measure of jobs to the time taken for their completion, or to make them commensurable with responsibility (Jacques, 1979). The latter takes the measure of responsibility to be decision-making. Jobs are then placed into decision bands which are further subdivided into grades. Productivity 'may be looked upon as the increase in the number of skilled decisions made by an employee per hour' (Paterson, 1981: 91).

Based on job documentation, interviews, observations and discussions, or through committees or scored questionnaires, jobs are analysed to identify information relevant to the criteria which have been identified. Each job's relative value is determined by the total points assigned to it, thus producing a hierarchy of jobs which are then allotted to grades. The process is essentially that of assigning quantitative factor points to a job description – a mathesis. In this way individuals are paid according to how their job contributes to the achievement of organizational objectives. A complication of these systems, however, is that when the points are added up they are unlikely to match the non-analytical 'felt fair' methods of the relative importance of each job, despite the selection of factors which reflect hierarchical systems. It is this which leads to the system of 'weighting factors', essentially to ensure the best fit between profiles and felt fair rank order (Hollway, 1984). Factors are then numerically scaled to produce degrees or gradations. Jobs are thus assessed according to factors, weights and degrees. Decisions on the number of steps in a hierarchy depend on the objectives of the management of individual organizations.

Table 2.1   *Potential compensable factors*

Skill	Effort
Accuracy	Concentration
Analytical	Fatigue
Complexity	Mental effort
Communication	Monotony of work
Decision-making	Physical effort
Dexterity	Pressure
Education required	Stress
Experience required	Visual demand
Initiative required	Volume of work
Interpersonal skills	
Motor skills	
Time required to learn job	
Versatility	

Responsibility	Working conditions
Accountability	Danger
Confidential information	Dirtiness
Contact with others	Disagreeableness of others
Co-ordination	Interruptions
Consequence of errors	Physical environment
Dependability	Out of town travel
Equipment and machinery	Stress
Money	
Policy making	
Quality	
Safety	
Supervision of others	
Supervision received	

Source: Weiner and Gunderson, 1990

Recommendations expressed in practitioner journals warn that too many grades in a salary structure induce the creation of artificial salaries (Richter, 1989), thus giving the impression that there is a 'natural' hierarchy which should be captured by job evaluation systems.

In the pursuit of more 'objective' ranking, some job evaluation schemes are based on ranking within compensable factors. They develop, in other words, a more elaborate taxinomia. This may be seen, for example, in the Hay scheme, one of the most widely known job evaluation schemes. This scheme identifies three factors which are claimed to be components of all jobs – problem solving, know-how and accountability – although the distinctly managerial bias of these factors has been commented on (Hollway, 1984). 'Working conditions' have also been added to the list. 'Know-how' (a compensable factor), the total sum of every kind of knowledge and skill, is classified in terms of managerial skills, human resource skills and practical procedures, with each having further gradations. Practical procedures has eight gradations. 'Managerial skills', which encompasses planning and organizing skills, has five degrees or dimensions, whilst 'human resource skills' or face-to-face skills has three dimensions. These dimensions are then combined to produce a matrix according to how much of each skill is required which is then scored on a further three-dimensional scale. Further dimensions of the taxonomy are also elaborated. Problem solving – the amount and nature of thinking required in a job – has two dimensions: the environment of thinking, that is, its degree of structure; and the challenge of structure, its novelty, complexity, etc. These are further subdivided, in the 'environment' eight gradations are identified, 'challenge' has five. Identification on this matrix results in a percentage score, which constitutes the percentage utilization of 'know-how'. Accountability, being answerable for action and consequences, has three components: freedom to act; magnitude (of decisions) measured in monetary terms; and impact (of decisions). The first dimension has eight gradations; the second, five; and the last, four. Final positions are then determined on a matrix which has three subdivisions in each category. Working conditions is equally subdivided according to physical effort (four gradations); physical environment (four gradations); mental stress (four gradations); and sensory attention (four dimensions). The final scores on each dimension are then compounded into an overall score – numerical scaling produces gradations, a disciplinary mathesis which determines what is to be seen in relation to what.

Although job evaluations are essentially quantitative systems and thus, given the legitimacy accorded to numbers or 'hard' data, have the appearance of fairness or legitimacy, they have been open to a range of criticism. For example, it is said they use too general and very superficial job descriptions; that there is a lack of standardized norms; that there are ambiguous factor definitions in systems using compensable factors; and that they are time consuming. Job evaluation systems have been criticized for potential for discrimination and gender bias (McShane, 1990; Mount and Ellis, 1987). Factors leading to discrimination include the choice of factors used in the job evaluation plan, factor definitions and anchor points, and the weighting of factor-points which favour male dominated roles (Arvey, 1986). Quantitative systems also have their drawbacks such as the lack of clear principles for the selection of items to be weighted; no clear guides on the selection of key jobs; and the lack of clarity about the need for differential weights and how they should be determined. Benchmark jobs may discriminate by being based on past practice. Equally the amount of information provided and the amount of training job analysts receive also influence the nature of the evaluations which are made (Hahn and Dipboye, 1988).

Whilst these criticisms are important they focus on 'technical' aspects of job evaluation, and are informed by its view as a system of remuneration designed to achieve considerations of equity, however defined, or a strategic compensation system. Viewing job evaluation as a disciplinary practice, however, illustrates other concerns. The whole process of job evaluation involves the creation of a series of equivalences, the construction of a matrix within which to locate positions. It is an exercise of power/knowledge often occluded in the way it constructs knowledge and the assumptions which sustain it. It rests upon job analysis and job content data, both presuppose the existence of a 'job' as a bounded set of discrete tasks, identifiable and articulable. Activities become constructed with boundaries, grouped or labelled into jobs. Jobs are then equated to each other through the construct of 'common' compensable factors. This presumes that the requirements of different work-roles of an organized system have a certain minimum similarity which enables them to be represented on a hierarchical continuum, and that differences in nature, type and extent of work being done, may be captured by each 'compensable' factor. It also assumes that there are 'benchmark' jobs to serve as reference points. These are the assumptions which sustain the process of standardization and homogenization. It further assumes that factors which make up the major elements of a job can be stated explicitly, identified clearly and that these factors are present in a finite number of levels. These assumptions will be considered in more detail in Chapter 3. Here it is useful to recall Schumpeter's remarks on the vertical mobility of labour power: 'Are abilities qualitatively different? Are "higher" abilities actually a "higher" form of the same abilities? Is there in fact any difference at all? All these abilities are ranked in some sort of scale, but how are they in reality related to each other?' (quoted in Offe, 1976: 48).

The process of job evaluation rests on a process of 'translation', involving not only the transfer of information for a series of discrete areas to a central decision-making body, but also its framing into specific vocabularies and methods of notation. There is the assumption of a common vocabulary, that each factor has the same meaning for everyone involved in job evaluations. The amount of translation involved is revealed in an IPM survey (Spencer, 1990). Job holders (88 per cent) and their immediate bosses (95 per cent) are almost always involved in providing information about jobs, sometimes aided by a job analyst (35 per cent) or an approved higher level manager (44 per cent). Job information is collected in the form of narrative job descriptions, often involving several stages of drafting and typing. It is therefore difficult to ensure that comparable information is collected about all jobs. The information is then subjected to further interpretation by 'expert' evaluators. Quaid's (1993) analysis of the introduction of a job evaluation system shows how job descriptions had to be rewritten because they did not meet the standards required by consultants. Job descriptions were no longer a process of 'putting down on paper what you do' (Quaid, 1993: 246). The emphasis on writing about a job in a certain way was part of the ritual to establish the belief that the system was rigorous. At the evaluation stage those closest to the job are involved directly by only just over a third of organizations, with most evaluations involving members of the personnel function with other line managers (Spencer, 1990).

Although aimed at evaluating jobs and not the behaviour of incumbents, job evaluation necessarily entails the use of personal judgement, although within formal processes, to describe the relative value of jobs to an organization. This occurs at each stage in the procedure: the description of the job; choosing compensable factors; rating jobs on these factors; giving weights, or assigning proportional value, to the factors to get the total points for each job; using points to set pay, which may be based on internal values or external survey data. Its role as the codification of a series of value judgements becomes lost, however, in an appeal to technicism and objectivity. The language accompanying its discussion is set against the background of presumed objectivity, thus 'sources of measurement errors' result from problems of implementation: the design of the job evaluation 'instrument'; the choice of factors not being sufficiently independent or comprehensive; the choice of degree-level definition being sufficiently inclusive and discriminatory; or the choice of weights. Data formatting and job rating are also sometimes called into question.

Implicit in job evaluation is the assumption that for each job there exists a true value. The notion of a 'correct' or 'accurate' method, as though this was verifiable against an extant measure, absent individual and social values. It is not accurate, however, to assume that any job evaluation method when correctly applied to a series of jobs will result in approximately the same rating classification as that supplied by any other method. The type of system used and their application by different analysts results in different relative worth scores (Madigan and Hills, 1988; Scheele et al., 1988). Different systems result in different ratings and concomitantly different hierarchies (Madigan, 1985; Madigan and Hills, 1988; Madigan and Hoover, 1986). Perhaps this is why personnel directors do not believe in the efficacy of job evaluation techniques for determining job worth or in the ability of personnel specialists in evaluating jobs equitably (Klinger, 1988). McNally and Shimmin (1984) also show how the choice of job evaluation method depends more on the recommendations of personal and business contacts than on a thorough analysis of available techniques and consideration of their relevance to the particular situation.

The essence of job evaluation is that it parades as a rational or just method of organization, founded on the presentation of language as representation, as the faithful reflection of organizational reality. This informs approaches adopted to the job evaluation committee. Divisions necessarily occur in job evaluation committees as factor points and weightings are disputed. Rather than being seen as a participative exercise which confronts directly the contentious issue of internal equity as seen by those who are closest to the daily functioning of jobs, the role of the committee and the disagreements it generates are portrayed as being either dysfunctional or the result of personality clashes (Benson and Hornsby, 1988; Benson and Hornsby, 1991). There is limited or no recognition that one function of job evaluation is to promote agreement and consensus among people by providing them with a common language. Instead, what is recommended, is its further removal from the social sphere with recommendations for the use of computerized systems. Computer aided job evaluation (CAJE) is recommended as an aid to decision making, providing standardized job evaluations and comparisons, giving consistency across functions, and promoting acceptability as computerized systems are equated with objectivity (Dufetel, 1991; Murlis and Pritchard, 1991; O'Neal, 1990). Point-factor evaluation lends itself easily to computerization with its administration based on questionnaire responses. CAJE systems include computer-aided job analysis, computerized data checking, and computerized evaluation. Job analysis questionnaires contain multiple choice or close-end questions which are fed into a computer, and closed-response questionnaires convert job data into a numerical format. The CAJE then scores responses according to how the work is valued, with the proviso that 'data verification is generally conducted by a compensation professional or other job expert' (O'Neal, 1990: 16).

The efficacy of job evaluation in providing a disciplinary matrix of organizations can be seen in the extent of their adoption. Job evaluations were first introduced in the 1920s in Westinghouse corporation which introduced a point-factor job evaluation (Sauer, 1989), and have been widely adopted in the US since. Some estimates are that between 60 per cent and 70 per cent of US firms use point-factor job analysis (Emerson, 1991). There was a movement towards the point-factor method in US public sector jobs in the 1970s away from position classification methods (Craver, 1977), with the introduction of a factor-ranking method to classify the 1.3 million white-collar, non-supervisory jobs in federal government (Epperson, 1975). The move was justified on the grounds that pay systems required a systematic examination of job elements and factors, and that this would therefore be an improvement. In the UK, a review of practitioner journals indicates that articles on job evaluation systems in the private sector begin to appear in the 1970s, coinciding with decentralized bargaining, white-collar union growth, and equal pay and discrimination legislation. Job evaluation techniques were recommended to 'liquefy attitudes, reduce misunderstandings and resolve conflicts in a way that is not resented' (Woods, 1976). High inflation levels and sectional wage disputes led, in management's eyes, to chaotic wage and salary structures, and in these circumstances job evaluation was advocated as a rational and fair system, which could promote a stable series of relationships. Indeed, motives cited for the introduction of job evaluation systems do not cite discrimination legislation but the desire to rationalize an unwieldy pay structure, a wish to overcome problems related to the erosion of differentials, and the desire to underpin a generally equitable pay structure (McNally and Shimmin, 1988; Spencer, 1990). Job evaluation is a process which rationalizes internal pay structures through the introduction of 'rational' company-wide pay scales. Patten (1977: 2) comments that 'its greatest success lies in the fact that it compels management to describe and classify positions'. It could transform, in other words, disorganized multitudes into organized multiplicities. It also allows for management at a distance. The value of its role as an ordered system imposed on a disorganized population is reflected in some calls in the late 1970s for a 'national' job evaluation scheme (Clegg, 1971).

Company level surveys indicated a rapid increase in their adoption in the 1970s and 1980s in the UK (Millward and Stevens, 1986). Between 1980 and 1990, there was also a rise in the number of work-places with schemes, especially in the public sector, private services and the newly privatized nationalized industries. About one quarter of all establishments have formal job evaluation schemes (Millward et al., 1992). About half of these schemes are point rating schemes, with ranking and factor comparisons being the next most popular (21 per cent and 15 per cent respectively). A 1989 survey by the IPM on job evaluation, updating an earlier 1976 survey, indicated that the proportion of new systems covering all job groups has doubled. At the same time there are almost no new systems being introduced for blue-collar or manual groups alone (Spencer, 1990). The extension of salary systems for blue-collar employees and integrated job evaluation schemes, introduced as employers move from the traditional hourly paid systems tied to narrow job duties to self-managed teams and flexible task allocations, also has the advantage of allowing for the population as a whole to be organized under a matrix.

There seems to be some indication of a change in job evaluation systems. As Penner (1983) notes, classification offers direct incentives to make organizations bigger and make jobs and organizations more complicated. Criticisms are made that job evaluation systems reinforce traditional bureaucratic styles of management. They are no longer considered adequate in circumstances where there is concern over productivity and costs. Other criticisms are that job evaluations measure what employees do rather than what they are capable of doing, and are seen to focus employees on moving up a scale, rather than performing effectively in their present job (Cummings, 1987), and are not flexible enough for 'modern' organizations desirous of product and service excellence, and with positions increasingly being defined in terms of the individual who fills them (Emerson,

1991; Lawler, 1986). Nor are they considered adequate given a changing composition of jobs. Point-factor job evaluation is considered inappropriate in high tech and creative work (Lawler, 1986). Work performed by technical and professional specialists such as scientists and computer software engineers are difficult to assess on traditional factors such as supervision and decision-making (Griffiths, 1981), and the view is expressed that job evaluation is more reliable in describing stable jobs involving primarily manual labour (Taber and Peters, 1991). Cross-functional teams also affect the use of traditional job evaluation schemes. The emphasis is on a broadly skilled workforce, reduction in administration, and the desire to pay the individual rather than the position.

As UK and US organizations reduce and simplify organizational structures, highly structured point-factor compensation systems are being replaced by simplified systems, for example, broad banding or salary banding (Jones et al., 1991). A broad band structure classifies jobs into a few wide bands rather than narrowly defined salary ranges. Suggestions are, however, that job evaluation should still be used to organize as a basis of internal equity, but be supplemented with other compensation systems which emphasize other elements, for example, individual productivity bonuses or pay-for-performance and profit sharing (Allen, 1990). This allows organizations to pay for individual skills, contribution and competencies rather than determine compensation through traditional job based evaluation (Murlis and Fitt, 1991). Even so there is the development of a matrix, for example, in the recommendation that organizations use an analytical approach which defines a range of skill factor requirements for the breadth of work involved. The definition of different levels for each factor produces a skills matrix for assessing individuals and mapping individual career paths (Murlis and Fitt, 1991).

There is some evidence in the UK that the function of job evaluation is changing from the industrial relations emphasis which heralded its introduction. There is now far less emphasis on traditional collective uses, revolving around formalized industrial relations and group pressure, and much more attention to the explanation of relativities across different categories of jobs. The use of job evaluation in the late 1980s and 1990s is as the basis of performance-related pay systems and as a source of management information systems in its own right (Spencer, 1990). Whilst there may be a change in the nature of compensation systems, that is, pay is no longer directly related to the position, with the desire to locate the individual more precisely, the overall requirement to locate populations and individuals within populations is still in effect. The matrix is still in place, although its immediate relationship to a financial matrix may have changed. Methods of locating the individual more precisely now come into function. It is for these reasons that job evaluation is presented here not simply as a type of payment system, but more importantly as a system which introduces a cognitive map thus forming the basis of the management and organization of a population.

Performance Appraisal

Performance appraisals are a systematic process of developing performance criteria for a job, and then assessing employees' job performance in relation to these. Designed to 'reinforce or redirect the work actions and results of every employee in the organization' (Cuddy, 1987: 20), they are a method for measuring employee actions against standards of acceptable performance. Performance appraisals are another mechanism through which a workforce may become differentiated through the art of distribution. Again this is effected through a process of ranking.

As the essence of performance appraisal is assessment of performance against defined criteria, it therefore requires the production of knowledge. As Miller and O'Leary (1987: 262) note, however: 'the efficiency of the person in the firm . . . is not something which can be observed with the naked eye. Indeed, one might say, it cannot exist until what is to be regarded as normal or standard has first to be constructed.' The knowledge required in appraisal involves the construction of a system of job factors (performance characteristics), evaluation standards, and performance descriptors.

Traditional appraisals were based on simple taxonomies designed to evaluate individual traits, personal qualities, personality and 'attitude', for example, loyalty, dependability, co-operation, initiative, self-confidence, etc. These were heavily criticized on several grounds, including the reluctance of managers to appraise, a high defensiveness amongst appraisees, and their failure to lead to improvements in performance (McGregor, 1972; Meyer, et al., 1965; Rowe, 1964). Assessment on personal traits, however, does not provide the basis for detailed intervention, the capacity for management is restricted as little change can be evinced in established traits. Received wisdom is now that the appraiser judges the work not the person, with trait-rating being replaced by appraisals which identify and measure some aspect of performance. This, however, introduces the problem of defining and measuring performance, whether this should include for example, skill, knowledge, potential and overall 'worth', etc., and the relative weight which should be attached to behaviour or results. These difficulties sometimes lead to arbitrary divisions between performance and trait-rating, as for example, in some manual employee appraisals which combine elements of activity and personal characteristics, for example, rating on knowledge, quality and quantity of work, initiative, dependability, judgement and relationships (Townley, 1989a). Most appraisals are based on hybrids of trait-rating, behaviour and effectiveness with generally an attempt to anchor the individual to some type of measuring system, be this behaviourally or numerically anchored.

Rating Scales

The basis of most evaluations is defined performance standards attached to a measurement scale. Based on 'subjective' or 'objective' standards, using results/outcomes, or process, appraisals reduce dimensions of the individual to numerical equivalents, a list of subjective performance dimensions (for example, the quality of work, attitude and interpersonal skills, initiative, technical skills, attendance, etc.) are reduced to graphic rating scales on which the employee is rated (for example, rank 1–6). Thus, for example, a performance dimension might be 'leadership ability' which might be graded on a five point scale ranging from well above to well below average (see Table 2.2, Scale 1, for an example). Measurement scales might be accompanied by verbal anchors (adjectival checklists or standard rating scales) which define the scales, (for example, Scale 2). More elaborate definitions may accompany a scale, for example, 'job knowledge' a performance dimension, might be ranked on a five-point scale ranging from 'extremely well informed about all aspects of the job' to 'misinformed or lacks knowledge on important job dimensions' (see Scale 3). Individuals may be classified as being 'outstanding', 'superior', 'satisfactory' or 'average', and 'below average'. Even where the professed purpose of assessment is for developmental purposes, they are not immune from the quantification of results with 'global rating' of performance or composite performance scores. Although checklists may be quite expansive there is evidence to suggest that there is difficulty in assessing employee performance levels when more than three categories are used, generally anything more than poor, average and good. Elaborations on these into unsuccessful, marginal, good, very good, and outstanding tend to be unsuccessful, leading some to suggest that it is easier to classify employees as average, distinguishing only those who are poor or outstanding (Girard, 1988).

Appraisal systems which specifically develop rating scales of performance levels 'anchored' to job related behaviours are Behaviourally Anchored Rating Scales (BARS), and a variant of this, Behaviour Observation Scales (BOS), which list performance-related behaviours. These concentrate on behaviours for achieving performance, rather than results per se, and developed out of the simple rating scales which assess a taxonomy of behaviour. BARS is evaluation against expected job behaviours. In this sense, these are more formalized than ratings against adjective checklists, anchoring scales with behavioural descriptions. The descriptions of behaviour serve as anchor points and are placed beside the scale at varying points, depending on the extent to which they exemplify the dimension under consideration. More specific than generic rating scales, they are based on activities required on the job.

Performance appraisal involves the production of a taxinomia and mathesis, a classification and numerical scale which evaluates individuals. It is

Table 2.2 *Examples of rating scales on quality*

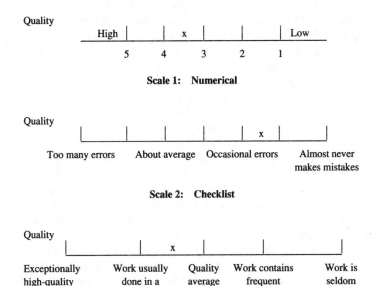

Scale 1:   Numerical

Scale 2:   Checklist

Scale 3:   Verbal anchors

a technology for reducing experience, characteristics and behaviour to linear scales. Complex impressions are calibrated by the use of rating scales. Performance appraisal also provides the basis for dividing practices. Overall performance may be based on generic dimensions, referred to as a global rating, or may be the culmination of various individual dimensions. These individual scores, however, provide the basis of comparisons with others. (Although measures may be absolute, for example, checklists, graphic rating scales, critical incidents, there is still the basis for comparisons to be drawn if there is a common assessment form. The only system which does not allow for this is the essay or narrative evaluation.) A matrix using common denominators of traits or skills allows for the process of distributing the individual within a population. The essence of the matrix is that it allows individuals to be compared to each other, to render them 'known', for their position to be related to the population of which they are a part. In this sense appraisal systems operate to individualize and standardize. The disciplinary aspect of the matrix is secured when appraisals are linked to the ranking process. This may take the form of paired comparisons (individuals compared with each other to provide overall ranking), and forced distributions (specification, for example, that 5 per cent of a population will be well above average, 20 per cent above average, etc.).

These are still engaged in despite their obvious detrimental effects on performance due to low morale, destructive effects on teamwork, etc. (Gabris and Mitchell, 1988; McBriarty, 1988). The advantage of ranking, however, is that it permits comparison across groups and the telescoping of data obtained in different groups (Miner, 1988). Its role in supplying a disciplinary matrix is perhaps another reason why appraisals are recommended as part of best managerial practice, despite a wealth of research data that appraisal reviews rarely achieve what they are designed to; that there is lack of consistency; little relationship between performance reviews and salary increases; a focus on performance of the last few weeks rather than the preceding year; and little follow up. From an elaborate taxinomia detailing performance levels, this is then open to being translated into a mathesis, a numerical ordering. Performance related pay is the final stage of the progress from taxinomia, to mathesis, to the latter being linked to a financial matrix. The overall effect of these systems is the organization of a disciplinary matrix, with, in the case of PRP or merit pay, its final correlation with financial or monetary equivalents.

Whereas job evaluation provides a matrix which differentiates between individual positions, that is, it organizes the spatial arrangement of jobs; performance appraisal provides a matrix which differentiates between individuals both in terms of actions and results. Job evaluation provides the standard or benchmark performance criteria to determine the position of the job within the population as a whole; performance appraisal assesses the improvement in an employee's performance during a given period. In this respect performance appraisal is a further embellishment or elaboration on a matrix which aims to locate more precisely the individual, thereby ensuring effective management of the population. Job evaluation and performance appraisal vertically segment the workforce. These may then be recorded on human resource information systems.

Human Resource Information Systems

Human resource information systems are another example of a personnel practice which acts both as a record of an organizational matrix which allows knowledge of both the population and the individual, and a system which allows further distributions to be calculated. These vary according to the depth of information and the degree of knowledge of the population they can supply. For example, simple, often manual systems, only provide basic population data often associated with payroll information, based on the simple partitioning of groups according to weekly and salaried staff, access to overtime, etc. More sophisticated systems dependent on computerization provide basic personal and employment data, thus allowing for a more specific analysis of the population in terms, for example, of age, sex, service, and educational profiles, or absenteeism and sick leave profiles according to groups. More detailed HRI systems may include information on employment history, individual work experience, training and development history, acquisition of critical skills, performance and potential ratings, again allowing for more complex population matrices to be produced. Other more detailed systems might include information on interests, self-assessment, and job preferences (Burack and Mathys, 1987).

HRI systems provide organizational maps of different scales. Small-scale maps provide only general outlines of the organizational population. Large-scale maps allow elaborate calculations to be derived including both average (the 'norm') and individual assessments in relation to this, for example, group and individual 'output' measures; relative returns on 'investment' with productivity measures analysed in terms of salary, access to training programmes, etc; levels of productivity based on 'output', absenteeism, illness, etc. Elaborate norms and matrices may be produced, where data include information on age, length of service, salary, job history, experience, qualifications, potential, performance and skills. A disciplinary organizational matrix is the result. It is perhaps for this reason that it is this area which is increasing in attention and activity, more so with developments in computer technology (Torrington and Hall, 1987).

Towards a Genealogy
To reiterate, the art of distribution is a method of ordering a population. It knows it in a particular way, making it open to intervention or management. It is reflected in a number of personnel practices. A Foucauldian analysis is concerned with how and with what effects boundaries become imposed, maintained, and breached – it is this which forms the focus of a genealogy.

The extent to which the art of distribution is engaged in varies enormously. A brief comparative sketch indicates a number of factors which would have to be considered as part of a broader genealogy of their use. For example, the larger Japanese companies place a greater emphasis on enclosure than their Western counterparts. Enclosure is secured through practices which include lifetime employment, seniority based payment systems, company based welfare schemes, and enterprise unionisms. A semblance of homogeneity within the enclosure is reflected in the use of company uniforms, and single status.

Dividing practices within organizations, however, may vary greatly. Work by Lincoln et al. (1986), for example, on a survey of American and Japanese manufacturing plants found significant differences in patterns of partitioning, with high occupational and functional differentiation in the former. Although there is a relative lack of occupational or functional differentiation in Japanese organizations there is a high degree of vertical status differentiation, the latter partly achieved through the primary salary system which is based on companies' grading systems based on skills.

The role of economic criteria in influencing the distributions used seems limited. For example, in their examination of labour market arrangements Baron et al. (1986) found only weak support for hypotheses linking internal labour markets (ILMs) to organizational or sectoral imperatives. They conclude that ILMs are heavily influenced by political and institutional forces inside and outside organizations, and suggest that research should be directed towards how ILMs become institutionalized, how and whether they become modified. Again, Baron et al.'s (1986) analysis of ranking through job ladders indicates that they could not be easily ascribed to the imperatives of firm-specific skills. Nor could Baron and Beilby (1986) identify efficiency factors as the cause of one organization structuring a given set of tasks differently from another. Their suggestion is that future research should examine the politics of how jobs come to be defined and how those definitions become institutionalized over time.

In the US and Canada, company practices were influenced by government policies. Job coding in both these countries was given an impetus by the Second World War, when, in the US, a job analysis unit was formed to arrange the coded jobs in a dictionary. Eventually the job analysis unit produced the *Dictionary of Occupational Titles*, a practice which also occurs in Canada. In Canada and in the US, there is a *Classification and Dictionary of Occupations*, giving descriptions of jobs assessed in terms of general educational level required; specific vocational preparation necessary; physical activities of the job; its environmental conditions; 'worker functions' in relation to data, people and things' aptitude factors; interest factors; and temperament factors required in relation to the job. All these are reduced to an accompanying code, thus giving a translation between jobs and their numerical representation. This practice is now used for the basis of national manpower planning predictions and analyses.

Ranking is also an important element of US employment practices, although it is achieved through different practices. There is a higher extent of job evaluation coverage than in for example the UK, Sweden and France, although job evaluation is increasing in the UK. French corporations, on the other hand, do not use job evaluation schemes to measure, compare and evaluate jobs (Craggs, 1990). The reasons for this difference in practice varies. Historically, management at Westinghouse Electric USA, where the first scheme was developed, was a strong advocate of Taylorism, time study and systematic job analysis. Technical agreements with Germany and Japan in this period influenced the spread of these management methods (Littler and Salaman, 1985). One factor, however, is the impact of the State through legislation designed to protect rights or judicial decisions on practices. Quaid (1993) notes how job evaluation has received the stamp of respectability from Parliament in both the UK and Canada, where it has been identified as an important component of

Employment Equity legislation. Although in the UK industrial tribunals have consistently refused to specify one type of evaluation as being more acceptable than another, in the US the courts have held that the position analysis questionnaire (PAQ) provides equitable standards for job evaluation and classification (Jeanneret, 1980). Judicial decisions rendered in relation to one area (employment equity) have implications for rankings which result. PAQ distributes according to certain criteria and would be different in outcome from other evaluations using different criteria. In the former Soviet Union, for example, greater emphasis was placed on working conditions in job evaluation (Quaid, 1993).

Ranking is also achieved through the use of performance appraisal systems. In the US, more than 80 per cent of companies surveyed indicated that they had a merit pay system for one or more of their employee groups (McGinty and Hanke, 1989). Another survey of appraisals of non-managerial city employees of 170 US cities indicates that rating scales were the most popular evaluation technique (England and Parle, 1987). In the UK, the Treasury wishes to extend performance related pay, at present covering 5 per cent of civil servants, to the whole of the civil service. Within such a system, civil servants would be rated according to their present five grades. Those rated in the top two grades would receive more than the standard increment, whilst those in the lowest grade would receive no increment – thus further extending the disciplinary effect through introducing a process of ranking.

The use of HRIS is influenced by access to and the degree of computerization. Evidence in the UK shows that computerization is limited (Hall and Torrington, 1986). In the US, however, computerization in personnel is far more advanced. Computerized systems are increasingly recommended to personnel practitioners for job evaluation and job analysis (Aho, 1989; Berger, 1986; Crandall, 1989; Ekholm and Subba-Rao, 1989; Kanin-Lovers, 1987). They are 'sold' on the basis of being more 'efficient', sophisticated, accurate in helping to minimize errors in data collection, and responsive to change. They aid 'objective statistical analysis' and the refinement of techniques (Finkelstein and Hatch, 1987; Milkovich et al., 1988), at each stage operating to facilitate further re-presentations. Legislation, however, also impacts practice. The 1991 Civil Rights Act, for example, introduces the concept of 'unintentional discrimination', where the legality of an employer's hiring and promotion decisions based on qualifications is determined by statistical analysis of the impact of the qualifications criteria on race, national origin and sex composition of the workforce selected (Cook, 1992).

Trade union actions may intensify the organization of populations and the individuals within this, as for example, protecting bargaining power and job security through the institutionalization of job demarcations. In the United States and Canada, the right of a union to exclusive representation of an appropriate bargaining unit reinforces vertical divisions within the workforce. This has developed even more strongly, allied to a whole pattern of bumping rights.[9] Equally, unions may resist certain disciplines. In the UK, there was strong opposition to job evaluation from the unions when it was first introduced. They have, however, shifted their positions from it being perceived as a serious threat to collective bargaining, to its now being a more accepted procedure provided that it is not used as the sole criteria for establishing wages or as a substitute for collective bargaining (Ghobadian, 1990; Ghobadian and White, 1988). Unions have been slow to develop positions on performance appraisal, often viewing these as the province of management. In other countries, Canada and the US, for example, unions are specifically prevented by public sector legislation to negotiate over performance appraisal, this being deemed to be within the ambit of managerial discretion.

All these factors illustrate the intersection of a range of influences on specific personnel practices – legislation, judicial decision, military practices, trade union policies, etc. Whilst they may have been introduced for a myriad of different reasons, their effect is to know a population in more depth, thereby enhancing its manageability. These factors indicate the importance of analysing these practices in detail and realizing their connection with different discourses. They also indicate the importance of the dissemination of practices, which become recommended, adopted, copied, and, in some cases, achieve institutionalized status of 'best' practice.

Notes

1 Attempts at sustaining the rigid division between work and non-work, however, is often breached, as is illustrated in Kanter's (1977) work on the 'office wife', Pringle's (1988) work on secretaries and Finch's (1983) illustration of how male careers are enhanced by their wives' social and entertaining skills.

2 Atkinson (1984) differentiates between a core group whose firm specific skills sustain employment conditions of career employees, as distinguished from first and second peripheral and external groups. These latter groups have general skills and are used to supplement the numerical and financial flexibility of the core groups' functional flexibility. Pollert (1987) illustrates both the ambivalence of these terms 'periphery' employees in terms of status, being 'core' in terms of their interaction with customers; and the way in which prescription has taken over from description.

3 Kerr (1977) identifies structureless markets (e.g. Californian harvest market) with few or no rules; communal (e.g. printing, trucking and construction) where employment rules were often organized by unions; and industrial where employment rules were heavily defined in terms of seniority and vertical movement. In his emphasis on institutional rules, Kerr (1977) is much more akin to Foucault than later analyses of partitioning have been.

4 Subordinate primary is distinguished from independent primary on the basis that work tasks are usually repetitive, routinized and subject to machine pacing, whilst still carrying risks of unemployment subordinate primary jobs still retain more protection in this area than those in secondary jobs. Edwards (1979) poses a direct link between control of the labour process and labour markets, with labour market segments being associated with different

types of control systems – simple, technical and bureaucratic.

5 Freedman (1976) identifies fourteen labour markets, including professional, managerial and submanagerial markets.

6 In *The Order of Things* (1970), Foucault traces what he identifies as different epistemes which underlay approaches to knowledge. He argues that there have been three transformations, from the Renaissance where knowledge of an entity advanced through the identification of resemblances; to the Classical episteme which was founded on representation; to the Modern in which the basis of knowledge is in relation to the transcendental subject. Taxinomia and mathesis are approaches to knowledge which typify the Classical episteme which saw the emergence of science and the scientific method.

7 The compilation of lists typified the work of Newton and Darwin, both of whom constructed elaborate lists as part of their daily lives. Bentham, as a social scientist, also kept elaborate lists and advocated this as an approach to social organization. For example, he proposed the codification (a term he invented) of legal decisions to form a Pannomian, in order to identify 'species' of offences (Dinwiddy, 1989).

8 Techniques for 'knowing' individuals and the criteria used in their organization are considered in Chapters 4 and 5.

9 'Bumping rights' are the exercise of seniority rights by workers to displace less senior union employees when business conditions require temporary layoffs or redundancies.

3

Control of Activity

HRM practices define the nature of work, organize the spatial and temporal dimensions of the labour process, and control the degree of effort required from the worker. These issues have tended to be analysed from the perspective of 'hard' technology – the tools and equipment of the production system, to the neglect of the 'software' of HRM. This chapter remedies this neglect.

For work to be manageable it must be known or rendered 'visible'. The dimensions of activity have to be named and inscribed. This is done by transcribing activity into a standardized and manageable format or taxinomia (as we have seen in Chapter 2). This requires that 'the labour process [be] articulated, on the one hand, according to its stages and elementary operations, and on the other hand, according to the individuals, the particular bodies, that [carry] it out' (Foucault, 1977: 145). Once dimensions of activity are known, they must be allied with time. Only then is it possible to specify how activities should be co-ordinated. This chapter examines the role of HRM in this detailed codification and enumeration of time, space and movement that organizes individual workers into a collective power or productive force (Sayer, 1987).

Inscribing Activity

The first stage in controlling work is to translate that activity into words by describing and analysing the 'job'. Job descriptions create an independent entity: the 'job'. They demarcate a set of activities from one another, establishing boundaries, however informally, around certain types of activities which then become further subdivided into, for example, job tasks and job dimensions. In doing so, they considerably narrow the meaning of 'jobs'. Originally this signified what was involved in work from the commencement of employment to its end, hence the reference to 'jobs of work' (*Oxford English Dictionary*). A job description is a process of translation, from a series of events to their depiction in adjectival phrases and 'descriptors'. Rodger's (1983) example of a head printer's job description illustrates what this involves. Journalists have instructions to deliver 'copy' for the following day's paper to his desk at varying times between 6pm and 9pm. Invariably the copy arrives two to three hours late and still has to be vetted by the legal department. The various actions associated with trying to receive copy on time are translated by the job description as 'to liaise with the editorial department'. Similarly, 'to supervise the work of compositors' involves nightly negotiations on a page-by-page basis of compositor's work as the paper awaits printing. We can see from this that, even in a job which is apparently more observable than others, there are severe problems in the process of inscription.

Job descriptions create 'jobs' in the sense that they designate job titles, the purpose of the job and its duties, essential functions and responsibilities, the identification of behavioural dimensions required to perform the activity successfully, technical knowledge, skills, physical abilities and other requirements which are necessary. They may also include a reference to job 'outputs', with some recommendations that descriptions include a set of measurements of how results associated with each major activity can be determined. One type of job description, for example, is the 'job effectiveness' description which describes a job in terms of output. It consists of a list of specific outputs expected for the position; measurement criteria for each output; and a statement of the authority of the position. It is the nucleus for an elaborate matrix as this then feeds into management information systems, appraisals, budgets, job specification, job evaluation, and compensation (Reddin, 1989). Advocated to enhance planning, selection, training, compensation and appraisal decisions, job descriptions form the basis through which the control of activity may become established.

Job Analysis

'Best practice' now dictates that job analysis is the prerequisite for a serviceable job description, although job descriptions functioned as a system of articulating activity before detailed job analyses came into prominence.[1] Job analysis is the systematic process of collecting data and making judgements about the nature of a specific job. It is the attempt to identify demanding tasks and the most important qualities needed for a job's completion, to access and articulate the individual's 'mental map' of the job (Smith, 1980). It reduces to words the things that people do at work.[2] It inscribes the activities of workers to create a visibility. However, as Hollway (1991) notes, identification of task functions has implications for the individual and leads to their gradation. It changes the focus from workers en masse to workers as individuals.

In job analysis, jobs are broken down into elements according to formalized procedures for data collection, analysis and synthesis. The first large scale job analysis was probably conducted by Denis Diderot the encyclopaedist. In 1747, Diderot was asked to undertake a French translation of Chamber's encyclopedia. To Diderot, Chamber's material, particularly in the trades, arts and crafts, seemed incomplete and lacking in unified purpose. After much consideration, he proposed a new investigation of job operations which until then had been unreported and considered to be trade secrets jealously guarded from rivals.[3]

The term first appeared in managerial literature very early in the twentieth century, reflecting the influence of Taylorism. In 1916, F.W. Taylor referred to work analysis as the first of four 'great principles' of scientific management in which 'traditional knowledge', that is, in the heads of workmen, would be recorded, tabulated and reduced to rules and laws and, if possible, mathematical formulae. This would also facilitate 'scientific' employee selection and training and employee motivation, through the use of both intrinsic and extrinsic rewards and job redesign. Under Taylor:

> Work study would define the best way to carry out each task; selection would assign the appropriate man for each job; training would inculcate the discipline of following methods laid down; scientific delineation of a fair day's work would allocate rewards to tasks to minimize dispute and maximize effort. The whole would be enforced by rigorous management of the minutiae of the workplace. (Rose, 1990: 57)

One of the principal concerns of Taylor was the importance of placing order on what was viewed as a confused mass. In this sense, Taylorism was part of a wider programme aimed at using scientific knowledge to enhance efficiency. It placed great emphasis on standardization. It did this 'by constructing norms and standards that accorded a visibility to previously obscure and unimportant aspects of the activities of persons, and by calibrating and governing these minutiae of existence in accordance with these norms' (Rose, 1990: 59). The ideas for the organization of production along these lines existed a lot earlier than Taylor, representing part of the classical episteme in an approach to knowledge and the practice of disciplines in a range of different arenas. In this sense, Taylorism represents an extension of the disciplines. It is the synthesis of science and administration based upon the classification and evaluation of activities and individuals. Taylor and Gilbreth began their study of jobs by focusing on tasks and analysing worker movements minutely. Work measurement and job fragmentation thus formed the basis for job analysis.[4] It was the attempt to produce a code which would control the acts of individuals.

Work study was introduced in the UK in the 1930s through the American Bedaux system. This formed the basis of payment by results systems prior to the Second World War, and was heavily promoted by the consulting firm of Urwick Orr. By 1959, there was a standard glossary of terms to be used in the area (Littler and Salaman, 1985). Some of the more comprehensive attempts at job analysis which developed later, however, were prompted by the work redesign movement of the 1970s. Hackman and Oldham, who devised the job diagnostic survey, identified one of the main problems in job redesign as being 'the inability *to measure, and therefore understand*, what happens when jobs are changed' (1975: 159 emphasis added). Although principally designed to assess factors which may be broadly described as affecting the quality of work, JDS was the development of a measurement tool.

Traditionally, job analyses involved narrative presentations. Despite the high user acceptability of the latter, they do not provide the form of information which lends itself readily to co-ordinated management, lacking as they do a comparable form. As a result, narrative job analyses have tended to be replaced by taxonomies (Gael, 1988), a descriptive ordering of activity, which, in some cases, might even be elaborated into a form of mathesis. Creating an inventory of activity necessarily requires that some form of taxonomic system is developed. However, the vocabulary chosen determines how language is to be used to record observations. A variety of different taxonomies have been devised to aid analysis: critical incidents technique (Flanagan, 1954); position analysis questionnaire (PAQ) (McCormick et al., 1972); functional job analysis (Fine and Wiley, 1971); task inventory – CODAP (Gael, 1988); job element method (Gael, 1988); ability requirements scales (Fleishman, 1975); threshold traits analysis (Lopez, et al., 1981).[5] These vary according to the extent to which they focus on the task (work characteristics, tasks and behaviour needed to produce an output or service); or take worker characteristics as their focus (knowledge, skills, ability, aptitudes and abilities of individuals necessary to perform job tasks and behaviours). Each system, however, results in differing job clusters, leading to different conclusions concerning job similarities (Cornelius et al., 1979).

Any taxinomia or measuring device is necessarily based on an underlying theory of what is important. Some taxonomies are relatively simple. The threshold traits analysis is a trait oriented approach to job analysis, based on a checklist of thirty-three a priori traits which include mental, physical, learned and motivational aspects of work. The analysis is designed to identify relevant traits, their levels and weights in relation to overall job performance (Lopez et al., 1981). Functional job analysis assumes not only that all jobs involve a relationship with data, people and things, but that these can be arranged hierarchically according to degrees of complexity. Activities are created and serially ordered, the activity of 'mentoring', for example, is deemed to be more complex than that of 'serving' (see Table 3.1).

Other taxinomia are more complex. For example, the position analysis questionnaire attempts to standardize a basic list of actions and behaviours that are common to all jobs, and is recommended to analyse any job or position. It has six subdivisions: the input of tasks; mental processes involved; relations with other people; the job context; manual activities and other job characteristics. These sections are then further subdivided. Manual activities, for example, is categorized in terms of: setting up or

Table 3.1   *Functional job analysis*

Data	People	Things
1. Comparing	1. Taking instructions – helping, serving	1. Handling, feeding, tending
2. Copying		
3. Computing/compiling	2. Exchanging information	2. Manipulating,operating– controlling, driving– controlling, starting-up
4. Analysing	3. Coaching, persuading, diverting	
5. Co-ordinating/innovating		
6. Synthesizing	4. Consulting, instructing, treating	3. Precision working, setting up, operating– controlling II
	5. Supervising	
	6. Negotiating	
	7. Mentoring	

adjusting material; manually modifying material; assembling or disassembling. Oral communications make reference to: advising; negotiating; persuading; instructing; interviewing; routine information exchange; nonroutine information exchange and public speaking. This system also includes estimates of time spent on various tasks, an analysis of the relative importance of each duty and the learning time taken for each task. These are ranked according to importance to the job varying on a five point scale from minor to extreme. On the basis of responses it groups items into factors and into families (Jeanneret, 1980), thus providing the basis for the hierarchical ordering or ranking of positions. All these techniques, however, elaborate the construct 'job' through the concept of job skills.

Other analyses introduce numerical components into analysis. Job task analysis (JTA), for example, involves a detailed analysis of each job task performed by employees, and includes reference to average time requirements for each component, as well as measures of its successful completion (Huettner, 1988). Quantification is introduced as dimensions of knowledge, skills and abilities are measured, or are represented numerically, in terms of their degree of importance and the prior experience required (Aho, 1989). From the original taxonomies, designed to aid clarification in description, there are the serial arrangements of elements giving the basis for comparison between positions – the basis for a mathesis becomes established.[6]

There are also recommendations that job analysis may be computerized (Aho, 1989). Jobs are separated into detailed functional components which then provide the basis of a questionnaire for employees to complete. Quantitative job analyses (QJA) – hierarchical cluster analyses, non-metric multidimensional scaling, canonical correlation, and univariate repeated measures – are offered as a means of reducing errors and limiting the reliance on the expert (Harvey, 1986). The core of most QJAs is a task inventory, essentially a structured questionnaire in which work and worker attitudes are listed. Such systems are 'more systematic, [rely] on computers for analysis and [are] less subject to error than conventional job analysis' (Milkovich et al., 1988). British Shipbuilders in the UK, for example, introduced an 'expert system' based on a computerized database, established through listing over two hundred possible dimensions of jobs. From this, all possible attributes of an individual required to perform each of the dimensions at the required level were identified (Green, 1987).

Job analysis proceeds from a number of assumptions. Its essence is that it gives a 'non-individualized impersonal definition' of the task. It is to be independent of the individual who performs it and must appear objective. Obtaining the 'requisite' information, however, inevitably involves observing or interviewing the job holder. Methods or techniques of accessing job information include interview and questionnaire, identification of critical behavioural incidents, a diary or log of activities, activity sampling, written records and training manuals, observation and work factor checklists or inventories. The type of methods used depends on the type of analysis being undertaken. Critical incident method requires substantial involvement by supervisors. The supervisor records in a specific format the behaviours of job incumbents that significantly contribute or detract from the accomplishment of organization or work unit goals. Work sampling typically involves observation by a trained job analyst, although incumbents have been used to record samples of their own job behaviour. In analysing managerial jobs, for example, managers may carry electronic beepers which sound at preset intervals during the day, when sounded individuals record the behaviour they are engaged in at that moment. In the interview approach, individuals are interviewed by one or more analysts asking incumbents, supervisors and occasionally subordinates similar questions about the job under analysis.

It is interesting to note that those involved in job analysis usually include the incumbent, first level supervisors, higher level supervisors, job analysts, technical experts, but rarely those in subordinate positions. (Munsterberg, an early pioneer of job analysis, believed that managers and supervisors were the appropriate source of job requirements information (Hollway, 1991).) An implicit hierarchy of knowledge is thus established. The technicist aspect of these technologies promotes the assumption that there is, if not a 'correct' interpretation of the world of work, then certain interpretations, in particular the analyst's, have greater credibility than others, most notably those who do the work. The need for an independent expert is also a function of the method of analysis. Even with a relatively simple taxonomy the process of 'extracting' information requires the services of a specialist job analyst who can help workers 'elicit' facts about a job, many features of which are tacit and taken for granted. In more complicated analyses their presence is mandatory. As Hollway comments

(1984: 42), 'it is as if what people know about their jobs . . . is taken away from them in the form of a job analysis. It is compared, scored, weighted, computerized and given back to them as objective and factual.'

Behind this is the view of the neutral observer or expert, who may remove the bias of self-reports and who offers 'objective', neutral, observation[7] (all the while trying not to make observation intrude upon the action undertaken). The advantages of the latter are held to be 'real time data', that is, it may be obtained as the work is being done rather than being retrospective; it is 'independent'; and more than one person can do it. Other justifications make reference to the 'expertise' of independent analysers, especially where employees are of a low educational level (Hackman and Oldham, 1975). There is, in all this, the easy slide into analysis being conceived of as revealing the natural, as a way to analyse 'reality', rather than the decision of an already 'encoded' eye (Foucault, 1970: xx). The premiss of job analysis is the existence of an extant 'job', having a definite and independent existence, which can be encapsulated by a sanctioned vocabulary.

Within organizations interpretations of categorizations inevitably reflect different perceptions. Employees and supervisors differ in how they view work, the distribution of time amongst tasks and the difficulties of tasks performed; supervisors and subordinates attach different meanings to work dimensions and possibly organize work differently. Equally, amongst the 'experts' there is disagreement, different 'subject matter experts' produce different job analysis outcomes. Cornelius et al. (1979) cite one study where, for 16 per cent of the tasks, supervisor and subordinates disagreed on whether or not a particular task was even performed as part of the job. Even where they did agree that the task was part of the job they disagreed considerably on the level of skill required to perform the task. In another study, incumbents and supervisors/analysts disagreed about whether certain abilities and other personal attributes were necessary for job performance. Older and less educated individuals tend to describe their work as less important and less complex; years in education rather than years on the job are more likely to produce comprehensive job analysis data. Analysts perceive and recall differential information; emphasize different things when seeking job information; the preselection of task inventories used in job analysis purposes have different emphases; and different information is generated about jobs by incumbents according to sex, age, and level of education.

Training is usually discussed in terms of its ability to improve the ability of an observer to discriminate among constructs, conveniently denying the crucial role that training plays in securing standardized observation. 'Observers can be trained in such a way that they will agree with each other and ratings on a priori scales will be consistent' (Jenkins and Lawler, 1981: 120). In other words, social agreement (training) on what the constructs 'mean', in terms of what they apply to, will ensure (be reflected in) consistency of approach. The practice of job analysis continually belies the personal and highly social nature of knowledge formation, for all its reference to an objective personnel technology. As Foucault (1970: xx) notes, 'there is no similitude and no distinction even for the wholly untrained perception that is not the result of the precise operation and of the application of a preliminary criterion'.

Job analysis privileges a particular approach to knowledge, one which favours the visible and privileges the judgement of the independent observer. The dangers of this, however, were recognized by Munsterberg, the 'father' of industrial psychology:

> we can see the psychological requirements of the particular occupation only in crude outlines. In a case of a well-known typesetting machine, I had the impression that the rapidity of the performance is dependent upon the quickness of the finger reaction, the managers on the other hand have found that the most essential condition for speed in the whole work is the ability to retain a large number of words in memory before they are set. The man who presses the keys rather slowly advances more quickly than another who moves his fingers quickly but must make many pauses to find his place in the manuscript and to provide himself with new words. (quoted in Primoff and Fine, 1988: 17)

There are many assumptions about how to categorize the world of work. The notion of a single scaling of importance of a skill for a task hides alternative interpretations that a single job skill (assuming one may be identified) may be required for a number of tasks, or that one task may require multiple skills. It denies that skill is not extant, but constructed, changing over time.[8] As Dex (1985) and Cockburn (1983) note, the nature of skill, far from being clear and unambiguously defined, is integrally bound up with the sexual division of labour, with certain factors in predominantly female jobs tending to be omitted from analyses. This is especially true of 'natural' female skills of dealing with upset people, dealing with the sick or disabled, and being responsive to the needs of others, as we shall see in Chapter 6 (Arvey, 1986; O'Rourke and Doyel, 1986).

The political dimensions of job analysis, however, are obfuscated, hidden behind a technicist cloak. Issues of hierarchy, power imbalance, socio-political determination of what constitutes activity and work are neglected. Job analysis specifies what constitutes a skill or ability, providing a technical and verbal matrix through which dimensions of organizational activity become known and manageable. Its practice also draws boundaries around the individual. As job requirements are primarily in terms of individual abilities or traits, it determines the unit of analysis as the individual. Its premiss is that of an individualistic conception of work, the description or analysis is of the individual position, denying the socially organized nature of work and the interdependence in the work environment. Its potential as a means of achieving consensus is denied.

Managerial Competencies

Managerial competency is a relatively new term which has replaced 'behaviour' as the key concept in the analysis of management development and training (Boyatzis, 1982). Although developed in the USA during the last twenty years, it reflects earlier attempts to capture the nature of management in taxonomic form. An early 1920s taxonomy, for example, identified management as being explosive, overanxious, obsessive, and self-controlled (cited in Rose, 1981). More recent academic taxonomies include Mintzberg (1973) and Stewart (1967). The appeal to competencies is born out of dissatisfaction with lack of precision which has characterized earlier attempts to classify the rather nebulous character of managerial work. Based on the work of McClelland at Harvard, is an attempt to introduce more 'scientific' methods to its study. In effect, it is job analysis applied to managerial work. In the UK, competency has been adopted for use in management education and development following the Management Charter Initiative. The idea behind the latter is that those involved in developing managers and preparing individuals to work in organizations should sensitize them to the nature of managerial work, developing competencies which will enable them to cope with and manage organizational variables. The appeal to management competencies is the basis of a structured approach to management development which individuals would then be able to use as the basis for individual development planning.

A competency is an observable skill or ability necessary to complete a task successfully. The aim of those supporting its use is systematically to identify critical characteristics which 'cause' or predict superior job performance. This is achieved through establishing 'criterion-related' factors of performance, based on an analysis of successful performance in managerial jobs and then isolating significant or important dimensions. Competency thus denotes dimensions of behaviour which lie behind competent performance. These then form knowledge bases. Proponents believe that it is possible objectively to identify clusters of competencies or sets of behaviour which differentiate a high performer, which are relevant across an entire organization and perhaps between organizations. Dimensions which might be identified include: problem-solving ability; ability to withstand pressure; decision-making ability; job knowledge; creativity and imagination; human skills; planning; organization; communication. The list of competencies, however, becomes very general, for example: self-awareness and self-knowledge; proactivity and vision; learning skills; staying power; interactive skills; team skills; analytical skills (Prideaux and Ford, 1988). For ICI, an organization specific model of competency derived five competency clusters: achievement, thinking, self-management, influencing others, and people management, each consisting of about six individual competencies, which break down into behaviour indicators capable of being observed (Arkin, 1991).

By implication at least, a set of competency measures could be used as the major reference point for a company's entire personnel management strategy. This was the intention of one organization adopting the competency initiative, in which the move towards decentralized management prompted the requirement for better ways of describing managers. Once armed with such a database it was then in a position to manage the careers of key players. From an initial menu of forty competencies the organization now has fifty in six clusters – 'the result is a dictionary of competence'. The goals of this particular programme are that every new employee should begin work with agreed development objectives, and that challenges, pressures and major changes should be described in competency terms (Glaze, 1989). As a practitioner commented:

> A small team of personnel colleagues has sought to inject the language through the arteries of traditional personnel activity, in the conviction that the disciplines of describing and quantifying managers are a prerequisite to more effective use of talent. As these disciplines have been absorbed into the bloodstream of the organization, a consistent understanding of commonly used behavioural statements has developed. (Glaze, 1989)

Making competencies visible provides the potential for a matrix, as, for example, their use in a system of assessment and development. The UK Government Information Service has developed appraisal forms to rate GIS members on competencies (Woodruffe, 1991). Competencies are also being advocated as the basis for payment systems with competency-based salary administration policies, where salary is based on demonstrated competencies within a particular job. Related to this are the development of competency exams. These require employees to demonstrate their understanding of new knowledge and new skills (Smith and Merchant, 1990). In some cases, knowledge bases have been incorporated into software packages. Structured computerized question and answer sessions enable the construction of a job profile, which is then used as the basis of performance evaluations (Rollins, 1991).

As a construction of knowledge, the competency initiative perpetuates a number of assumptions. As an approach to understanding management, it is informed by a mechanical rationale based on the assumption that understanding human performance involves 'taking it apart', analysing its basic constituents and then reassembling it. In this sense, it is an approach to knowledge which emphasizes enumeration and the imposition of a classificatory order. The purpose of the competency initiative is to identify clusters of behaviours that are specific, observable and verifiable and that can be reliably and logically classified together. There is a constitutive role to these technologies. They privilege the visible, the ability to observe behaviour bringing with it the prerequisite to measure it and include it as a dimension of performance. They emphasize cognitive rationality and measurable or verifiable facts, and downgrade those abilities or qualities incapable of direct observation and measurement. This emphasis on 'technical' aspects of management and its consequent neglect of important qualities – creativity, sensitivity and intuition, the 'soft' qualities, which are difficult to measure – has led to attempts to include the latter in competency-based assessment. Despite this attempt to redress the balance, however, there is the danger that the importance of ethics and moral values become lost. The emphasis on the use of 'scientific' methods creates a rather narrow view of managerial behaviour, and provides a relatively partial view of performance (Jacobs, 1989).

Nor is there an acknowledgement that important managerial strengths and weaknesses arise from personal meaning systems, that is, an understanding of individual behaviour from the perspective of what qualities and attributes individuals and colleagues think are important in a particular setting, and how individuals perceive what they are doing. The attempt to standardize norms of behaviour denies that people perform successfully for different reasons, at different times under different sets of circumstances. The need to take more account of the different values and social processes and the difficulty of defining performance, conflicts with the view that managerial performance can and should be defined and measured uniformly. The context specific nature of understanding brings into question the prospect of addressing development needs in a single uniform way. It is this which partially informs the current controversy in the UK around the 'universal competence approach' versus the 'process approach', that is, whether a generic list of competencies may be identified or whether these are context specific to organizations (Hamlin and Stewart, 1990).[9]

There is also a danger that the competency initiative perpetuates the model of formal rationality in its depiction of managerial work and activity. It is a model which practising managers do not identify in their own work experience. For example, there is rejection of the views that managers are self-starting and autonomous; that they know what their jobs really entail; that they know how well they are performing; that they seek information they need; that goals are an effective guide for managerial action; that competition among managers is good for business and for managers; and that formal performance appraisal adequately monitors and guides managerial performance (Longenecker and Gioia, 1991). Issues about the nature of managerial work involve the inevitability of interruptions, the range of possible activities, and the discontinuous nature of the work, differing perspectives of work organizations, 'proficiency for superficiality', and the difficulties involved in delegating (Willis, 1989). It also singularly ignores not only the importance of the political dimension of the job, but also the gender and racial imbalance of most organizational hierarchies and the implications that this has for what gets identified as requisite behaviour.

Control of Effort

Having identified dimensions of activities, the next stage is to co-ordinate and control this activity. This requires that activity be co-ordinated and controlled through time, ideally with a precise specification of how activity is to be achieved within this temporal framework. In essence, what is required is the specification of effort – activity through time.

The Subdivision of Time

A primary technique for controlling activity through time is the timetable. It introduces established rhythms and regular activities to divide up the day. It was first associated with religious orders – 'specialists in time' – and their monasteries. This practice was extended into the daily routines of schools and poor houses. Thompson (1974) has explained the importance of a more detailed partitioning of time in early factory organization and administration, where temporal discipline was further developed and elaborated, by dividing time into quarter hours and minutes. Thompson gives an example of Crowley Iron Works in 1700, with its use of the time-sheet, the time-keeper and a system of fines. The partitioning of time was not important when manufacturing was conducted on domestic or small workshop scale, but it increased in importance under capitalism and was adopted towards the end of the century in early cotton mills.

The timetable expresses the principle of non-idleness, it is 'forbidden to waste time, which was counted by God and paid for by men' (Foucault, 1977: 154). This principle attempts to ensure that time is used efficiently. 'It is a question of constituting totally useful time' (Foucault, 1977: 150). The modern notion of efficiency is premised on a commodified sense of time; time is measured and paid for. Efficiency rests on a quantitative conception of temporality and its equivalent or exchange in activity or production.[10] Time is a scarce resource which has to be maximized: time is money, time is no longer passed but spent. It is a commodity to be traded like any other. The subdivision of time is the organization of social time in terms of economic production and profit, and with it is the attempt to state specifically how an employee's activity through time (effort) is to be organized, used and measured.

The timetable provides a temporal framework for work (Blyton et al., 1989). The 'working day' itself is segmented and work is assigned within discrete time periods – day shift, night shift, split shifts, overtime, and so on – and regulated through the time card and the time clock. There is 'bankable' time in flexi-hour programmes. There is 'billable' time in the accounting and legal professions, where the hour, divided into quarter hours, or tenths, becomes a mechanism of control of the services provided and the time spent with clients. Professional groups which have not worked under the discipline that 'time is money' are also under pressure to prove an adequate return on time; in some cases it being directly incorporated into the employment contract. For example, in the UK under new conditions of employment school teachers contract annually for 1265 hours, 195 days per year of which 190 are dedicated to teaching with a notional thirty-five hour week. The response in some cases has been a withdrawal of goodwill and the work-to-contract, as activities which are not part of the contract are no longer undertaken. In the case of hospital consultants, aspects of work previously covered by salary are now to be separately contracted and paid for (Starkey, 1989).

In both cases, the quantification of work is seen as an attack on the professional status of these employees. In the case of the latter, claiming and justifying overtime payments which are open to administrative scrutiny is construed as the first step towards the quantification of work and the specification of time norms for standard forms of activity. This leads to the erosion of the professional freedom to allocate clinical teaching and research and managerial activities as the individual consultant sees fit. However, the reverse is also true. These practices are not essential, as may be seen in the attempt by hospital doctors to restrict the unregulated voluntarism which at present controls their time, with the demand for a more closed contract with specific limits of hours worked.

These examples illustrate the attempt to introduce discipline through the incorporation of time into the employment contract. There are other mechanisms, however, through which time is used to control or supervise activity. The introduction of time into job evaluation was recommended by Jacques' 'time span of discretion', in which he advocated that job size may be measured by using the significance of time in management. This was advocated for the design of systematic pay structures and flexible organizational structures for managerial roles. Time spans are deemed to change as the level of work changes, and are held by Jacques to be more objective than other measures, applying to all jobs and being a uniform measure for all jobs. 'Time span is measured in concrete terms with every task having a concrete time for being completed' (Jacques, 1979: 126).

The use of time as a measure has been partially adopted and incorporated into compensation policies. For example, an occupational learning difficulty index incorporates time by introducing a measure of the difficulty of work by aggregating workers' evaluations of task learning time. Taking task learning time indexes as measures of occupational difficulty are recommended for inclusion in, for example, job evaluation (Mumford et al., 1987). Time-targeting in compensation systems involves assessing the time taken for a competent employee to become fully proficient in a job (England and Pierson, 1990). The resulting time standard determines how quickly employees at various performance levels should move to and beyond their salary midpoints, and how far above the market rate the company is willing to pay for long-term superior performance. It is recommended that these factors are included in the salary grade structure and the merit matrix (England and Pierson, 1990), to form a complete disciplinary matrix.

The Temporal Elaboration of the Act

Whilst the timetable is the general framework for activity, it does not ensure the continuous application of activity to time. It does not ensure 'quality' time. As Foucault notes: 'time measured and paid must also be a time without impurities or defects; a time of good quality, throughout which the body is constantly applied to its exercise. Precision and application are, with regularity, the fundamental virtues of disciplinary time' (Foucault, 1977: 151). An extension of temporal discipline is secured through what Foucault terms the 'temporal elaboration of the act', a mechanism which breaks down gestures and movements and adjusts the body to temporal imperatives. It constitutes an anatomo-chronological schema of behaviour, whereby: 'The act is broken down into its elements, the position of the body, limbs, articulations is defined; to each movement are assigned a direction, an aptitude, a duration; their order of succession is prescribed. Time penetrates the body and with it all the meticulous controls of power' (Foucault, 1977: 152).

The example Foucault provides is that of the drill of troops, where the elaborate detail of the act of marching is specified in terms of the time to be taken for each movement. From this develops the correlation of body and the gesture – a relation between a gesture and the overall position of the body, thus ensuring its efficiency and speed – 'in the correct use of the body, which makes possible a correct use of time, nothing must remain idle or useless: everything must be called upon to form the support of the act required' (Foucault, 1977: 152). Discipline also defines the relations that the body must have with the object that it manipulates. This requires the specification of the parts of the body to be used, the parts of the object to be manipulated, which are then correlated into a number of gestures to be exercised in succession. All these mechanisms lead to the control of activity through the principle of exhaustive use.[11] The body, in other words, is made susceptible to specified operations. It becomes the basis for useful training.

This body–machine complex at work was achieved initially through constant supervision. Through Taylorism it became incorporated into work organization and technology. For the latter, the control of actions and activity through time – the anatomo-chronological schema of behaviour – has been most readily associated with the study of the physical organization of work and the incorporation of control through technology. This, however, would be to neglect the 'soft' technology of personnel practices which also act to control activity through time.

The control of activity is perhaps most apparent in some training programmes. An example is a training programme based on a manual skills analysis of fish-filleting, which details some of the actions involved: 'hold knife against first and third joints of the fingers. Place upper part of thumb, first joint, against lower blunt edge of knife and the lower part of thumb against upper edge of handle. Do not grasp knife tightly. Do not curl tip of fingers into palm of hand.' Whilst this is being done with the left hand the right hand should 'pickup knife with thumb and first, second, third, and fourth fingers around handle. With sharp edge of blade to right of filleter.' In addition the individual should 'glance ahead for knife position on board' and 'glance ahead for fish position on trough' (Kenney et al., 1981: 80). Efficiency of movement is ensured through a training schema where the act is broken down into its elements, the position of the body and limbs is defined; each movement is assigned a direction and their succession is prescribed. It involves the prescription of how bodies should act; the nature of gestures and co-ordination which should be used; a detailed specification as to how the body should engage with physical objects. Through minute and detailed regulation, disciplines attempt the meticulous control of the body. The individual becomes subject to habits, rules and orders, with the intention that they operate as 'one wishes, and with the techniques, speed and efficiency one determines' (Foucault, 1977: 138).

This application is not restricted to manual tasks, as the following example of an interpersonal skills analysis training illustrates. In this case, training is designed to teach individuals how to handle customer complaints, and involves the detailed articulation of the series of gestures which occur in a social interaction, so that they may be explicitly recognized and incorporated by the trainees.

> Manageress (sic) smiles to make initial welcome contact, manageress makes subjective judgement about type/mood of customer and looks for signals . . . Manageress smiles warmly with direct eye contact . . . watches customer's reactions . . . notes customer's embarrassment by lack of eye contact . . . keeps eye contact with customer, nods when customer makes valid point. Manageress gives customer full attention . . . smiles, offers money back immediately . . . avoids too much eye contact to allow customer to relax. (Kenney et al., 1981: 82)

In this case, 'behaviour and its organized requirements gradually replaced the simple physics of movement' (Foucault, 1977: 156). In some cases, control over activity is supplemented by procedures manuals, a more detailed guide as to how a job is done, elaborating the broad idea of functions given by the job description (Rathie, 1990). For example, McDonald's 700 page training manual, details not only the physical requirements of the task, but also when and how the employee is to interact with the customer.

Control of activity through training creates several problems. It is difficult to transfer training recommendations into work areas with well-established work patterns. Over time, idiosyncrasies develop as individuals become familiar with their work and develop their own methods of achieving it. Control over activity requires that individuals be intermittently reminded of the desired behaviour and degree of effort to be achieved. Performance appraisal is a personnel technology which helps fulfil some of these functions.

Performance Appraisal
Performance appraisal is a systematic process of developing criteria by which to assess employees' job performance. Its purpose is to reinforce or redirect behaviour and performance of employees in the organization. As a method for measuring employee actions against standards of acceptable performance, performance appraisal is perhaps one of the most obvious controls of activity in which organizations engage, especially when used as a basis for improving performance, productivity and efficiency through their use in salary and promotion decisions. Performance measures also introduce the commodification of time, they trace the nature of activity through time and therefore act as the monitoring of time commitments.

Although appraisal of individual traits is now eschewed in favour of evaluating work performance, there are difficulties of defining and measuring performance. For example, whether this should include skill, knowledge, potential and overall 'worth', etc., and the relative weight which should be attached to behaviour or results. Some of these difficulties have resulted in performance appraisal systems which emphasize the results or outcomes of performance, as for example management by objectives.

Management by Objectives
Although identified by French and Drexler (1987), as part of Sloan's management practice at General Motors in the mid-1920s, management by objectives (MBO) is most associated with Peter Drucker. Three aspects characterize MBO systems: participative decision-making, goal setting and objective feedback. It is an appraisal system designed to enable managers and individuals to define achievable work objectives which would form the basis of subsequent appraisals. The objective of this system is to remove some of the arbitrariness and inconsistency in other appraisal systems. Its thesis is that resistance to performance appraisal was in part

due to the lack of involvement of individuals in establishing their goals. Supported by pronouncements in social science, which decreed that individuals were goal directed, and the importance of motivation through the establishment of clear, attainable and desirable goals (Vroom, 1964), all management was required to do was to make outcomes desirable and the link between action and outcome clear. The emphasis of the MBO programmes is therefore employee participation in goal setting, in essence, participating in deciding appropriate levels of effort. In addition to assessing current and past performance, MBO was also future-oriented. It also has the advantage of being related to specific jobs as opposed to general schemas designed to be applied to a range of jobs. Based on specific, largely quantitative criteria within the context of a formal objective-setting procedure, it was held to be more 'objective', and therefore, more acceptable.

In its broadest interpretation, management by objectives involves the establishment of institutional goals, which are then translated into departmental objectives, with the latter forming the basis of discussions of individual objective setting (Drucker, 1964; Seyna, 1986). In this sense, it is designed to focus attention on long-term objectives, rather than day-to-day output. It is also recommended for giving employees a sense of direction, a focus for priorities and improved morale. Justified in the literature recommending its use as providing 'a focal point' for behaviour (Harper, 1988), in essence, it ensures that the highest levels of the organization are linked to individual activities, through a goal or activity matrix. An example would be the system used by Wang Laboratories, Strategic Measurement Analysis and Reporting Technique. This involves a four level pyramid of objectives and measures which relate strategies to operations. The first level is the 'vision for business'; the second is the objectives for each business unit defined in market and financial terms; the third defines more tangible operating objectives and priorities; the final level is performance measures defined in terms of quality, delivery, process time and cost (Cross and Lynch, 1988). This strategic aspect of MBO systems has tended to be forgotten with the result that recent emphasis is placed on concepts such as 'Performance Management', a process which emphasizes the definition of an organization's mission, aims and values, which should then form the basis of individual objectives (Fowler, 1990).

The emphasis of management by objectives is that the action plan specifying what is to be achieved should include time limits for particular activities, and in this we have the basis for the temporal elaboration of the act. The process involves the goals for each employee being set at the beginning of the review period, involving subordinates' identification and development of performance standards, objectives and measurements. (The extent of this participation differs in principle as well as practice, varying from being the mutual agreement of superior and subordinate to employees having complete responsibility for self-established goals.) The success with which these have been achieved are then evaluated at the end of the period. In some cases there may be a mid-period review to see how progress is going. At the end of the period past performance is assessed with new objectives being set for the future period. The actual periods chosen may vary between a few months, with quarterly or semi-annual appraisals, to a year or possibly longer. In many cases this may be influenced by accounting practices within the organization. The appraisal date, however, may also be 'personalized', based on the anniversary date of the individual joining the company.

Control of activity comes through the emphasis on goals being specific. Clarity is associated with conciseness, which is associated with impartiality. There is also a requirement that goals be achievable, realistic and timely, and is often accompanied by acronyms, for example, SMART – specific , meaningful, ambitious, reachable and trackable (Crane, 1990); or the 3 Rs – realistic; relevant to the company's goals; and relative to the individual (Quick, 1990). Most important is that they are expressible in measurable terms. There is a strong emphasis on the quantification of performance goals, the automatic equation of clarity and comprehension with measurement, even to the extent that if objectives are not measurable they should be changed (Wilkinson, 1987). This is reflected in recommendations such as the following:

> objective measures of performance usually take the form of an expression that interrelates two or more of four factors: quantity, quality, time and cost. Job description tasks must be refined to sets of criteria on which the employee will be evaluated. Each criterion must be simply and specifically delineated so that it is possible to provide either a precise measure of task performance in quantifiable terms or a simple two-choice or three-choice judgement indicating the evaluators' assessment of the employee's level of success. (McConnell, 1991: 70)

In some cases, this may just translate into a statement of objectives in financial or monetary terms, the equivalent of sales projections, a consequence which has led to criticisms of MBO systems. Other controls of activity are more elaborate. For example, job descriptions for a position may be divided into several areas of responsibility, with supervisor and employee working together to define specific goals and objectives to be achieved in each area (Goodnough, 1990). Goals become targets which each individual is expected to attain within a given time-frame with measures of progress made towards achieving these goals being established.

Criticisms levelled at MBO systems are that they have a tendency to focus too strongly on the individual, to the detriment of broader organizational objectives; and that they encourage short-term myopia, with an emphasis on the achievement of objectives over all other considerations.

Other problems are conflicting objectives; conflicting views on the appropriateness of objectives; and the extent to which these are mutually agreed upon. Subordinates may set low targets or may not be encouraged to exceed targets. Inevitably there are disagreements about reasons why objectives were not achieved (Kane and Freeman, 1986, 1987). Modifications and suggestions for improvement have included the attempt to try to 'capture' process as well as outcomes and may be seen in the development of the Productivity Rating Index (PRI). This is a combination of a time-based index (TBI), the achievement of time-related goals; and a quality index (QI), an assessment of how well, rather than just whether, these goals were achieved. The PRI combines the TBI and QI into a single measure to stress the quality of the task. An average PRI summarizes evaluation over a period (Bordman and Melnick, 1990). Other variations of MBO systems are MBQO – management by quality objectives, recommended as a system which incorporates MBO with Deming's fourteen basic principles for achieving productivity through quality, and arranging Deming's principles (relating to general goals, production and production support goals, and training goals) into sets of functional quality goals (Stein, 1991).

An important dimension of the MBO system is that it constructs a job in a particular way. It correlates activity with time, the temporal elaboration of the act, especially if the system is supplemented by monthly progress reports. It defines activity as the clear, concise and 'objective' statements of responsibilities and authority. In this it equates activity with visible action. Its effect is the provision of an individual activity mathesis through the exercise of goal-setting. It also defines boundaries around individuals, groups or departments as they become the unit of evaluation. All these have the effect of allowing the extent to which targets have been achieved to be assessed at a distance, or as one professional journal claimed, enhancing 'pyramid performance monitoring' (Erban, 1989).

Also within MBO is the principle of exhaustive use, another dimension Foucault associates with control over activity. It is not acceptable to say that goals for the coming period will be the same as or even less than before. A goal is something a person is attempting to accomplish. Doing what has been done before is therefore not sufficient. 'The process involves a cycle of setting and achieving clear-cut objectives that point the way to perfection and not to minimum standards of performance' (Beckert and Walsh, 1991: 79). Some systems specifically establish the number of goals which should be set for the period, for example, four to six objectives for a one year period. Goals become further differentiated into routine goals – an extension of what is already being done; problem-solving goals – focusing on shortcomings or weaknesses; innovative goals – the introduction of something which has not been done before; and personal development goals. Nor are goals simple objects, but may have several attributes, for example: goal specificity, the degree of precision or clarity with which the goal is defined; goal difficulty, the level of proficiency or performance sought; goal intensity, the process employed for setting a goal and the process utilized in determining how to reach it (Vilere and Hartman, 1991).

Although an elaborate MBO system may not be in operation, objectives-based performance appraisal systems or individualized goal-setting, with their emphasis on clear and realistic indications of work which must be accomplished, and performance expectations have become more current. These approaches to appraisal may, however, be combined with some kind of assessment of behaviour.

As mentioned in Chapter 2, Behaviourally Anchored Rating Scale (BARS) and Behaviour Observation Scales (BOS) list performance-related behaviours. They are advocated over traditional results based evaluations based, for example, on number of sales calls or financial or unit volume which may be used in the evaluation of sales personnel, because they are based on activities required on the job and thus capture the 'process' involved in the activity. They involve the identification and definition of major areas of performance, formulated by supervisors and workgroups, or with the completion of a job analysis, and a standard for judging these areas of performance. Critical incidents representing very good and very poor performance and illustrations of effective and ineffective behaviour, are then gathered for each job dimension. These are then rated on a good/bad continuum, with ambiguous examples being discarded. The descriptions of behaviour serve as anchor points and are placed beside the scale at varying points, depending on the extent to which they exemplify the dimension under consideration. In the case of a departmental manager supervising sales staff, an example of behaviour rated low on the scale would be, for example, 'could be expected to make promises to an individual about salary even though this is against company policy'. Examples of highly rated behaviour might be 'the ability to instil confidence and responsibility in sales staff through delegating important jobs to them'. Behaviour dimensions of waiter or waitress service may include, for example, whether the individual 'knows the menu and can inform customers what each item is, how it is served and how it is prepared'; 'asks customers how they would like their meat and eggs done, brings rolls to the table promptly', etc.

A development or extension of this control of activity is performance related pay which relates compensation to the level of performance rather than the fact of employment. Early systems based on the measurement of performance included incentives tied to productivity – piecework. Piece-rate, however, offers little control over activity, controlling as it does output alone, and research by NEDO and IPM indicates a change from piece-rate systems, with one quarter of all those existing before the mid-

1980s having been withdrawn. Performance related pay (PRP) offers potentially greater control of activity through the practice of relating pay to aspects of individual performance at work. Under such a system, salary increases are totally or partially dependent on an appraisal or merit rating. Its action, however, is retrospective with no guarantee of future performance. Some performance related pay systems act to specify future desired performance standards, in some cases specifying the particular compensation which may be expected if these standards are met. Some packages also attempt to influence individual contribution to the group, through rewarding team contribution (Kinnie and Lowe, 1990). It is also recommended as a means of encouraging individuals to become involved in total quality programmes (Botterill, 1990). One of the difficulties arising in translating such a performance appraisal into a salary adjustment is that the calculation of performance payments becomes more complex (Fowler, 1988), with the result that statistical packages are now being introduced to calculate them (Wagel, 1988).

Performance appraisal is a process of controlling activity through its emphasis on formalized procedure, 'goals', 'standards' and 'rewards', and linking these to time, or its specification of behaviours for successful performance. It is thus placed at the nexus of several disciplinary practices or matrices – allocation of rewards, identification of skill deficiencies, promotion potential. This helps explain why appraisal has been described as an important dimension of 'a well-defined, consistently managed, ongoing programme linking business objectives and individual performance' (Cuddy, 1987: 22). Its versatility in fulfilling several functions including the ranking of individuals, indicated in Chapter 2, is reflected in the following recommendations in a trade journal:

> A combination of three existing approaches, Management by Objectives (MBO), Behavioural Observation Scales (BOS), and Forced Choice ratings, creates an appraisal system that is superior to any one of the approaches used alone. MBO allows for 'bottomline' types of measures and contributes to the planning, control and motivational processes. BOS reveals to the subordinate the job-related behaviours that lead to goal accomplishment and makes it possible for the superior to evaluate subordinates on behaviour that contributes or detracts from goal attainment. The Forced Choice evaluation, used to appraise personality traits required for certain jobs, should be added to the performance appraisal when evaluating job applicants and when an employee is being considered for promotion. (Muczyk and Gable, 1987)

The relative value placed on performance appraisal systems as a means of improving overall managerial and organizational performance may be seen in the resistance to upward appraisal or subordinate appraisal of supervisors or managers (as we shall see in Chapter 6).

Employees at work benefit from clear and realistic indications of work expectations and required work performance and performance appraisal fulfils some of this function – how successfully is debatable. For example, criticism has been levelled at errors of human judgements, raters, criteria, format, namely the potential for gender bias, as, for example, the proportion of females in a particular workgroup affecting performance ratings (Drazin and Auster, 1987; Sackett et al., 1991); the importance of other factors such as similarity to the supervisor, level of knowledge of the employee, experience of the appraisee as a supervisor, etc. (Clement, 1987). This, however, would be to address appraisal as a representational function, that is, with the assumption of an extant, objectively knowable performance and as a system which records or reflects 'performance' more or less accurately. Addressing appraisal in this way creates the illusion of its being a technicist science, a portrayal reflected in the recommendations on the importance of training – 'it is critical that supervisors are properly trained to rate employees accurately'. Uniform or homogeneous interpretations of the social, through the translations which are established in the process of reducing experience and social interaction to adjectival or numerical checklists, have implications for the systems of governance which come to operate in organizations. This stresses the importance of gaining a democratic consensus on what is meant by the terms used.

The Organization of Geneses

The previous sections have outlined how activity is rendered visible, and, once visible, is then articulated with time. Aligning activity with time, although providing some basis of control of activity, is insufficient by itself to provide a disciplinary matrix through which both individuals and populations may be co-ordinated. This final stage is achieved through the 'organization of geneses' (Foucault, 1977). It involves a new technique for 'taking charge of the time of individual existences' (Foucault, 1977: 157). It is a mechanism by which individuals are organized to form an efficient or productive power or force. In this, Foucault attempts to delineate the mechanisms of organizing a productive power the effect of which is superior to the sum of the elementary forces composing it. For example, a perfect army is a disciplined mass of docile and useful troops who act as meticulously subordinated cogs of a machine. Foucault writes:

> Discipline is no longer simply an art of distributing bodies, of extracting time from them and accumulating it, but of composing forces in order to obtain an efficient machine . . . The individual body becomes an element that may be placed, moved, articulated on others. Its bravery or its strength are no longer the principal variables that define it; but the place it occupies, the interval it covers, the regularity, the good order according to which it operates its movement. *The soldier is above all a fragment of mobile space before he is courage or hon-*

our . . . The body is constituted as a part of a multi-segmentary machine. (Foucault, 1977: 164, emphasis added)

In essence what is being described are the mechanisms or disciplines which are called upon to organize a population and the individuals who comprise it, more exactly or with greater precision.

The example Foucault uses to explain the organization of geneses is the gradual dissolution of the apprenticeship system and its replacement by a systematic, standardized, detailed and disciplined approach to knowledge and time. Traditional apprenticeships, which were not just restricted to skilled crafts, involved training under a master over a period of time, after which the individual had achieved mastery of a particular area. Within the apprenticeship system there was no systematic programme of instruction, no set aspects of knowledge to be imparted by a particular time, nor, apart from a final rite of passage, were there formal examinations. The system of instruction was essentially based on an informal system of copying, watching, following and practice. Within the traditional apprenticeship, time and knowledge were divided along simple binary lines of initiation or training and 'adult time'; one was an apprentice or a master. This system was replaced in favour of a more systematic and standardized approach. Thus, the period of time of the apprenticeship became subdivided into successive or parallel segments, each of which was to end in a specific time. These periods were arranged according to a linear succession, from the most 'elementary' to the most 'complex'. Thus a hierarchy in terms of 'complexity' of knowledge was arranged and correlated with time. These temporal segments, set periods of time within which knowledge was to be assimilated, concluded with an examination.

From a pattern of overall time, one master and one exam, disciplinary time 'substitutes a multiple and progressive series' (Foucault, 1977: 159), with different stages, separated from one another by graded exams; a programme of stages involving increasing difficulty, whereby individuals are qualified according to how they pass through the series. To ensure that both time and activity are rendered productive there is the organization of activity into a series or in a temporal sequence, with each stage successfully graded from the other and leading to a seemingly logical progression. The series identifies the individual, 'according to his level, his seniority, his rank, the exercises that are suited to him' (Foucault, 1977: 158). What Foucault identifies is the seriation of time and the 'progress' of individuals. Thus a matrix is provided of activity through time, upon which a population and individuals within it may be located. 'Each individual is caught up in a temporal series which specifically defines his level or his rank' (Foucault, 1977: 159). It is the operation of a disciplinary matrix, one which enables the individual to be located *vis-à-vis* the population – 'the collective, permanent competition of individuals being classified in relation to one another' (Foucault, 1977: 162).

The hierarchizing of stages in small steps introduces the concept of 'development' and 'progression'. As a mechanism of organizing, it is now so familiar that it is regarded as normal, for example, in schools (children progressing through grades or forms) or the military (progression through the ranks). It may equally be identified in work organizations, most notably in hierarchical job ladders, career paths, each premised on an assumed difficulty of task; with progression or promotion dependent on the requisite training (the exercises for each level in the series), and satisfactory performance in the examinatory performance review. In each case it is the use of time, and activity associated with time, through its hierarchical organization, 'which does not culminate in a beyond, but tends towards a subjection that has never reached its limit' (Foucault, 1977: 162):

> the seriation of successive activities makes possible a whole investment of duration by power: the possibility of characterizing, and therefore using individuals according to the level in the series that they are moving through; the possibility of accumulating time and activity, of rediscovering them, totalized and usable in a final result, which is the ultimate capacity of an individual. Temporal dispersal is brought together to produce a profit, thus mastering a duration that would otherwise elude ones grasp. Power is articulated directly onto time; it assures its control and guarantees its use. (Foucault, 1977: 160)

What is achieved is a new way of organizing time, one which makes it useful, by 'segmentation, seriation, synthesis and totalization' (Foucault, 1977: 160). The time which these mechanisms introduce, however, is a linear time: 'whose moments are integrated, one upon another, and which is oriented towards a terminal, stable point; in short an evolutive time ... the discovery of an evolution in terms of "progress" ' (Foucault, 1977: 161). The act of tying activity towards a terminal state, makes it possible to characterize the individual either in relation to this term, in relation to other individuals, or in relation to a type of itinerary.

The operation of the organization of geneses may be identified in a number of HRM practices, most particularly in the organization of careers. It may also be identified in other programmes, for example, skill-based pay systems and training and development programmes, wherever there is the assumption of linear hierarchical movement in staged progression.

Skill-based pay systems which reward individuals based on the number, type and depth of skills mastered are an example of the system described in the organization of geneses. It is centred on redefining jobs in terms of skills and establishing reward structures based on skill-determined career paths. Employees are paid according to the range, depth and types of skill they are capable of using, the ability to perform an operationally related array of tasks or skills, rather than for work performance at any given time. Knowledge-based pay systems reward employees for their range of knowledge, the number of business-related skills mastered, the level of those skills or knowledge, or some combination of level and range.

Progression through knowledge-based systems is based on the employee acquiring additional knowledge and skill within the same job category. Workers are hired at below market rate. As the person acquires enough skill or knowledge the level of base pay is increased. Pay increases are then available as new skills or knowledge are mastered. For example, pay-for-skill schemes may operate by dividing production teams into twelve skill levels, each defined in terms of performance required, area knowledge and technical knowledge. All skill levels are considered equal in value, training time and compensation. This defines all skill blocks as being of equal value to the operation as well as facilitating job rotation. Considerable training is required to advance through the entire pay system with employees taking four to five years to reach the top plant rate (Ledford and Bergel, 1991).

Although introduced with reference to job enrichment and empowerment, the incentive for their use lies in the move away from rigid job classifications to taxinomia based on skill classifications, and, as such, these are adaptive to a flatter organization structure. It reflects some of the changes which are going on in terms of decentralized planning and decision-making and the use of multidisciplined teams. They are advocated for increasing workforce flexibility and the capacity to respond to changing demands and schedules – the improvement of productivity without capital investment (Krajci, 1990). They are also introduced where traditional promotion paths are blocked or restricted. In some cases they are an integral part of a competitive portfolio as, for example, the pay-for-knowledge system at Federal Express. This system directly ties what employees know about their job to what they earn. The employee's knowledge is 'measured' every six months by a job knowledge test. Managers, directors and vice-presidents also take periodic knowledge tests (Galagan, 1991). The philosophy behind the scheme is that superior job knowledge translates into superior customer service. The system is supported by a large training budget and an interactive video network which delivers job training and testing to 45 000 customer contact employees, couriers and ground operations staff.

Training and development programmes also have within them aspects of the organization of geneses. They assume a 'measurement of progress'. The notion of growth and development is especially evident when allied to the setting of objectives and goals, and aspirations of personal development, or individual action plans. The process establishes the agreement of goals as individuals identify the elements that they feel they need to develop (hierarchized if necessary), feedback, followed by a series of steps to try to improve performance (performance improvement plans). The premiss behind goal-setting is a form of geneses: time is partitioned, objectives are set in relation to time, the end of the period is marked by an 'examination' to see if goals have been attained or not. If successfully attained, further, slightly more difficult goals are set, and so one advances further up the steps in a perceived hierarchy of 'worth'. (The metaphor of progression is evident in the recipes for 'plateauing'.) Personal goal plans are a means of achieving progress on the stepping stones and may be identified in career planning recommendations. Realizing personal goals often establishes personal geneses for the individual to complement the organizational system. It is the further division of established organizational hierarchy of job titles and compensation,

At the national level, in the UK, the effects of the organization of geneses can be identified in the reforms which are taking place in national training schemes. These have been prompted by criticisms of traditional apprenticeships because of the latter's unsystematic nature, and failure to conform to classical patterns of the synchronization of knowledge with time. Reforms of training are premised on the classical pattern of a hierarchy of knowledge and a series of levels, marked by examination.[12] National vocational qualifications (NVQ) are currently being developed across all sectors of industry for both craft and operative workers. Based on industry-defined, nationally recognized standards they introduce into many occupational sectors assessment in the work-place by first line supervisors. The standards are precise descriptions of work performance, based on knowledge and skills necessary to do the job and the application of these skills at work. Units of competence or modules define what people need to be able to do and incorporate standards which reflect the overall competence in a job. Performance is evaluated against these standards.

NVQ identifies grades or levels of competencies. Thus NVQ 1 is defined as competence in the performance of a range of work activities which are primarily routine and predictable, or provide broad foundations, primarily as a basis of progression. Through stages, the individual 'progresses' to NVQ 4 which is competence in the performance of complex, technical, specialized and professional work activities, including those associated with design, planning and problem solving, normally carrying a significant degree of personal accountability. In addition, the Training Agency in the UK is considering the feasibility of a national network of local centres for competency assessment (Dulewicz, 1989) – a disciplinary matrix for a population is effected. As indicated earlier, at the managerial and supervisory level also there has been concern to recognize and identify core transferable managerial skills which are common across industries with the Management Charter Initiative.[13]

These examples illustrate the organization of geneses, the notion of gradual progression or evolution, the acquisition of knowledge in 'lumps'. They thus enable the individual's activities to be co-ordinated with those of the workforce. At their premiss is the view that knowledge comes in readily identifiable segments, with each building on each other. As an approach to knowledge this is a relatively modern approach to its acquisition, certainly not the basis for the organization of knowledge which characterized earlier educational practices (Cohen, 1982). It also acts to introduce linear concepts of time. It introduces, in Clark's (1990) terms, a homogeneous chronological code – 'an objective, singular system containing defined, measurable units of highly stable lengths . . . which can be atomistically ordered in a linear and/or cyclical pattern'. With its emphasis on the unilinear and its implication of progression, each sequence leading to a higher level of development, it may severely limit the recognition of different ways of ordering (Burrell, 1992).

Towards a Genealogy
As with the art of distribution, outlined in Chapter 2, mechanisms adopted for the control of activity vary greatly and are influenced by a range of discourses. For example, in Japanese work organization, individual work roles lack the specificity and definition typical of Western organizations. Individual employee positions and roles, job boundaries, are rarely specified as employees are expected to perform a range of job functions, with the tradition of work teams which incorporate managerial and maintenance functions. Equally, there is an emphasis on overlapping managerial jobs and collective authority. Groups, networks of collective units, rather than the individual, are the elementary functional units. There is also evidence that Japanese work organizations, as with many in the East, use different time codes. There is not the Western preoccupation with homogeneous chronological codes (Clark, 1990). In contrast, in the US a strong emphasis is placed on the individual position and job requirements, an emphasis which has been reinforced by legislative and judicial requirements. The 1990 American with Disabilities Act, for example, requires that job descriptions reflect the actual physical and material requirements needed to perform a job, and that judgements regarding job qualifications are based on the realities of the individual skills necessary to perform specific jobs, rather than on traditional assumptions of what is required to perform the work (Meng, 1991). The 1991 Civil Rights Act emphasizes the role of job descriptions supported by job analyses (Cook, 1992). The strong emphasis placed on job ladders and job families also indicates a strong commitment to the principles underlying the organization of geneses.

Control of activity through the systematic application of pay-for-performance also varies. It is higher in the US than in the UK and Sweden. In one survey in the US more than 80 per cent of companies surveyed indicated that they had a merit pay system for one or more of their employee groups (McGinty and Hanke, 1989). But US derived systems are being more frequently and extensively taken on in the UK than Sweden (Cameron, 1985). A survey in the UK found that MBO was the most common method of performance appraisal in manufacturing companies, followed by forced choice and Critical Incident Systems (Forbes and Anaya, 1980). A variation on the MBO system is administration by contract, an agreement by supervisor and subordinate which sets targeted goals for improvement in a given time frame. It is encouraged in the US through the Civil Service Reform Act (Schor, 1981).

Government reinforcement of the disciplines can be identified as a factor in the increase in performance-related pay. In the UK, the Conservative government's Citizen's Charter refers to the importance of explicit standards and the role of performance-related pay. Formalized performance appraisal systems, for example, have been introduced for teachers, university staff, public servants and hospital administrators, each providing examples of the attempt to control activity through replacing professional personnel systems, with their infrequent but elaborate processes for promotion. Merit pay for public sector employees, especially teachers, was also a feature of the 1992 US Presidential campaign. In some US States the performance appraisal system is determined by law. The 1978 US Civil Service Reform Act introduced a merit pay system, later to be modified by the Performance Management and Recognition System, which stressed the importance of goal setting and feedback (Perry and Petrakis, 1988).[14]

Judicial and legislative decisions may impact the nature of appraisals, their degree of specificity and potential for control. The US Uniform Guidelines on Employee Selection Procedures requiring the validation of selection procedure has now been interpreted by the courts to apply to performance appraisals. Court judgments have led to recommendations that pay should be closely linked to job outcomes (Goddard, 1989); and that staff involved in their conduct are fully trained (Nobile, 1991). Other recommendations include formal appraisal systems based on job analysis, behaviour-oriented questions, specific written instructions to raters, and feedback to personnel (Eyres, 1989; Townley, 1990). The elaboration of what constitutes acceptable performance in appraisal ratings has also been reinforced by court decisions on discharge cases (Barrett and Kernan, 1987).

The degree of specificity of practices is also influenced by the nature of labour-management relations. In the US, for example, union certification procedures exclude managerial employees, thus requiring judicial clarification of the definition of management (an articulation of its activity), as well as organizational descriptions of activity. The juridified nature of labour management relations in the US has resulted in quite elaborate documentation of both dividing practices and control of activity. The asymptotic nature of trying to make the intangible tangible, the seemingly insatiable drive towards greater clarification is a feature of North American practices. Inevitably, however, meanings and discursive practices are constant sites of struggle. Definitions, clauses, codes, etc., rather than replacing texts, merely add to them. Ultimately the attempt to articulate the analytical space in the employment relationship by trying to impose definitive and unambiguous meaning may result in chaos: for example, the fragmentation of bargaining units; backlogs in grievance systems; the proliferation of job classifications with demands for job regrading; the bureaucratization of payment systems through appeals on merit payments, etc. – the general rules of managing (Kochan et al., 1986). It is the dysfunction in the degree of rationalization which the disciplines introduce, in particular, in North American personnel and IR, that has stimulated the search for alternative systems abroad.

Notes

1 Pressures for job analysis come from the desire for more effective utilization of employees in improved 'manpower' forecasting and planning, improved control of personnel-related costs, increasing interest in performance measurement, as well as compliance with government equal opportunity requirements. It provides the basis for other aspects of personnel activity, especially recruitment and selection, training, job evaluation, performance appraisal and career planning.

2 Job analysis comes with an elaborate vocabulary, for example, US uniform guidelines specify:

> work behaviour: an activity performed to achieve objectives of the job. Work behaviours involve observable (physical) components and unobservable (mental) components. A work behaviour consists of the performance of one or more tasks. Knowledges, skills and abilities are not behaviours although they may be applied in work behaviours.
> observable: able to be seen, heard or otherwise perceived by a person other than the person performing the action,
> knowledge: a body of information applied directly to the performance of a function
> skill: a present observable competence to perform a learned psychomotor act
> ability: a present competence to perform an observable behaviour that results in an observable product.

3 This would coincide with Foucault's identification of the sciences of the classical episteme as the drawing up of taxonomies.

4 Wales, the chief examiner of the US Civil Service Commission, emphasized the impetus given to job analysis by the scientific management movement: 'much as the scientific management theory in industry has been attacked or condemned as an attempt at Prussianizing, it has at least one good result in forcing employers of labour, especially the larger corporations, to consider methods of employment, to make job analyses and to ascertain as closely as possible the ultimate cost of their method or lack of method in employment' (Primoff and Fine, 1988: 17).

5 A survey by Levine et al. (1983) found there was no consensus amongst job analysts on the schemes. Choice of system is influenced by factors such as suitability, objectives, level of standardization, sample size, respondent/user acceptability, training required, reliability, cost, quality of outcome (Ash and Levine, 1980). The main criteria influencing its acceptance are organizational factors such as cost, time taken to complete, standardization of

application, reliability, whether it is available off-the-shelf and its degree of acceptability to those who are subject to it. Those systems requiring short training time, low cost, and a short time period to completion were all scored highly. The logistics of the questionnaire is also important with an emphasis on key measurable dimensions of jobs being identified in the minimum amount of time.

6 The 'reduction' of tasks or jobs to numerical representation is perhaps epitomized at the national level by governmental classifications and dictionaries of occupations.

7 This is reinforced with reference to job analysis techniques becoming more 'comprehensive' or 'objective'. This is to neglect, however, the four dimensions on which analyses vary: the types of descriptors or elements used to describe jobs; the forms in which job information is obtained or presented, with the choice of analytical method adopted significantly influencing job hierarchy and pay structure outcomes (Madigan and Hoover, 1986).

8 Distinctions are usually drawn between technical skills and interpersonal skills. Such distinctions do not necessarily reflect different types of jobs, but may be highlighted within individual jobs, for example the shift from 'technical skills' highlighted in tellers' jobs in banks, to the 'interpersonal skills' of the newly named 'customer service representative' as the finance sector emphasizes customer service as part of their competitiveness.

9 The complexity of operating in social settings highlights the dangers of generalizing too much beyond particular situations. Some large bureaucratic organizations, operating in relatively stable and predictable business environments, for example clearing banks and oil companies, in their adoption of these systems reflect the belief that performance can and should be defined in a single, company-wide way. Universal management competencies are identified as the ability to deal with people, activity management skills, personal effectiveness, and sensitivity to environment or external factors (Jones, 1990). There are indications that process skills tend to be more enduring than content knowledge, but the important determinant of effectiveness of process skills is the nature of the paradigm from which they derive. Quantitative skills based on a deterministic view of the world tend not to be used in practice, but diagnostic skills, where human nature and organizations are probabalistic, indeterminate worlds of multiple interacting variables are more useful and enduring (Bunning, 1992).

10 According to Marx, time is the underlying constitutive component of both goods and labour that permits their common existence as interchangeable commodities. The objectification of labour power through the quantification of time is the foundation for the exchange of commodities.

11 Foucault writes: 'it poses the principle of a theoretically ever-growing use of time: exhaustion rather than use; is it a question of extracting from time, ever more available moments, and from each moment, ever more useful forces . . . This means that one must seek to intensify the use of the slightest moment, as if time, in its very fragmentation, were inexhaustible or as if, at least by an ever more detailed internal arrangement, one could tend towards an ideal point at which one maintained maximum speed and maximum efficiency . . . the more time is broken down, the more its subdivisions multiply, the better one disarticulates it by deploying its internal elements under a gaze that supervises them, the more one can accelerate an operation, or at least regulate it according to an optimum speed' (Foucault, 1977: 154).

12 In the UK, the MSC advocated the grouping of skills as part of manpower mobility and training programmes, principally in response to a deteriorating employment situation for young people, and labour market imbalances. Its intent was to identify and better understand underlying skills needed to perform jobs so that they might be compared and grouped. This was designed to enable career and education courses to be better structured to give young people skills relevant to career interests. It was also designed as an aid to employers for man-

power transfer and retraining (Townsend and Freshwater, 1978).

13 The American Management Association also has a Competency Programme aimed at practising managers. They have identified eighteen generic management competencies clustered into four groups: goal and action management, directing subordinates, human resource management and leadership. The Competency Programme includes a Master of Management Degree Programme, a two to four year graduate level education programme designed to help managers acquire the competencies in the model and then use these on their jobs (Evarts, 1988).

14 Although a recent study indicates that ratings have been concentrated at the highly successful and outstanding end of the ratings, with merit increases becoming fairly automatic (Perry et al., 1989).

4

The Individual as Object

HRM practices focus on the individual: an observable reality with an essential identity. He or she is a given, which the employing organization recruits, selects, appraises, trains, develops and compensates. From this perspective the function of personnel practices is to discover or uncover some essential knowledge about the individual to aid rational decision-making, by indicating which individual should be recruited, how they should be trained and appraised, and so on. To be effective personnel practices must become less 'subjective' and more 'accurate'. A Foucauldian analysis rejects this presentation. The individual is not a 'given', essential identity but is actively produced. One mechanism for this is to construct the individual as an object of knowledge and power. This chapter examines the role of HRM techniques in this process of constituting individuals as objects.

The Examination

To be manageable, workers must be known; to be known, they must be rendered visible. Chapter 2 explained how disciplinary mechanisms act to organize the workforce, so that individual positions are identified *vis-à-vis* the whole. Chapter 3 showed how the activity of individuals becomes known and controlled. The art of distribution and control of activity, however, do not permit identification of the individual per se. They articulate an individual position and determine the activity involved but do not specify which individual is placed in which role or the nature of the selected individual. It is the individual qua individual who is placed in a disciplinary matrix. Individuals themselves remain unidentified. Knowledge of the individual is necessary, though, in order to gain productive service. Work organizations require systems to inspect workers, to observe their presence and application, inspect the quality of their work, compare them with one another, and to classify them according to skill and speed: 'power ha[s] to be able to gain access to the bodies of individuals, to their acts, attitudes and modes of every day behaviour' (Foucault, 1980a: 125). What HRM mechanisms are available for this?

A start in answering this question is to recognize that the individual is a relatively recent object of knowledge:

for a long time ordinary individuality – the everyday individuality of everybody – remained below the threshold of description. To be looked at, observed, described in detail . . . was a privilege . . . The disciplinary methods reversed this relation, lowered the threshold of describable individuality and made of this description a means of control and a method of domination. (Foucault, 1977: 191–2)

As a result of these disciplinary methods, the formation of individuality was no longer achieved through historical ritual, but became increasingly the province of science: 'the normal took over from the ancestral, and measurement from status, substituting for the individuality of the memorable man that of the calculable man . . . All the sciences, analyses or practices employing the root "psycho" have their origin in this historical reversal of the procedures of individualization' (Foucault, 1977: 193).

One of the technologies which lowers the threshold of describable individuality and achieves the objectification of the individual is the examination. Essentially a system of marking and classification, the examination, through the simple device of questions and answers, provides the basis for judgement and measurement. In this, it is both a system of knowledge and a system of power. Examination has two meanings: to look closely or analytically at; and to judge according to a rule. These two meanings correspond to two techniques: hierarchical observation and normalizing judgement (Marsden, 1993).

Hierarchical observation allows those far removed to 'know' the individual in detail. It permits the close 'examination' of individuals by others. Through this, individuals are open to observation, constantly being seen, or being able to be seen. Foucault illustrates the effects of hierarchical observation in his discussion of architecture and the physical layout of military camps and hospitals. They reveal that the physical ordering of space is a means through which individuals are rendered more visible. Surveillance, or hierarchical observation, is a feature of many organizations, incorporated not only through physical and architectural arrangements but also through information systems. Through these mechanisms, visibility is no longer focused solely on the powerful. As power becomes more anonymous and more functional, 'those on whom it is exercised tend to be more strongly individualized' (Foucault, 1977: 190).

The examination, through its use of standardized documentation and comparative measures, also facilitates the process of normalizing judgement. Unlike the law, which is based around a bifurcation of prohibited and allowed, normalizing judgement is based on a distribution between a positive and a negative pole. Instead of behaviour being good or bad, 'all behaviour falls in the field between good and bad marks, good and bad points' (Foucault, 1977: 180). In an examinatory system, individuals become known in terms of their mark or the score they achieve, which fix individual differences. Such a system distributes individuals according to aptitude and conduct. In doing so it offers what Foucault (1977: 180) terms a penal accountancy, a 'punitive balance sheet of each individual'. Each individual may be rewarded or punished on the basis of his or her individual position on the grid. 'It is the penal functioning of setting in order and the ordinal character of judging' (Foucault, 1977: 181). Given the possibility of attaining higher ranks and places, it simultaneously exercises a pressure on individuals to conform. The examination provides a lens through which individuals may be viewed, judged and compared. It is through the exercise of observation, and comparative measures, that the examination becomes the centre of procedures which 'constitute the individual as [an] effect and object of power, as [an] effect and object of knowledge' (Foucault, 1977: 189).

The examination is the means by which behaviour can be categorized and measured. A standardized format and common documentation allows for the classification and arrangement of individuals in a particular sequence, reflecting a hierarchy indicative of quality or quantity. In this sense, it serves to distribute and classify individuals, differentiating them from one another. As a process of ordering and systematizing, the examination facilitates ranking. It allows individuals to be placed on a hierarchical grid and permits the fixing of differences. Although a 'tiny operational schema' (Foucault, 1977: 185), the use of the examination has become so widespread – 'from psychiatry to pedagogy, from the diagnosis of diseases to the hiring of labour' – that its effects are barely noticed or remarked upon. It is as Hoskin and Macve (1986: 107) note, a way 'of writing the world (in texts, institutional arrangements, ultimately in persons) into new configurations of power'. Through scientific method and quantification individuals become potentially 'knowable' and 'governable'. Foucault writes of the examination: 'it provides a way to know where and how to locate individuals . . . to be able at each moment to supervise the conduct of each individual, to assess it, to judge it, to calculate its qualities or merits. It was a procedure, therefore, aimed at knowing, mastering and using' (Foucault, 1977: 143).

As a disciplinary technology which allows comparisons to be made between individuals, the examination simultaneously individualizes and totalizes:

> Thanks to the whole apparatus of writing that accompanied it, the examination opened up two correlative possibilities: firstly the constitution of the individual as a describable, analyzable object . . . and secondly the constitution of a comparative system that made possible the measurement of overall phenomena, the description of groups, the characterization of collective facts, the calculation of the gaps between individuals, their distribution in a given population. (Foucault, 1977: 190)

Individuals may be measured and known in relation to one another. In this it facilitates the 'objective' calculation of the total population made up of individually 'calculable' subjects. By referring individual actions to the 'population', it makes it possible to form categories and determine averages and calculate 'gaps' between individuals, as such it allows for the individuals and their respective positions *vis-à-vis* the population to be known. The 'rule' or 'norm', once established, may then act as a minimum threshold, an average to be respected or an optimum to be attained or achieved. It thereby becomes possible to enmesh the individual in a series of calculative norms and standards, and to identify those who do not live up to the rule or the norm.[1] In providing standards for 'proper' conduct, it simultaneously offers the prospect of correcting deviations from the norm. 'The disciplines characterize, classify . . . they distribute along a scale, around a norm, hierarchize individuals in relation to one another and if necessary, disqualify and invalidate' (Foucault, 1977: 223). As a calculative technology, the examination enables individuals to work out where they are and where they should be. The possibility of setting limits, to define what is acceptable or normal over time, normalization also reinforces the process of conformity and standardization – 'the norm introduces, as a useful imperative and as a result of measurement, all the shading of individual differences' (Foucault, 1977: 184).

The examination is therefore a disciplinary process which makes the individual an object of both knowledge and power. It refers his or her actions to a whole which is at once a field of comparison, but simultaneously differentiates individuals from one another. Judging individuals according to comparative scalar measures simultaneously indicates membership of a homogeneous social body, and also ensures a process of classification, hierachization and distribution of rank. There is differentiation within homogenization. As such, examining operates as a system of governance which individualizes and standardizes. It measures the individual in quantitative terms and hierarchizes the population according to their value, abilities, level and nature. It differentiates individuals, hierarchizes and normalizes through the process of judgement.

This objectification of the individual through individualization, that is, making the individual more identifiable *vis-à-vis* others through a process of identification and differentiation, also relies on the process of individuation, the attempt to identify, label and measure 'components' of individuality. Objectification is the process of dividing individuals not only from others but also *within themselves*.

Making individual differences and capacities visible, also allows for these differences to be inscribed or noted through writing, listing, numbering and computing. Through these techniques, the individual can be evaluated, measured, compartmentalized, and reported upon for the purpose of administrative decision-making. The individual is constituted as potentially a knowable and calculable individual. With knowledge comes the opportunity for intervention. 'It is the individual as he may be described, judged, measured, compared with others, in his very individuality; and it is also the individual who has to be trained or corrected, classified, normalized, excluded' (Foucault, 1977: 191).

The Individual Examined

The means used to make the individual an object of knowledge are only now attracting the attention of scholars (Hollway, 1991; Rose, 1990). Initial studies of differentiation of individuals were influenced by studies of 'madness' which developed early testing techniques designed to differentiate the 'feeble-minded'. This was the basis for the development of the first intelligence test devised by Binet and Simon in France (Hollway, 1991). Testing on this basis was later taken up by the emerging eugenics movement (Rust and Golombok, 1989). The First World War, with its requirements for the selection of 'officer material', raised the problem of the means by which a large population might be handled. With its need for mobilization and placement, and with little time for training, the war saw the development of various examinatory procedures. In the US, intelligence tests designed to identify the mentally incompetent and select the competent for responsible positions were used in the screening of recruits. These tests were further refined during the experience of the war and were administered to nearly two million recruits (Rose, 1990). Recruits in the UK, however, were not tested. After the war, in the 1920s, the National Institute of Industrial Psychology was concerned with selection testing and its work became increasingly dependent on psychometric measurement (Hollway, 1991). This contributed much to the refinement and standardization of selection testing (Rose, 1990).

The war also stimulated research into productivity. This tended to concentrate on the physical body, with research into fatigue and the effect of 'environmental factors' of heating and lighting on the individual, and on productivity. The body was conceived of as a psychophysiological mechanism, and it was only later that the mind or psyche became identified as a key to gaining knowledge of performance. Human relations 'discovered' the importance of sentiments, attitudes and emotions in shaping individuals' responses to things going on around them, and motivation was recognized as an important dimension of performance. The recognition that productivity and profit could be enhanced by attention to these factors led to the increased interest in the dimensions of the worker, with 'behaviour' gradually replacing 'the simple physics of movement' (Foucault, 1977: 138). As Foucault (1977: 138) notes, disciplines create an 'aptitude' or a 'capacity' of that which they seek to increase. New dimensions of subjectivity – attitudes – were thus introduced which helped bridge the external world of conduct with the individual's internal world (Hollway, 1991; Rose, 1990) – another dimension of the individual to be observed, identified 'known' and ultimately managed. The internal world of the psyche had to be rendered more intelligible and, more importantly, predictable. 'The advantage of the notion of attitude was that it provided a language for talking about the internal determinants of conduct and a means for thinking out how these determinants could be charted' (Rose, 1990: 28). 'Attitudes' were factors to be specified, investigated and measured.

The Second World War advanced understanding of the individual in terms of notions of morale and attitude, and individual differences became the province of personality as much as intelligence. Rose (1990: x) comments, 'While World War One had stimulated the development and deployment of intelligence tests, World War Two led to the invention of a range of devices for the assessment of the psyche . . . New dimensions of subjectivity, especially "attitudes" and "personality", were grasped in thought and utilized in practice.' From the beginning of the war, procedures of selection, allocation and promotion increasingly deployed psychological and psychiatric criteria. There was a desire 'to act upon the efficiency of the fighting forces by administrative means' (Rose, 1990: 40). This was a move towards the composition of forces, the maximization of effort through the efficient combining of individuals, supported by an underlying rationale of the importance of matching the individual to the job. Although not welcomed by the military, there was greater involvement of psychiatrists and psychologists in devising selection for recruits – including Alec Rodger, whose seven point plan for recruitment and selection would later be taken up and advocated for industry. Recruits were now given intelligence and aptitude tests, and the basis of 'scientific selection' was laid.

Character and personality testing developed rapidly during the Second World War, where large populations meant that statistical techniques could be developed and applied. The new device for mental calibration was the scale, a process whereby responses on certain issues were likely to give a high predictive indication of responses on other items. Further investigation into personality developed when Eysenck applied factor analysis to its perceived dimensions. Personality was deemed to consist of 'a small number of dimensions assessable through the application of psychometric techniques' (Rose, 1990: 233). Large-scale factorial studies of personality, based on questionnaires and rating scales, were checked against small-scale experimental studies of personality factors. From the premiss that particular acts could be grouped into habitual responses, thus identifying traits which comprised the general factors of personality, psychometric testing would be able to identify 'suitable' individuals. Described by Hollway (1991: 57) as providing a 'unique cocktail of "scientific" measurement, mass regulation and the claim of enhanced productivity' psychometric testing has a clouded history. Of particular interest is its relationship to the eugenics movement, with the view that individual differences are based on genetic inheritance (Rust and Golombeck, 1989). For Eysenck, the axes of personality were neuroticism and introversion–extroversion, dimensions which would allow the observer to predict those individuals who would be able to learn from environments and stimuli and those who would be unable to cope with stress. Through quantification of individual responses and derived scores which were compared with others, and with the belief that populations are distributed on a normal curve (thus conflating statistical and social norms), statistical methods and the laws of probability produced 'norms' and 'deviants'. 'Means' served as standards or norms for benchmark comparisons and concepts of normalcy gained credibility (Hacking, 1990). Whereas psychology had previously limited itself to the study of behaviour, tests were now designed to measure the mind. Personality thus became inscribable and quantifiable, and the basis for management and administration (Rose, 1990). As Rose (1990: 85) notes, 'the internal world of the factory was becoming mapped in psychological terms, and the inner feelings of workers were being transmitted into measurements about which calculations could be made'.

The techniques of scaling further introduced the subjective dimensions of individuals to the sphere of knowledge and regulation. Other research into personality generated projective tests and factorized personality tests in the attempt to isolate those dimensions of the individual which might be identified, measured and acted upon. The Minnesota Multiphasic Personality Inventory, and Cattell's Sixteen Factors Personality Questionnaire[2] were an outcome of this work and introduced a standardization to personality.

In the UK, research emphasized the importance of assessing candidates in their accomplishment of tasks, on the grounds that traits were not constant qualities of individuals, but moderated by the context in which individuals found themselves. The qualities needed for officer material would, therefore, only be displayed in the roles which officers would be required to take. Organizational effectiveness was conceived in terms of an interplay between social solidarities and individual personality dynamics. Bion's leaderless group test emerged from such an approach. Other aspects of the individual which became 'known' was the importance of the relationship with the group. From the Hawthorne experiments and research into the behaviour of soldiers, the informal or primary group was identified as the important moderator between the individual and the organization. Productivity was the product of a sense of cohesion, and beliefs – a series of 'phenomena' to be rendered into a conceptual and ultimately quantifiable framework. 'The minutiae of the human soul – human interactions, feelings, and thoughts, the psychological relations of the individual to the group – had emerged as a new domain for management' (Rose, 1990: 72).

Another aspect of the individual to be identified was the importance of goal-setting. Influenced by those who had worked with concentration camp survivors, the setting of goals was identified as an important dimension of well-being (Rose, 1990). This subsequently became the basis of work by Argyris, Vroom and Herzberg, and the establishment of clear, attainable and desirable objectives was quickly established as the basis of successful management. External controls could be dissipated as individuals were given the opportunity to self-actualize. Individuals might be categorized into theory X and theory Y types, and the self-directions of individuals were to be incorporated into the production process. The individual was to become compartmentalized into further classificatory systems, human nature increasingly objectified, and action reified. Human 'types' were created: actions are performed because an actor is an 'X' type person, or 'X' type persons perform such actions. Certain work arrangements suit individuals with high 'need to achieve' or 'type A' individuals.

Gradually, human subjectivity emerged as a complex phenomenon to be understood, transcribed, and, ultimately, acted upon. Testing was now designed to identify Maslow's needs of safety, love, esteem and self-actualization. Thus individuals may be high-power people or low-power people (Tjosvold et al., 1991), with high or low self-esteem. They have high or low needs for achievement, affiliation or power. Leaders may be directive or supportive, and may display actions which are directing, coaching, supporting and delegating. Employees can be assessed in terms of behaviour, motivation, interpersonal relations, problem solving, adaptability, risk-taking and rebelliousness, to name but a few. The process of enumeration produces attributes of individuals. There is a choice of over fifty rating scales which measure sensory, perceptual, cognitive, psychomotor and physical performance (Fleishman, 1988). Thus there emerges a scale for practically every eventuality – scales of 'morningness', the individual differences in circadian rhythms which influence an individual's propensity for daytime activity, enabling individuals to be classified according to evening, intermediate or morning 'types' (Smith et al., 1989). The effects of these processes recalls Foucault's (1977: 173) comments about hierarchical observation: 'these mechanisms can only be seen as unimportant if one forgets the role of this instrumentation, minor but flawless, in the progressive objectification and the ever more subtle partitioning of individual behaviour'.

The essence of knowledge encapsulated in psychology is not that which is common to all humans, that is, their humanity (Cixous, 1992), but that which gauges differences amongst them. Rose notes that 'The conceptual systems devised within the "human" sciences, the languages of analysis and explanation that they invented, the ways of speaking about human conduct that they constituted, have provided the means whereby human subjectivity and inter-subjectivity could enter t. lations of the authorities' (Rose, 1990: 7). It must be noted, howe the individual who is rendered the object of discourse and inter through these techniques is genderless. The composition of the Hawthorne groups, although commented on, did not enter into conceptual evaluation (Kanter, 1977; Mills, 1988). The overwhelmingly male population which provided the large populations for research during the war, and the largely male personnel which formed the basis of institutes, did not prohibit the formation of universal statements. Some of the more blatant voyeuristic and sexist stereotyping which informed the basis of Maslow's theorizing on motivation and categorization of self-actualization, not only remained unnoticed, but formed the basis of future theorizing (Cullen, 1992).

This Foucauldian overview of how the attitudes, needs and innate motivations of individuals are constructed has implications for traditional distinctions used in the area. Most commentaries recognize a shift from Taylorism to human relations. Hollway (1991: 73), for example, states that in the US the emergence of the latter represented a shift 'to a social-psychological paradigm for understanding the individual at work and to recommendations for management practice which stem from this approach' (Hollway, 1991: 68). For Hollway, it represented a radical departure because of the way it constructed the individual, changing from a psychophysiological, or mechanical, model of the employee, to a socio-emotional one. The individual was formally discovered to have sentiments. Related to this is the shift from the body – 'hands', or the interface between body and job – to the intervening variable of 'attitudes' between working conditions and work activity (Hollway, 1991). Hollway describes the shift as being from the coercion of bodies to the attempted production of self-regulated individuals.

But the privileging of attitudes or 'sentiments' over physical characteristics is based on a mind–body distinction which does not concur with a Foucauldian concept of the body. It is a distinction based on the nature or content of knowledge rather than how it is produced and its effects. Attitudes constituted another dimension of the body which science discovered and incorporated into a mechanism designed to secure its effectiveness. In this sense, it does not fundamentally differ from characteristics such as physical strength. The approach to the body taken by human relations was to make it known, to act upon it, make it manageable, that is, productive and increase its utility. Certainly, knowledge of the individual expanded. Human relations 'discovered' the importance of the group for individual behaviour: the relation of the individual to the work-group, the relations between work-group as well as the group's relationship with management (Rose, 1981: 157). But this does not constitute a radical departure from the underlying trajectory of all these practices, to make the individual an object of knowledge, to locate him or her in a power/knowledge construct for the purposes of making them manageable. It is a process of objectification – the reduction of individuals to standardized, describable and measurable dimensions. Human relations, although presented as recognizing the human side of the employee, is merely the intensification of knowledge. Measurement and performance are not downgraded but merely take different forms. In this sense there was no paradigm shift, merely an *intensification* of the processes involved. Both Taylorism and human relations were simultaneously involved in the will to knowledge.

The Examination in HRM

These new ways of interpreting the individual, and the burgeoning of scientific research into this new object of knowledge, stimulated the disciplines of organizational behaviour, industrial and occupational psychology. Some of this research has become incorporated into personnel practices,[3] and may be identified in technologies which make individual differences and capacities visible, inscribing or noting them in legible forms. This section considers some of these practices.

Selection
Selection procedures are an obvious form of examining. Selection testing – a systematic procedure for observing an individual's behaviour and describing it with the aid of a numerical scale or category system – is an important means of 'knowing' and managing employees. Such techniques, however, are only required when there is a need for the co-ordination of large numbers of people, and the ability to differentiate among them. The latter is dependent upon the emergence of large-scale manufacturing and the growth of labour markets. Prior to industrialization, recruitment on a large basis was limited. Individuals were not 'known' in 'themselves', but only through a proxy, for example, owning a parcel of land, or belonging to a particular family. The monasteries accepted anybody to join them who could bring a small endowment, or were known because they belonged to a particular family. Once in the organization, a probationary period of a year enabled the abbot to 'know' if the individual was appropriate or not (Lawrence, 1989). Recruitment at court, if not based on feudal obligation, was usually on the same basis of proxies of land or family. Selection was based on the process of avowal, the process of vouching for others, based on the ties of family, allegiance, and protection. Recruitment into the officer class of the navy and the army also was based on this method.

The early factories acquired their workforce from workhouses, orphanages and prisons. Recruitment and selection evolved as a factor when these forms of 'captive' labour could no longer be relied upon. In craft employment, recruitment was largely handled through the unions, with successful completion of an apprenticeship the necessary basis for employment. Hiring fairs were held for farm servants in search of annual paid employment, from the fourteenth to the twentieth centuries, with as many as 15 000 attending some hiring fairs in the nineteenth century (Catt, 1986; Roberts, 1988). Here enquiries were made about background, where the individual was born, the service they had been in and the work done. Other 'clues' included physique, cleanliness, dress and clothing. With intermittent employment in the nineteenth century, factory recruitment was random, the foreman at the gate hiring the quantity of 'hands' required,[4] or through a reliance on the proxy of the family. School and university networks also became 'proxies' for knowing individuals, more so with the development of an education system in the nineteenth century.[5] It was only in the late nineteenth century that the civil service introduced a formal examination as the basis of selection into its ranks (Anstey, 1971a,b).[6]

There was little knowledge of, or interest in, the individual in the largely undifferentiated population in early factory organization. Making aspects of the labour process more visible, however, had direct implications for constituting the individual. Control over activity necessarily involves the delineation of the individual, as it specifies the relation of the body to the object. Making activities more visible, through the codification of action, necessarily renders the individual 'known' – the one functions to produce knowledge of the other. Taylorism's attempt to control activity introduced a greater differentiation amongst individuals. Taylor recognized that workers had sentiments, particularly those which dissuaded them from working to their utmost capacity,[7] and it was this which contributed to differences in efficiency. He advocated the 'scientific' selection of the individual, in the belief that certain tasks would be more suited to certain types of individuals. As Taylor specified, 'one of the first requirements of a man who is fit to handle pig-iron as a regular occupation is that he shall be so stupid and phlegmatic that he more nearly resembles in his mental make-up the ox than any other type' (quoted in Rose, 1981: 36). From Taylorism came the importance of differentiating individuals in work. It required that the activity of men, their skills, 'the way they set about their tasks, their promptness, their zeal, their behaviour' (Foucault, 1977: 173), be taken into account. Taylorism advocated that individuals should be selected, trained and paid in accordance with their ability to perform specific tasks, thus creating dimensions in which the individual was to be rendered knowable. Undertaking a 'complete' job analysis laid down the dimensions of the individual or the criteria necessary to do the job,[8] but as Hollway (1991: 65) notes, individuals' aptitudes and abilities become known 'in terms of the requirements of machine-based manufacturing industry'. Greater differentiation arose in early classification systems derived largely on the basis of observable factors such as skill, age, performance, and behaviour, etc. Systems of classification, partitioning and ranking also contributed to the enumeration of the capabilities of organizational members.

Testing

The basis for selection is premised on fitting the person to the job, finding the 'best man' for the job.[9] In other words, the worker is 'to be individualized in terms of his or her particular psychological make-up and idiosyncrasies, the job analysed in terms of its demands upon the worker, and human resources were to be matched to occupational demands' (Rose, 1990: 67). It is the psychological calculation of suitability. Supported by a belief that employees who are carefully and appropriately matched to their jobs are satisfied and productive, skilled job-matching involves defining the job, that is, the content and the required behaviours of the job (the job description, the policies and procedures of the organization, the positions, goals, and the listing of tasks). From this is developed a taxonomy of essential and desirable qualities and skills the preferred candidate should have, including education, work experience and qualifications, and minimum levels in these to be attained. Also recommended is that categories are established to assess how well candidates meet these requirements. These are then ranked in order of importance. Thus a matrix is established which assesses candidates in relation to job criteria, sometimes with recommendations that each individual should be scored according to the identified criteria. This disciplinary matrix allows the individual to be related to the population, to be accepted or eliminated accordingly. Sometimes this procedure is quite elaborate with the development of skill profiles, a composite of traits and qualities which exist in the 'best' employees, which is then used as the basis of comparison. Again, the disciplinary matrix is suggested as a method for using this material, for example, the advice that managers should: write down desirable skills; summarize the skills in ten or twelve major categories; rank the skills in order of importance; determine which skills can be taught; set an acceptable level for each skill on a scale of one to seven to determine a minimum score a manager will accept (Trow, 1990). The repertory grid technique also recommended as a basis for the person–job match in selection (Anderson, 1990), is a more sophisticated technology but principally works on the method just outlined, whereby dimensions, criteria or constructs underlying rationales are articulated.

Competency-based selection is an extension of this process and is based on a system of interviewing outstanding and average employees, to determine behaviour patterns present in the outstanding group. These behaviour patterns are labelled 'differentiator competencies', and the whole premiss of the selection process is based on the accurate definition of the criteria most critical for job success. Often, performance indicators are clustered into groups, for example, problem-solving may include: problem identification, judgement, practical sense, decisiveness; administration: planning and organization, control, strategy, organizational know-how, specialized knowledge; supervision: behaviour to individuals, management of the group as a whole, and so on.

Any assessment procedure used to make decisions regarding a job applicant's qualifications is a test, although the specific format of some 'tests' make them more identifiably so. This is especially the case where there is a systematic procedure for observing an individual's behaviour and describing it with the aid of a numerical scale or category system. In this sense tests may include application forms; personality inventory tests; aptitude tests which aim to determine an employee's potential in a specific discipline; proficiency tests, which measure whether an individual has achieved proficiency in a particular area or discipline; perception-tests and knowledge-based tests; trainability tests and work-sample tests (Robertson and Downs, 1989); honesty testing (used in pre-employment screening especially in the States to ensure against 'employee counter-productivity') requires disclosure of information about inner attitudes and past behaviour (Sackett et al., 1989); self-assessment or effectiveness tests; and graphology.

Most testing advances by the means of a taxinomia or grid, the use of which allows similarities and differences among people to be recognized. The very act of enumerating attributes in a programmatic or codified manner allows for the amount of a particular attribute or quality to be measured and thereafter compared with others. Through grids, individuals are rendered observable, measurable and quantifiable. There is the mathematization of difference (Hacking, 1990; Rose, 1988). No matter how informally conducted, selection tests fulfil the function described by Rose (1988) of providing 'a grid of codeability of personal attributes', and enhance the calculability of individuals by placing them on a comparative scalar measure.

Formal testing procedures are now incorporated into the selection procedures of many private corporations, although the extent of this practice is an under-researched area. A survey of large firms in the UK indicates a growing use of psychological tests, biodata and assessment centres, although the interview remains dominant (Shackleton and Newell, 1991).[10] The following brief description of some of the main selection devices indicates how they act as an examinatory technology.

The preliminary screening device is normally the application form or curriculum vitae. In reading or screening these employers act to constitute the individual in a particular way, constructing profiles around stability of employment history; consistency of positions and responsibilities; achievements, experience and education. The use of biographical data to construct the individual and predict future behaviour has a long history. In 1894, in the US, the Washington Life Insurance company suggested the selection of potential life insurance agents could be improved by insisting that all applicants answer a standardized list of questions relating to age, residence, marital status, previous experience and career history (Mackay, 1988). The responses of good and bad salesmen were related to the various items of an application blank or form by Woods in 1915 (quoted in Ferguson, 1963), and in 1917 Scott included a personal history record in his list of 'Aids in the Selection of Salesmen' (quoted in Mayfield, 1964). Biographical data has become more formalized with the development of biodata, a systematic method for assessing job applicants on the basis of personal history, which is premised on the use of past behaviour to predict future performance. In the Second World War, the scored biodata form was used extensively by the armed forces. Parish and Drucker (1957) report the results of a sixteen year research programme by the US Army in which biodata had been the most consistently successful tool for predicting ratings of leadership (Mackay, 1988).

Biodata is a particular type of selection device which has gained some popularity in the UK (Townley, 1989a). It standardizes the historical information which is collected and establishes a clear scoring system tracing patterns of behaviour over time.[11] Factors which are identified include home background, school environment, family socialization, educational achievement, economic stability – 'positive early socialization experiences'. Existing employees' responses are used as the basis for identifying patterns which differentiate 'good' from 'bad' performers. Scores are determined according to the responses of successful incumbents by analysing the relationship between the responses on biographical items to measures of job performance (e.g. absences, productivity, turnover). Information pertaining to an applicant's personal history is given a mathematical weight to produce a 'score' for each individual. One scoring method is the horizontal per cent method. For example, if 60 per cent of a sample of incumbents indicate that a particular biographical detail is common and 45 per cent of this group are successful, a similar response by future applicants receives a weight of 75 per cent (45/60). One version of this, the weighted application form, is a rapid scoring device which is scored 'capitalizing on the three hallmarks of progress in selection: standardization, quantification and understanding' (Milkovich et al., 1988: 394). As a procedure, however, this works against the importance of achievements in non-occupational settings, as for example what is understood by the criterion 'experience' in the evaluation of women's application forms when returning to the workforce after raising a family.

Other selection devices include personality and interest tests. Focus on personality is based on the assumption that individual differences in personality, moderated by ability, have their effects on performance. Thus statements are made that personality variables are significant predictors of job performance if they are matched carefully with the appropriate occupation and organization (Day and Silverman, 1989). The premiss that 'personality' affects job performance has led to measures of its supposed constituent components, the attempt to quantify 'all the qualities of the human soul' (Rose, 1988: 194). Taxonomies of individual dimensions are constructed: for example, restraint, aggressiveness, sociability, emotional stability, friendliness, objectiveness. The most famous of these personality tests is Cattell's 16PF test, subsequently superseded by the Occupational Personality Questionnaire which tests for additional categories of empathy, being 'active', 'planful', and 'contesting'. Some of these tests become specialized for occupations, such as the Myers–Briggs Type Indicator for success in sales which measures empathy, ego-drive (persuasiveness) and ego-strength. The Myers–Briggs Type Indicator, for example, summarizes an individual's personality based on the degree of extroversion, an inclination to focus on specifics or generalities, whether decisions are based on logic or emotions, and the speed of decision-making. It rests on a system of binary divides which of necessity values one characteristic over the other, most specifically, extroversion rather than introversion, logic rather than emotions. It should be noted that there are a number of assumptions underlying these criteria which reflect what the ideal candidate should look like – quick at making decisions based on logic, able to see the general picture, and extrovert. The gender implications of such models should not be ignored. Ipsative personality tests are other examples of the examination of the individual. Essentially these are self-appraisal personality inventories, typically employing forced-choice, ranked-scale format. Although not valid for inter-individual comparisons, they cannot be used for comparing individuals on a scale by scale basis, they are used to determine personality 'types' or 'syndromes' (Johnson et al., 1988). Other tests include IQ, critical thinking and interest tests, which, when combined with biographical information, are deemed to give a picture of a suitable candidate. Temperament profiles assess an individual's character, leadership qualities and likely performance in various job roles.[12]

Testing contains a number of problematic assumptions: that the individual can be matched to the job; that job descriptions capture the nature of work; that there is a relationship between the functions of the job and personal characteristics; that 'attributes' are distinguishable and isolable, and are directly related to a 'job'; that 'jobs' pre-exist rather than being organizational constructs (see Smith and Robertson, 1989). Personnel practice concentrates on managing these problems. But this is to miss their significance. These tests function as a means of measuring and evaluating individuals, 'differentiating between them for the purposes of prediction and control of behaviour' (Hollway, 1984: 40). They render individuals calculable and manageable by 'representing in standard forms, human mental capacities and behavioural characteristics which previously had to be described in complex and idiosyncratic language' (Rose, 1988: 195).

As Taylor (1986: 76) comments, 'to try to bring it (the individual) under the control of reason is to divide what should be a living unity'. Not only this, the individual is constructed in a particular way. There is a specific view of the individual as an 'essential' personality which does not change according to situation nor is it manifest in a 'relational' context reflective of interaction. The individual is assumed to hold the same, or broadly similar, criteria of judgement or similar preferences, over time. He or she bears the consequences of their past actions, as the past and future actions are linked together. Society, in other words, is conceived 'as a population of preconstructed, pre-labelled individuals each a bearer of interests that he will seek to enhance' (Pizzorno, 1992: 204). It becomes the task of the employing organization to 'discover' these dimensions of the individual. Individuals become known in comparison to others, not in their own right. Identity is constituted through its relation with a matrix. This is, perhaps, the ultimate objectivization.

The examination has been considered in the context of selection, but its actions may be identified in a range of personnel activities. It is equally applicable to an analysis of performance appraisal techniques, which aim to evaluate an individual on specific dimensions, according to some comparative scalar measure. The appraisal form and documentation, for example, constitute knowledge of the individual in a particular manner (the quality of work, attitude and interpersonal skills, initiative, technical skills, attendance, etc.). Their standardized nature operates to individualize and totalize. As with selection tests, they establish a process of differentiation and judgement locating efficiency or productivity at the level of the individual. Again, based on 'subjective' or 'objective' standards, using results/outcomes, or process, there is a tendency to reduce dimensions of the individual to numerical equivalents. Individuals may be classified as being 'outstanding', 'superior', 'satisfactory' or 'average', and 'below average'. This examinatory procedure, which translates individuals into 'numerical equivalents', operates as a system of governance which may often become incorporated into an individual's subjective assessment of themselves.

Assessment Centres

A more elaborate examinatory procedure can be seen in use in assessment centres. The assessment centre, a more elaborate version of the examination, owes its origins to War Officer selection boards (WOSBs), which were used during the Second World War for the selection of officers. They were established in 1942 when the supply of 'suitable' recruits known through the proxies of universities and public schools was no longer sufficient for recruitment purposes. Over a period of three days, candidates were given a number of tests, including intelligence and personality tests, interviews, biographical and medical questionnaires and practical tests. Following the war, the Tavistock Institute for Human Relations developed these procedures for the recruitment and development of managers. They were also adopted for selection in the Civil Service. Although primarily designed for selection and promotion decisions, they are also used for career planning, self-development, succession planning and organizational development – all processes which require an indepth knowledge of the individual as the basis of rational decision-making.

Assessment centres consist of a standardized evaluation of behaviour based on many inputs. They involve a series of exercises and tests conducted over a few days, in which candidates have to demonstrate knowledge, skills and abilities considered to be most important to the new position. The exercises are designed to simulate job conditions realistically, and elicit behaviour important to the role. They are based on job analysis and skill identification of major activities, responsibilities and tasks associated with a position.[13] Thus, for example, if it is decided that the essential skills are leadership, interpersonal communication, problem solving and persuasion skills, a series of structured exercises including collaborative and competitive situations are established, with the goal of eliciting a wide range of behaviours which assessors may evaluate. Exercises include presentations, group decision-making or discussion, in-basket exercises, simulation exercises, and leaderless group exercises. There is usually also an interview. Assessors rate a different number of dimensions in the exercises. For example, in-tray or in-basket exercises may test listing, prioritizing and action planning from a set of letters and memoranda.

In addition to multiple assessment techniques, there are also multiple assessors who are trained in recording and observing behaviour, usually with the aid of behaviour checklists. There is also a separation of evaluation from observation. Final assessment is based on an 'overall assessment rating', that is, there is a final 'mark' placed on the individual – the numerical translation of an individual into a number, for the purposes of action at a distance. Debate is in terms of whether final scores should be mechanically or judgementally combined, with some evidence suggesting superiority of mechanical over judgemental combination (Feltham, 1988; Lowry, 1988).

The advantages claimed for assessment centres is that they place candidates in realistic settings (a lot of the assessment is conducted in groups, which is supposed to characterize managerial work), in which they must prioritize activities, make decisions, and act upon these. In operation, however, there may be inadequate specification of 'target competencies' against which participants are assessed, which may be loosely defined in non-behavioural terms which may be overlapping (Dulewicz, 1991). There are also low correlations of dimension rating across assessment centre exercises (Gatewood et al., 1990). Other concerns are that assessment centres measure situation-specific performance rather than cross-situational managerial skills (Bycio et al., 1987), measuring exercises rather than traits (Robertson et al., 1987). Suggestions for improving assessment centres are given in technical terms, increased training, more precise definitions of what is being measured, adequate job analyses, etc. But there is a number of broader questions which are raised.

The assumptions behind the examination are that there is a set of verifiable, predictable management characteristics. As indicated in Chapter 3, management or management potential is a nebulous concept. Standard descriptors of planning, organizing, leading and controlling are rarely reflected in behaviour. There is the danger that dimensions identified reflect the *image* of management, rather than what managers actually do, raising questions as to whether it is congruence with expectations of a managerial role which is being assessed (Smith and Blackham, 1988).[14] Kotter (1982), for example, notes how the apparently accidental way in which a manager operates is efficient, providing essential information, understanding and contact. Whilst there are many benefits of assessment centre procedures, for example, clarifying the nature of jobs and articulating implicit values which underpin these, and individuals may learn a great deal from them, it must be recognized that these models are founded on the rational model of organizations, where complete or optimal knowledge influences rational decision-making.

Several other dimensions are also missing from the assessment of the job, principally that it takes place within a hierarchy in which not only power but personal politics is an important dimension of 'skill'. Failure in a position is not necessarily because of incompetence, but a failure to fit the peer group or dominant managerial philosophy. Assessment centres also reinforce hierarchy, validation is against a hierarchical evaluation of performance or success. What is being recorded is the effectiveness of perpetuating an in-built hierarchical evaluation, especially as assessment centres have an impact upon candidates' post-assessment attitudes towards the organization and their jobs (Robertson et al., 1991). Although evidence indicates that assessment centres predict future performance reasonably well (Iles et al., 1989), another 'predictor' of success is subordinate appraisal. In one study ratings by subordinates outperformed assessment centres as predictors over a two to four year period, and were as accurate in predictions over a seven year period (Anderson and Shackleton, 1988). This latter method of forecasting managerial talent, however, is rarely advocated. Also missing is the recognition that these senior hierarchies are usually male dominated and that what is being assessed is not only an image of management, but also a very gender specific model of what is involved (Calas and Smircich, 1991). The racial composition of managerial hierarchies also has implications for what is understood as leadership characteristics (Morouney, 1991).

The purpose of the examination is to make the individual an object of knowledge and power. This is achieved through reducing the individual to a physical or emotional component of their identity which is then evaluated and measured. Once a dimension of the individual is identified it may then become the object of management intervention. An example of the latter is Hochschild's (1983) analysis of Delta Airline's inflight service programme, deemed to be one of the best in the airline industry, which places a high premium on service.

Hochschild describes the training flight attendants receive, and illustrates how one particular facet of the individual becomes isolated and placed under examination. As airlines are ranked in well-publicized customer evaluations by the quality of service their personnel offer, this ranking influences the training of flight attendants. The aspect of the individual which receives close attention is the stewardess's smile.

> The value of the personal smile is groomed to reflect the company's disposition – its confidence that its planes will not crash, its reassurance that departures and arrivals will be on time, its welcome and its invitation to return. Trainers take it as their job to attach to the trainee's smile an attitude, a viewpoint, a rhythm of feeling that is, as they often say, professional. (Hochschild, 1983: 4)

Smiles are part of flight attendants' work. The company lays claim to the attendants' emotional actions – 'corporate logic creates links between competition, market comparison, advertising, passenger expectations and company demands for acting'. The smile becomes an extension of recorded music, airplane decor and make-up. Its effect is to estrange workers from their own smiles. The worker becomes estranged or alienated from an aspect of self, even to the extent of workers talking about smiles being 'on' them.[15]

The Inscribed Subject

The examination also introduces individuality into the field of documentation. The same process which places individuals in a field of surveillance, also situates them in a network of writing; 'it engages them in a whole mass of documents that capture and fix them' (Foucault, 1977: 189). Individuals become 'cases' to be measured, described, evaluated, examined and compared, 'real lives are converted into written case notes' (Burrell, 1988: 226). Documentation registers the services and value of each individual and acts as an integral part of the process of objectification. As with the specific mechanisms used to elicit information, the recording of knowledge is not a neutral process. As Pym (1973: 233) notes of appraisal, 'the most damaging aspect of the activity is the need for written formalization, the supposition that relationships and personal performance can be encapsulated in a static framework. There is something final and irreversible about what is written.' The very act of recording has a control effect because records are kept 'the organization members presume that they are being kept for some purpose (or at least that their existence will induce some purpose for them)' (Cyert and March, 1963 quoted in Cooper et al., 1981: 178). 'Documentation, a whole meticulous archive, is no longer a monument for future memory but a document for possible use' (Foucault, 1977: 191).

Documentation, the individual file, is an important aspect of personnel. The first stage in formal disciplinary procedures, for example, involves entering details on a person's file. Recording negative information has a long history – the Book of Hours in monasteries recorded individual deviations from the monastic rule (Lawrence, 1989). Enmeshing the individual in documentation occurs throughout the employment relationship. The idea of an individual record card was used in Cadbury's early Bournville factories, in which each 'girl' had a record card on which was inscribed offences or points of special merit (Hollway, 1991). The introduction of specialized personnel systems evolved from practices introduced in the First World War, in which tables of occupational requirements for units and specialist skills of recruits were registered. 'The system thus had the capacity to link the one with the other and to distribute the skilled specialists in a systematic and rational manner to the places where they were required' (Rose, 1990: 18).[16] Other personnel records, references, test scores, performance evaluation records, potential assessments, all contribute to an enumeration of the capabilities of organizational members. Foucault (1977: 191) notes, 'these small techniques of notation, of registration, of constituting files of arranging facts in columns and tables that are so familiar to us now, were of decisive importance in the epistemological "thaw" of the sciences of the individual'. All are familiar tools which register 'human resources'.

The coercive effect of individual documentation becomes evident when it is incorporated into systems of registration which link it to the details of others. As individual data is integrated into a cumulative system, so the individual is located on a general register and concomitantly affects overall calculations. Not only is the individual linked to the general but the nature of the general is affected by the actions of the individual.

This opportunity for governance is enhanced with the growing recommendations that databases be computerized, including the computerization of job descriptions and job information (Boelter and Olsen, 1991).

Computerized human resource information systems, and their ability to develop sophisticated systems and be able to update them, provide the basis for personnel to adopt a consulting support to the organization. They provide the basis for decisions to be taken at a distance in centres of administrative power. The methods used for collecting the statistics on activity are easily transported to 'centres of calculation' (Latour, 1987) where judgements are made. The bridging of physical distance, however, is only partially accomplished. The information will be assessed in a context quite different from that in which it has been gathered, with the increased likelihood that the information will be interpreted reflecting different sets of interests. The information supplied denies the physical processes and social relationships which engendered it.

Towards a Genealogy

The aim of the examination is to objectify the individual through procedures of standardization, description and measurement. Its use varies greatly. The relative lack of visibility of the individual is reflected in Japanese selection procedures, which are more heavily dependent on school grades and the honours system of references than detailed selection testing (Marx, 1988). The emphasis on the individual is a role taken over by the educational system with its highly competitive emphasis and concentration on examination results. Without the firmly established proxies of the educational system to rely on in selection procedure, however, Japanese companies abroad constitute the individual as an object through the use of very detailed selection procedures. For example, Toyota locating in Kentucky in the US used technical skills assessment, interpersonal assessment, leadership assessment, technical performance assessment, 'Toyota' assessment and health assessment. More than 60 000 applicants were considered over a twelve month period (Cosentino et al., 1990). Detailed selection procedures were also used by Nissan when they established a plant in the north of England (Townley, 1989a; Wickens, 1988).

The intense objectification of the individual in elaborate testing and examination procedures is also a feature of US systems. This practice has been heavily influenced by legislation and judicial decisions. Anti-discrimination law and the judicial decisions stemming from it has restricted the type of selection tests and appraisal systems which may be used in the US (Rust and Golombok, 1989). It is in violation of Title VII of the Civil Rights Act to use any employee selection method which is not related to job performance and has a disproportionate impact on a protected group (Sobol and Ellard, 1988). This also applies to 'subjective' hiring practices, that is, interviews. The doctrine of negligent hiring or negligent retention in the US has also influenced the type of selection processes which are used, and the extent to which the individual is to be 'known' (Petersen and

Massengill, 1989). Equally, these factors influence the degree to which the individual becomes an inscribed subject. Anti-discrimination legislation in Japan, on the other hand, has not had this impact. The 1984 Equal Opportunity Law which emphasized equal treatment for men and women at the time of entry into employment does not benefit those already employed (Adachi, 1989; Hosni, 1990), and has not impacted on the type of selection procedures which might result. Generally, trade unions have not mounted much criticism or opposition to the use of psychological measurement for selection purposes (Hollway, 1991), nor do they seem to have thought out policies on these issues.

As Jacoby (1988) notes, the diffusion of behavioural science through-out industry has been positively related to its perceived profitability and inversely to its cost. But whilst organizational interest in social science is 'an effort to obtain knowledge which can be used to augment labour pro-ductivity' (Rose, 1981: 16), an economic rationale cannot account for the variation in social science 'truth' which accompanies it and the difference in practices that this entails. The variation in the development of various techniques, for example, owes much to the development of industrial psy-chology, which differed from the US to the UK (see Hollway, 1991; Rose, 1990), influenced by the difference in the funding of higher educational establishments, where much of the research was carried out,[17] and because of the disciplinary practices already in place to which these techniques were applied.

The role of the military in providing the basis for personnel techniques is also an important, if neglected, aspect of its history. The organization of work in itself owes a lot to military models with many management terms, for example, line and staff, coming from this sphere. Co-ordination of the war effort required the development of principles for organizing a popu-lation on a large scale. A doyen of military psychology described its tasks as 'job analysis and adaptation of machinery and equipment, characterol-ogy and personnel selection, training [and] morale' (quoted in Rose, 1990: 19). A lot of the taxonomies for analysis, which originated from the mil-itary, were later incorporated into corporate policies (although the military still funded and funds a lot of the research into 'perfecting' these tech-niques). In both the US and the UK the army was important in developing selection techniques, and the technology for mass psychometric selection developed out of the war. Rose also (1990: 48) notes that 'the invention of the "group", the concept of "social" or "human" relations as key determi-nants of individual conduct, were the most consistent lesson of the psychological and psychiatric experience of war.' The Tavistock Institute, which became influential in industrial and occupational psychology, had its origins in the Second World War. Early research on leadership was funded by the military in the US, from whence it became transferred to organizational hierarchies at work (Hollway, 1991: 111). Baron (1986) also illustrates how the personnel function enhanced its role as the result of wartime legislation, an enhancement which also occured in the UK (Niven, 1967). Once established there is then a professional interest in maintaining this position.

The dissemination of social science knowledge by personnel professionals and consultants is another dimension which affects personnel discourse and practices and the extent to which the individual may be constituted as an object of knowledge. The role of the behavioural sciences in developing personnel management as a profession has been an important dimension of its development. Lupton's IPM text *Industrial Behaviour and Personnel Management*, first published in 1964, reprinted six times before being reissued in 1978, is a case in point. He states in its preface, 'personnel management must increasingly become the application of behavioural sciences to problems of the structure and functioning of industrial and commercial organizations'. In the efforts to gain in status from being a relatively minor administrative aid to management to being an industrial profession, personnel management is described as being a 'technology of these sciences' (Lupton, 1978: 1). The special skill which is advocated as being the realm of the personnel professional is 'the capacity first to recognize human needs' (Lupton, 1978: 5). Having identified how this may be frustrated or enhanced in organizations, administrative and other procedures can be devised to ameliorate or mitigate their effects. The personnel manager thus becomes the 'expert in the analysis and diagnosis of the social structure and functioning of organizations' (Lupton, 1978: 5). Requirements for this are psychology, social psychology, sociology, and social anthropology, thus: 'He [sic] must also have a method of analyzing human social behaviour so as to be able to say with reasonable certainty, or at least with more certainty than others, what the consequences of managerial decisions are likely to be for relationships within the company' (Lupton, 1978: 19). Whilst such a skill may be picked up 'by trial and error . . . what is surely required is a more general skill, rigorously and systematically taught and applied' (Lupton, 1978: 19).

As with any profession, there has been an attempt to ensure technical standards of performance with collegiate control over these. Legitimate knowledge with its systems of measurement, classification, recording and calculation, offering scientific, research-based, rational 'answers' to managerial problem-solving, has become defined through publications, professional journals, meetings and the operation of professional associations generally. Control over examination syllabi also serves to promote particular views of the profession's role. Early in its history the IPM established associations with universities for training programmes and in 1955 developed its own examination scheme and regulations. In 1975, these courses included statistics, psychology, sociology, economics and a general personnel option: training and development, employment/

employee services and IR. In Japan, by contrast, HR management is not usually considered a profession, rather managers are rotated in the various functional areas, HR being one of these. The HR manager is also expected to know more about employees in Japan than, for example, in the US. This involves knowing the individual in a different way from the examined individual of close observation (Overman, 1990).

A continuation of this is the recommendation that practising managers should adopt 'advances' by occupational psychologists, and that psychological testing and assessment centres have to be developed with the aid of a qualified occupational psychologist, by organizations desirous of developing systematic selection techniques (Anderson and Shackleton, 1990). The organizational psychologist is thus the expert who can diagnose a problem (assuming that a 'problem' exists and is merely waiting to be discovered) and generate possible alternative solutions (Warmke, 1988). As Rose (1990: 95) notes of the psychologists of work, they provide 'a vocabulary and a technology for rendering the labour of the worker visible, calculable and manageable, enabling it to be integrated into the rational economic calculus'. It is the portrayal of knowledge for technical advantage – technicist 'solutions' for the enhancement of productivity, despite pronouncements of welfarist or best interest statements. Expertise, especially with its claims to rationality, fairness, and a 'scientific' approach, may parade as being in the interests of all – an authority 'on' rather than an authority 'over'.[18]

The danger of an emphasis on the technical is that there is the virtual monopolizing of an area to the exclusion of those who do not have specialist training to interpret results, who are usually those most directly concerned with the outcome. An example is the emphasis on 'scientific' selection techniques and the recommended rejection of those which are shown to have less validity, despite their popularity. Technologies are offered as facilitating, or even categorically proving a particular action or decision. They are mechanisms which are somehow divorced from the structures of domination which provide the basis for conceptual mediation. Technicist views of knowledge are in danger of creating a role for the expert, with its appeals to accuracy and objectivity, as though they are simple empirical mechanisms to access a predetermined world, and remove the political and ethical element of such procedures. This is not to argue, however, that discrimination and the reinforcement of stereotypes may not occur in the more 'popular' procedures, rather to argue that these problems can be alleviated through other means, training for example, rather than restraining participation. They necessarily close down avenues of participation and involvement.

The individual as object is premised on the view that knowledge of the individual is an important dimension of productivity and profitability for the organization, and that social and psychological attitudes are important factors in the 'production' process. It is also based on the belief that the 'full' knowledge of the individual is necessary in order to ensure the most productive capacity. The individual as object is premised on the view that knowledge may be obtained from the examinatory technologies which 'observe' behaviour, attitudes, etc. Constructing the individual as an object of knowledge, therefore, involves the delineation of components of individuality identified through these technologies, enabling the individual to be located on a matrix. Literally, the individual becomes an object of knowledge, and an object to be commanded. But it would be a mistake to assume that the individual is a passive participant in the constitution of identity. The process of constructing an identity also influences how the individual sees him or herself, that is, how they view themselves as subjects. It is to the individual's active role to which we now turn.

Notes

1 Thus organizations devise micro-penalties around time (lateness, absences); activity (inattention, negligence); behaviour, speech, the body.

2 The identified components of personality are reserved, outgoing; less intelligent, more intelligent; affected by feelings, emotionally stable; submissive, dominant; serious, happy-go-lucky; expedient, conscientious; timid, venturesome; tough-minded, sensitive; trusting, suspicious; practical, imaginative; forthright, shrewd; self-assured, apprehensive; conservative, experimenting; group dependent, self-sufficient; uncontrolled, controlled.

3 This new knowledge was also incorporated into practices for knowing the family and the child, see Rose (1990).

4 This practice remained in some areas into the early decades of the twentieth century and was one of the bases of unionization drives.

5 The use of these proxies for labour still continue, as for example in manufacturing (Maguire, 1986) and the 'old boys network' in managerial jobs.

6 Examinations as the basis of selection have a long history, with the earliest recorded being at the court of the Chinese emperors. In 1115 BC the emperor required all applicants for government positions to take examinations in horsemanship, archery, writing, arithmetic, music and the required ceremonies or rites (Mitchell, 1988).

7 This was not elaborated in terms of the psychology of individual differences because this was poorly developed at the time of his writing. It was not necessarily the lack of recognition of sentiments, but rather the inability to make them the objects of knowledge, that is, to place them in a matrix in which they could be known, and more importantly, managed. This came with the 'technological' developments of the First World War.

8 The individual, however, becomes 'known' in a particular manner as illustrated in the following: 'The Directorate for Selection of Personnel had undertaken a complete job analysis of the multitudinous tasks in the different arms of the Service, and as a result was able to lay down the standards of intelligence and other aptitudes necessary for each job, thus providing the basis for the correct posting of men in certain proportions to each type of unit' (quoted in Rose, 1990: 42).

9 Hiring for the organization, rather than the job, extends the type of analyses which is required, thus organizational analysis supplements job analysis; and personality attributes may be screened in addition to skills, knowledge and abilities. 'Fit' is now required between personality and climate–culture, between work environment and the 'type' of person required (Bowen et al., 1991).

10 An important dimension here is the dissemination of these selection devices in trade journals.

11 Biodata receives a relatively high degree of validity, indicating that some items appear stable across time independent of knowledge, skills and abilities (Rothstein et al., 1990). Biographical information is thought to be a useful predictor of several criteria for salespeople and top-level managers (Russell, 1990), and the training success of professionals (Drakeley et al., 1988). For example, for occupations requiring security clearance criteria which seem to be important include getting into trouble in school, reasons given for considering quitting school, employment experience, measurement of grades and participation in school clubs, criminal activity (i.e. arrests), and the measurement of socio-economic status (McDaniel, 1989).

12 It is interesting to note that in a survey of US human resource managers, over half reported that they would automatically reject a job applicant who refused to take a personality test (Blocklyn, 1988).

13 In the US there are professional guidelines which have replaced a 1979 Standards and Ethical Considerations for Assessment Centre Operations, which specify the job analysis role, clarify the kinds of attributes to be assessed, delineate the methods of observation, evaluation and aggregation of information, as well as specifying training.

14 It is perhaps for this reason that construct validity of assessment centre dimensions is rarely obtained, and the reasons for its success are hard to distinguish (Klimoski and Brickner, 1987).

15 De Michiel's (1983) analysis of health and safety provides another example of how the physical body of the individual becomes objectified. She analyses how health and safety discourses – policies, practices, the way issues and individuals are viewed – exhibit tendencies to fragment and objectify the body. The idea that parts of the body can be separated from the whole person allows them to become not parts of the body but products to be purchased. Through fragmentation and objectification parts of the body are made interchangeable with protective equipment. The inevitable extension of commodity production is the translation of individuals into numerical equivalents, the epitome of which is described by de Michiel (1983) in her study of occupational health and safety policies, which act to commodify the body 'supervising its sale'. Through the operation of these schemes and following a medical examination, the left little finger is the equivalent of $6723.78 (Australian), a leg $22 000. In Canada reference is made to the 'meat chart'.

16 As the person who introduced this scheme states, 'a cynic might even say that the psychologist's greatest contribution to the war effort was the introduction of a system of colour-coded celluloid tabs indicating occupational skills on the army's personnel cards' (Rose, 1990: 18–19).

17 Industrial psychology emerged earlier in the US than the UK, and the growth in applied psychology initially derived from its ability to be able to understand the 'market', that is, individual consumers (Rose, 1981: 91). On a related issue, the role of educational establishments in influencing the type of practices which may proliferate is an important one, see, for example, Hoskin and Macve (1986) on the role of Westpoint Military Academy on the dissemination of the examination.

18 As Anthony (1977: 261) notes: 'A great deal of management education, that part of it concerned with behavioural science, is in fact theocratic, it is designed to establish a sense of unity of purpose and of values, largely by providing managers with a common language and a system of concepts. Management education is truly ideological in this sense, that it aims to influence behaviour by inculcating beliefs and expectations. Dissemination of an ideology by way of management training has these two latent functions: it helps to promote the internal solidarity of management and it helps to justify its authority over subordinates.'

5

The Individual as Subject

The presentation of the individual in HRM stresses the importance of recognizing inherent needs and attitudes which have to be managed for the effective organization of work. It assumes the existence of an alienated individual whose potential lies repressed, waiting to be unleashed or self-actualized when his or her true nature is uncovered. A Foucauldian conception of the subject emphasizes the constitutive role of practices in forming an identity. The techniques that make individuals objects of knowledge and power also constitute them as subjects. They provide individuals with self-knowledge and a sense of identity.[1]

This chapter examines three types of HRM techniques which constitute the identity of the individual worker. Firstly, those practices by which individuals try to locate and identify themselves. Secondly, the practices which are directed at reconstituting the subjectivity of the worker. Thirdly, practices which attempt to construct an identity of the productive subject and thereby establish the individual as an active agent in a productive role.

The Confession

The individual is both an object and a subject of power and knowledge; these two sides corresponding to two notions of 'truth' and methods for its discovery. As an object, the 'truth' about an individual is amenable to the conventional methods of positivistic social science. This is 'surface' knowledge, truth as it appears to others through observation, that is, empirical knowledge. As a subject, the 'truth' about an individual is hidden from view and must be accessed through other methods which delve deeper.

A belief in this hidden knowledge is reflected in some management literature related to knowing the individual:

> the individual knows . . . more than anyone else about his own capabilities, needs, strengths and weaknesses, and goals . . . no available methods can provide the superior with the knowledge he needs to make such decisions . . . ratings, aptitude and personality tests, and the superior's necessarily limited knowledge of the man's performance yield at best an imperfect picture. (McGregor, 1972: 136)

McGregor advances this position as a justification for changing performance appraisal systems from the examinatory or judgemental ethos to a developmental one. His statement recognizes that the individual is not just an 'object', but is tied to self-knowledge. The individual as subject entails a belief in an authentic self which lies hidden within, which, through the aid of correct technologies, will reveal itself. The idea of truth which underlies the individual as subject is that 'truth' is not immediately accessible to empirical knowledge, that it is somewhere else, out of reach, located within the individual, a buried secret which has to be accessed. The assumption is of a known truth, usually residing in the consciousness of the knower, which may be forgotten or may slip away from notice, but which may be retrieved through an effort of memory. This truth must be brought into speech and conveyed by the speaker; such a view of the individual would permit the operation of 'pastoral' power. 'This form of power cannot be exercised without knowing the insides of people's minds, without exploring their souls, without making them reveal their innermost secrets. It implies a knowledge of the conscience and an ability to direct it . . . It is linked with the production of truth – the truth of the individual himself' (Foucault, 1983: 214).

Discovering this hidden truth about the individual requires a new technology. The calculative practices of the examination are based on an inadequate psychology. Special emphasis is placed upon the psychological features of 'the producing subject', not as they are 'known' through (social) science, but as they are affirmed by the individual. The individuals must 'own' the understandings of their actions. The spiritual subject has become the object of knowledge (Miller and O'Leary, 1987), and the self-direction of individuals must be incorporated into the 'government' of the organization. But what technologies are required to set up a relationship with the self, 'for self-reflection, self-knowledge, self-examination, for the deciphering of the self by oneself' (Foucault, 1991c)?

The principal technology for producing self-knowledge of the subject is the confessional (Foucault, 1981a, 1988a, 1988b, 1990, 1991c). One of the most ancient Western traditions, the confessional is 'one of the main rituals we rely on for the production of truth' (Foucault, 1981a: 58). It is worth quoting Foucault at length on the role of the confessional:

> The confessional became one of the West's most highly valued techniques for producing truth. We have since become a singularly confessing society. The confession has spread its effects far and wide. It plays a part in justice, medicine, education, family relationships, and love relations, in the most ordinary affairs of everyday life, and in the most solemn rites; one confesses one's crimes, one's sins, one's thoughts and desires, one's illnesses and troubles. One goes about telling with the greatest precision, whatever is most difficult to tell. One confesses in public and in private, to one's parents, one's educators, one's doctor, to those one loves, one admits to oneself, in pleasure and in pain, things it would be impossible to tell to anyone else, the things people write books about. One confesses – or is forced to confess. When it is not spontaneous or dictated by some internal imperative, the confession is wrung from a person by

violence or threat; it is driven from its hiding place the soul, or extracted from the body. (Foucault, 1981a: 59)

Although the confessional is most often associated with religious practices, it may be identified in activities as diverse as consultations, autobiographical narratives, and interrogations, and operates in education, in medicine, and also – as I shall now show – at work.

The confessional operates through avowal, the individual's acknowledgement of his or her own actions and thoughts. From its original meaning of being the guarantee of the status, identity and value granted by one person to another, avowal came to signify acknowledgement of one's own actions and thoughts. It is a process which confirms identity. Through the act of speaking, the self is constituted, tied to self-knowledge which has been uncovered through prior self-examination. Identity is affirmed at the point of speaking. Furthermore, 'in compelling, persuading and inciting subjects to disclose themselves, finer and more intimate regions of personal and interpersonal life come under surveillance and are opened up for expert judgement, normative evaluation, classification and correction' (Rose, 1990: 240).

Confession rarely takes place alone. It requires the individual to break the bounds of discretion or forgetfulness. It is based on the verbalization of thoughts, intentions, consciousness, to a 'master' by virtue of the latter's greater experience and wisdom. Although the very act of articulation, producing truth, serves to act upon the individual – 'it exonerates, redeems, and purifies him; unburdens him of his wrongs, liberates him and promises him salvation' (Foucault, 1981a: 61) – the confession itself requires the presence of an interlocutor or confessor.

> The truth did not reside solely in the subject who by confessing, would reveal it wholly formed. It was constituted in two stages: present but incomplete, blind to itself, in the one who spoke, it could only reach completion in the one who assimilated and recorded it. It was the latter's function to verify this obscure truth: the revelation of the confession had to be coupled with the decipherment of what it said . . . The one who listened . . . was the master of truth. His was a hermeneutic function. With regard to the confession, his power was not only to demand it before it was made, or decide what was to follow after it, but also to constitute a discourse of truth on the basis of its decipherment. (Foucault, 1981a: 67)

Truth is not only assessed in relation to what is told, it is also assessed in relation to how it is told. The role of the confessor is required by virtue of the difficulties experienced in expressing truth. Generally, the greater the obstacles and resistances it has to overcome, the more truthful is the knowledge. The confessor is a verifier of what is confessed. His or her role is that of the authority figure who intervenes in order to judge, punish, forgive or console.

The Confessing Individual

The role of the confessional in HRM can be traced to the non-directed interview of the early Hawthorne studies which provided an insight into factory life. These discovered that sympathetic interview techniques could elicit valuable information for management, information which was not easily accessible and in some cases had not been expressed before. 'One could thus get at the thoughts, attitudes, and sentiments among workers, foremen, supervisors and so on that gave rise to problems, dissatisfactions and conflict' (Rose, 1990: 71). With the disclosure of the information in itself there might be a change in employee attitudes, the airing of grievances was seen by the researchers, and some sections of management, as being therapeutic.

The interviewing programme at Hawthorne led to the development of a range of recommendations as a guide to interviewers (Hollway, 1991), often repeated as the basis of recommendations for selection interviewers today. It became the basis of an indirect type of interviewing which 'was preferable if the spontaneous convictions of the worker were to be obtained' (Roethlisberger and Dickson quoted in Hollway, 1991: 81). This finding illustrated the importance of internally held beliefs. The weight of sheer numbers, however, entailed more standardization in its operation, as seen for example in the use of attitude surveys.

Attitude Surveys

The simplest and most restricted mechanism for accessing the thoughts, views and opinions of individuals is the attitude survey. This technique was first developed by Houser in the US, who was concerned about management's lack of information about employee morale and attitudes. His book, *What the Employee Thinks* (1927), developed quantitative attitude tests as a means of accessing this information (Jacoby, 1988). This, and the use of political opinion polls in US politics in the 1930s, encouraged their introduction in industry (Rose, 1990). They were also encouraged by the mass counselling schemes developed by the Hawthorne studies, as a means of handling mass data (Hollway, 1991). They were adopted after the Second World War, mainly in response to fear of unionization but are now considered an integral part of US communications policy, especially in their identification of some of the causes of turnover and absenteeism (Gallup, 1988; Townley, 1989b).

Employee attitude surveys are used to 'uncover' information about the effectiveness of existing policies and programmes. They question such issues as commitment to the organization, supervisory relationships, workgroup relationships, organizational climate, etc. Most operate through the use of self-completion questionnaires which, once measured, form the basis of remedial action, such as the modification of programmes or the implementation of new policies (although lack of follow up is a frequent complaint of such systems (Feuer, 1987; Sheibar, 1989)). However, IBM, which has used attitude surveys to poll its employees for a number of years, has now developed a computerized system with questions appearing on each employee's screen. The IBM survey also includes an unstructured 'write-in' section. This automated survey gives management access to responses according to specific skill groups and geographical areas (Read, 1991).

Attitude surveys are introduced as a method of overcoming the inevitable dysfunctions of hierarchy. They are a method by which senior managers gain access to the information which employees have. 'Managers must know how and what their employees are thinking in order to manage them successfully and elicit the best performance from them' (Drennan and Walker, 1987). The view which informs them is that of the confession, but the technology is that of the examination. It is, as Rose (1990) notes, a means whereby the internal world of individuals becomes inscribable and calculable, with the Likert scale operating as a device to render attitude quantifiable. Attitudes can now be measured, made known and policies made in the light of this. The degree to which employees are candid, however, is heavily linked to the degree of anonymity that these systems have. The nature of the information, however, is usually highly restricted in terms of the range of topics which are involved and the structuring of the format of the interaction. It does not engage the individual, being a rather passive method of interaction. It also reflects a view of the population as an aggregate of individuals, with views which might coincide, but are in no way representative of a collective interest. It also, as Jacoby (1988) points out, fosters a hierarchical, technocratic approach to solving problems.

The Selection Interview

Knowledge of the individual is important at the point of entry into the organization, and it is here that a number of confessional technologies operate. Pre-screening processes prior to interviews often incorporate this as part of their procedure. Application forms, for example, may conceal such an approach by requesting that the individual acknowledge their main weaknesses or strengths; how they cope with success or disappointment; pleasures or regrets over past decisions. Other selection devices, for example, pre-screening inventories, ask the individual to be as open and as accurate as possible in acknowledging what words or phrases characterize them. 'Life style inventories' ask the individual what is 'like you most of the time'; 'like you quite often'; and 'essentially unlike you'. As part of the progress to humility and perfection in the identification of 'sin', the individual is asked to admit their responses to the following adjectives and adjectival phrases: being proud, self-sufficient, considerate, encourages others, concerned with status, worries a lot, upset if not accepted by others, says what's expected, good listener, usually thinks ahead, honest and direct in feelings, suggestible, concerned with what others think, etc. These inventories, the administration of which are strictly timed, have included in them honesty tests or traps to try to assess the legitimacy of the confession. Other pre-screening inventories ask individuals to rank descriptions of attitudes, as for example the following used as a selection device in an organization which has recently introduced team-working: 'I focus more on my personal relationships with my peers and my supervisor than I do on my relationships with my subordinates'; 'I spend time and effort developing and improving my personal relationships at work'; 'I develop personal relationships at work only when they help me complete my work tasks' or 'I enjoy being perceived as a team member'; 'belonging to a specific team is not a priority with me'; 'I enjoy my individuality, being seen as a team member does not interest me'.

Another confessional device is the interview. This appears a normal, innocuous procedure, but is actually an important part of personnel activity, upon which large decisions may ride – the appointment of individuals to positions, merit pay or promotion decisions based on the appraisal interview, dismissal based on a disciplinary interview. The interview has stimulated a lot of research in trying to decipher its dynamics, for example, the role of managers' impressions in assessments (Kinicki et al., 1990); physical attraction (Morrow, 1990); similarity to the interviewer (Anderson and Shackleton, 1990); the time taken to reach a decision (Buckley and Eder, 1988). Its persistence, particularly in selection, is a continual frustration to those who wish to see it replaced with more 'reliable' and 'valid' procedures. It is in the interview, however, that the confessional plays a central role. Selection interviews require the individual to divulge education and work experience, professional goals, activities and interests, and so on. Indeed, exhortations include: 'the supervisor must attempt to determine how the applicant interacted with former supervisors, colleagues, superiors, and the public, as well as the applicant's achievements, likes and dislikes from the previous job' (Talson, 1987) – all in one job interview.

Interviews operate on the basis of avowal. As such, a lot of emphasis is placed on the importance of interview techniques and their perfection – as though technique alone would hide or dissolve the inherent tensions and ambiguities of the process, transforming confession into dialogue. Recommendations are made that interviewers should get the candidate to talk openly, and to do most of the talking, for example, between 70 to 90 per cent of the time (Martin, 1989). There is a view of the individual as harbouring a secret truth, access to which is through interrogation by a privileged speaker – the interviewer. Practitioner journals recommend the most suitable methods for accessing the truth: creating an 'interviewing environment' in which candidates feel safe enough to talk about strengths and weaknesses; putting the candidate at their ease; establishing a comfortable rapport; asking probing questions 'to get the candidate to talk openly' (Swan, 1990: 96); establishing 'congruence', demonstrating 'acceptance' (Kowal, 1990). Alternatively, 'prodding, either with direct questions or through the use of silence, usually generates more details' (M.L. Smith, 1990: 11).

The interviewer is the interpreter of the inner meaning of the outward sign. His or her craft is the patient observation of surface expressions which reveal the inner truth. Thus, 'individuals reveal themselves not only through their verbal communication, but by their mannerisms and reactions to others. Interviewers need to be more aware of these nonverbal clues' (Kowal, 1990: 68). As an interpreter of signs, he or she uses the outside body to know the inside, and gradually leads the individual to divulge hidden secrets, whilst at the same time keeping his or her responses hidden ('keep any emotional reactions from surfacing' (Half, 1988)). Perhaps the epitome of using outer signs to distinguish inner truth is research into eye movement in relation to truthfulness. Looking to the left is indicative of recalling of past events and telling of truth; eye movement to the right, however, is indicative of future thought and may suggest fabrication and deceit (as this is related to left brain–right brain distinctions complications may arise with left-handed people, in which case the pattern may be established from a response to a question for which there is no reason to lie) (Johnson, 1987).

The interview must be seen in relation to the view of truth about the individual it implies. The idea is entrenched in HRM that truth is unitary, there is one truth, which, like a commodity, is possessed by the individual until it comes into the possession of others, either through cross-examination or testing for the purposes of disproof or refutation. Accessing this hidden truth, requires the operation of various techniques, 'patience, sometimes payment of gifts [performance related pay], sometimes seduction [promise of promotion], sometimes violence [now banned, but there is the threat of disciplinary action, demotion, the loss of a potential increase]' (DuBois, 1991: 106). It is interesting to see how the nature of interviews changes in relation to views on hierarchy and truth. The 'ordeal' element of the interview is a more accepted procedure or practice for those who are lower in the hierarchy. Servile status is not guaranteed to produce a pure statement spontaneously. However, the validity or truth of what is divulged by those who are interviewed for positions higher in the hierarchy is ensured through a code of honour.[2] These views are to be contrasted with the view of truth as a dialectic, as process, as the making of truth in time, between people, but not as the revelation of something lost in the past but as the production of something in the present (DuBois, 1991: 107).

Other variations of the standard interview include structured interviewing, situational interviews and patterned behaviour description interviews (BDI). Here there is the emergence of an examinatory technology used in conjunction with a confessional view of the individual. Behaviour description interviewing or situational interviewing is designed to obtain the most information about past behaviour as it relates to specific job skills. It is based on the principle that the best predictor of future behaviour or performance is past behaviour or performance in similar circumstances. The more recent and the more longstanding the behaviour, the greater its predictive power. BDI is based on an analysis of those events or behaviours which define 'successful' job performance, in the eyes of peers and supervisors (rarely subordinates). Managers are asked to list essential characteristics for effective performance, for example, ability to set priorities or delegate responsibilities. These are then used to develop specific interview questions for a given job position. Those characteristics deemed to be consistent with corporate focus and vision are then the focus for the interview, with structured behavioural questions developed to elicit examples of past behaviour indicative of the critical characteristics. The interviewer asks for actual situations or events from work history or experience, to see how the individual has handled 'real-life' incidents. The 'trick' is to get the individual to be accurate or relate in sufficient detail the particular experience cited.

Large organizations are encouraged by HRM literature to use behavioural descriptive interviews as part of their managerial selection process. One multinational corporation, for example, identified six characteristics of the successful manager: demonstrated leadership, ongoing learning, self-starter, creative problem solver, team player, and effective communicator. It recommended the following 'confessional' questions. Where the critical characteristic is 'demonstrated leadership', questions prompted included: 'Describe a recent event in which you needed to stand up and influence the people around you on a certain issue or idea, what obstacles did you overcome?'; for 'self-starters': 'Tell me about a time when you showed the most initiative'; for 'creative problem solvers': 'Tell me about your toughest assignment and how you approached it'; to recognize 'team players': 'Give me an example of a group project in which you differed with the rest of the group, how did you resolve these differences?' or 'Tell me about the most trying time you have had with a co-worker or fellow student'; for 'effective communicators': 'Tell me about the last time you had a really good idea and had to persuade someone to accept it.' Although there is recognition of the subject in this process, as a final part of the process all these answers were then reduced on a graphic rating scale to a final cumulative total.

BDI is similar to structured interviewing where questions are based on job analysis and the same questions are asked of each candidate, with recommendations that interview panels record and rate answers (Campion et al., 1988). The scales for scoring answers are 'anchored' to examples of behaviour. Further 'refinements' lie in the form of scorable interview tests. Based on a test and retest basis, these interviews score 'winners' and 'losers' at interviews, ensuring predictive validity of the evaluation technique in relation to future performance data (Mercer and Seres, 1987). There is evidence that these interviews have a higher correlation with performance on the job (as reflected in performance appraisals) than traditional interviews lacking situational content (Robertson et al., 1990; Stohr-Gillmore et al., 1990; Weekley and Gier, 1987). In essence, however, it is the attempt to introduce a more examinatory technology into the process in order to systemize the selection interview, with some suggesting that this type of structured interview acts more like an orally administered intelligence test (Wright et al., 1989).[3]

Self-assessment

It is in the operation of developmental appraisals that the confessional may be most readily identifiable. Self-assessment or self-evaluation is an important dimension of developmental appraisals. It is based on the view that the individual has certain beliefs and ideas about what the job requires and what needs to be done to achieve job requirements. Since these beliefs affect on-the-job performance, accessing this information is an important aspect of being able to control the latter. Participation in performance appraisal through self-assessment and self-reporting becomes an important means by which these ideas may be accessed.[4]

These schemes ask questions on, for example: job satisfaction – is this area of your work satisfying? are your skills overstretched or underused? have any recent changes affected your job satisfaction? achievements – are you are pleased or displeased with any feedback you have received? obstacles – what particular obstacles are in the way of your professional goals and targets? what particular factors impair your job performance?or have you any hidden talents which are not at present being utilized? Recognizing that the context of the divulgence – normally within a hierarchical relationship – will inevitably constrain the extent of that which is confessed, there is an emphasis on inducing the individual to confess and to make more visible his or her innermost thoughts. There is an emphasis on the role of the appraiser as trying to access hidden knowledge, with recommendations that they adopt a counsellor role rather than a judgemental one, to help reduce anxiety. A heavy emphasis is placed on the importance of building or creating 'trust', and putting the individual at ease.

Confessional appraisal systems designed for professional development are considered unsuitable for performance assessment or monitoring because they do not provide the simple measures of the examinatory system (Carley, 1988). In the search for control, these systems are easily dismissed as 'soft' human relations techniques. Such an assessment, however, ignores the nature of power operating in the procedure. Whilst the power-knowledge dyad and the mechanisms whereby the individual is objectivized are more discreet in the confessional appraisal than in its examinatory counterpart, they are not absent. A power structure operates but remains obscure.[5] The appraisee may be, for example, encouraged to reflect on performance and in collaboration with the head of department (the confessor) to discover areas of individual potential. The views of the confessor are then shared with the individual who, it is hoped, will come to share these perceptions and see themselves in this way.[6] As Miller and Rose (1990: 19) note:

> To the extent that authoritative norms, calculative technologies and forms of evaluation can be translated into the values, decisions and judgements of citizens in their professional and personal capacities, they can function as part of the 'self-steering' mechanisms of individuals. Hence 'free' individuals and 'private' spaces can be 'ruled' without breaching their formal autonomy.

The confessional appraisal attempts to harness personal wishes and desires of the individual with the aim of creating an internalized self-discipline based on evaluation. Through the adoption of organizational norms the individual is required to attend to his or her deficiencies.

Part of the value of the confession is that it produces information which becomes part of the individual's self-understanding. It is important to notice that these practices shade into others based not merely on accessing the individual, but on allowing or training the individual to access themselves. Training enables individuals to 'identify what is happening within themselves' in order to become more 'effective'. Thus, for example, the suggestion that if individuals know their managerial style, personality type, job placement strengths, and compatible personalities, they will be less likely to make a serious 'wrong' decision (Kahler, 1987; Lee, 1991; Levasseur, 1991). Awareness of personal styles, strengths and weaknesses and differences among individuals then provides the basis of a programme of adjustment. Personality pattern inventories, for example, enable individuals to come to this self-knowledge, and through training, individuals may gain clues to identify what is happening within themselves by examining speech patterns, personal attitudes and physical reactions. In addition to understanding themselves, one of the intentions of such schemes is that they also aid understanding of others. Self-knowledge facilitates understanding of the inherent personality characteristics of others, and the ability to motivate them according to their needs. In addition to being able to interpret their own inner drives and motivations the individual takes on the burden of examination and normalization (Miller and O'Leary, 1987). They participate in the discipline of themselves.

Reconstituting the Subject

The first role of the confessional is to access individuals' deeply held knowledge of themselves. Its second role is to change, or reconstitute, individuals or aspects of their behaviour in a way which is more productive. In HRM, the process of constituting the subject is evident in orientation, socialization and induction programmes; training; appraisal systems which try to inculcate the correct behavioural norms (Townley, 1989a); health and safety and employee assistance programmes where the individual may be encouraged to adopt certain types of behaviour or postures which accommodate them to the work environment (De Michiel, 1983). Some equal opportunity programmes, in which women are treated 'as if' they were men, also function in the same way. Equally, the individual may be constituted through *proscribing* certain aspects of identity. Disciplinary procedures most obviously define the parameters of acceptable and non-acceptable behaviour. Other mechanisms are more subtle. Hochschild (1983), for example, in her analysis of training programmes for flight attendants illustrates its emphasis on managing 'negative' emotions and summoning the ubiquitous smile. This attempts to constitute the individual in a particular way by denying aspects of self.

Reconstituting the subject via the confessional, however, relies on more substantive changes than these mechanisms allow. From accessing 'truth' via surface or hidden knowledge, reconstituting the individual involves the *creation* of truth. Foucault (1988b: 49) notes, 'from the eighteenth century to the present, the techniques of verbalization have been reinserted in a different context by the so-called human sciences in order to use them without renunciation of the self but to constitute, positively, a new self'. It is a process which goes beyond being tied to an identity through self-knowledge, it involves a reconstituting of self through the creation of a new identity. It is a process whereby individuals 'by their own means or with the help of others, acted on their own bodies, souls, thoughts, conduct and way of being in order to transform themselves' (Martin et al., 1988: 4). The transformation which is sought has oneself as object. In this case, however, the individual is not compartmentalized, components of personality are not identified for the purpose of stimulating or increasing productivity, rather the individual is conceived of holistically and actively. The subject through his or her own will can actively and creatively engage in what is required.[7] It is perhaps in the area of training and development that there is the most recognizable form of reconstituting the subject.

Employee Development
An increasing number of organizations are moving towards a system of developing potential through encouraging employees to enhance skills and capabilities through self-development (Huntley, 1991). This has

received encouragement from the recent initiative in competency based management education and development, and the importance of total quality management (TQM), which emphasizes the need for continuous improvement in organizational productivity. Continuous improvement has now been expanded to include an individual's personal and professional development (Wille, 1990). Management development places an emphasis on the identification of individual skills and knowledge required for the organization to meet its strategic objectives (Berry, 1990; Miller, 1991). Personal 'growth' is with a view to the wider purpose of adding value to the firm and enhancing its future security (Hunt, 1990; Mitchell, 1989). Management development becomes the management of careers in an organizational context (Burgoyne, 1988). The definition of managerial skills in terms of competencies (see Chapter 3), however, allows the two levels, individuals and organizations, to be related, as the 'organization's' development needs are translated into individual key competencies (Mandell and Kohler-Gray, 1990). This provides the basis of a matrix which enables the individual to be seen in terms of organizational needs.[8]

Employee development is usually set in the context of an active and positive staff appraisal programme designed to identify future needs in training and development. At its basis is some form of self-assessment, or avowal of identity which takes place with the aid of career counselling and development planning. 'Self-assessment is necessary to formulate realistic development plans and to evaluate progress' (Boak, 1991: 23), and it is on the basis of responses to these initiatives that a development plan is created. There are many different methods of development including experiential learning, observation of practice, formal on-the-job training, seminars and workshops, coaching, professional conferences, degree programmes, special work groups, continuing education and job rotation – an array of methods which reflects evolution and pragmatic trial and error. Each method assumes different assumptions about learning, in terms of both content and process (Burgoyne and Stuart, 1991). Each is aimed to some extent at reconstituting the individual. A more 'mechanical' approach to the latter is the system of behaviour modification.

Behaviour modification techniques are stressed for their potential for enhancing self-management skills and helping individuals gain control of their feelings and behaviour. The process works through self-inspection. Individuals 'audit' themselves through a systematic self-monitoring and record keeping to identify desired and undesired behaviour. Once an assessment has identified strengths and weaknesses the individual is then in a position to be able to intervene and change themselves. In some cases the individual may be encouraged to follow more acceptable forms of behaviour. The mechanisms for this type of skills training is similar to the organization of geneses seen in Chapter 3, where advancement is in the form of following a series of steps. Through a ranking of achievable goals, the aim is gradually to transform conduct,[9] 'not through airy and overambitious hopes, but through little steps, with achievable goals, each followed by rewards' (Rose, 1990: 237). Thus, for example, training and development programmes come with the following advice: '1. Make a list of areas of self-development 2. Take them on individually 3. Put them in writing and publicize the effort to improve' (Odiorne, 1988). There are recommendations, for example, that individuals desirous of 'supportive facilitation' should communicate genuine concern and interest; maintain composure; practice active listening; make non-judgemental remarks; focus on the ability of employees to help themselves; avoid open anger and hostility; use suggestions to help employees reorganize perceptions and understanding; and allow employees to build competency (Davidhizar, 1990) – the recipe approach to human relations skills, based on adherence to a code of behaviour. Advice to trainers states, for example, determine what the trainee needs to accomplish and present the appropriate skill model; show examples of the skill model and smaller skill elements that comprise the whole; shift the emphasis away from the model and towards how to execute the steps within it; drill each skill element until the learner has mastered it well enough to succeed in a real-life situation; teach trainees how to coach one another for reinforcement back on the job (Georges, 1988: passim).

Behaviour modification is a process of self-modelling, conformity to a series of actions maintained through constant self-monitoring. This process of knowing oneself, however, is based on an assessment according to given ideas of how one should be. As Rose (1990: 11) notes, 'through self-inspection, self-problematization, self-monitoring and confession, we evaluate ourselves according to the criteria provided for us by others'. Essentially a process of self-examination and evaluation these techniques also institute a constant self-doubt, a constant scrutiny of how well one is performing, 'the construction of one's personal part in social existence as something to be calibrated and judged in its minute particulars' (Rose, 1990: 239). Rarely is the voice heard that intervention through targeting specific traits for modification is ethically suspect, not least in its violation of the integrity of the individual's personality.

Interpersonal skills training is a more 'sophisticated' approach aimed at changing individuals by interpersonal skills training. 'People skills' – the 'soft' skills which are resistant to clear articulation or quantification, including communication skills, and the ability to relate to others – lie at the centre of successful management. 'For people to be effective their social skills must be as well-developed as their technical knowledge' (Kizilos, 1991: 66). Interpersonal skills training was initially championed by the Tavistock Institute in the 1950s and 1960s through T-group training, although as Hollway (1991) notes the techniques of T-groups are now used in team-building. The T-group, or training group, method reveals the dynamics of small group interaction experientially. It places people in an unstructured setting in order for them to understand how groups function, how individuals come into conflict, or work to co-operate, whilst at the same time encouraging individuals to examine their own assumptions, expectations and attitudes. They are also encouraged to project themselves into the roles of others. Through these activities the T-group is designed to make managers more aware of their own experience and feelings and their impact on others. Managers are to learn sensitivity, awareness, trust, openness and sharing. The consultant acts as interpreter of group dynamics to individuals, a skill which is reincorporated into the social competence of the group members, influencing both self-evaluation and self-presentation (Rose, 1990).

Like behaviour modification, these systems were designed to effect fundamental change in the ways of relating with others. However, the emphasis is not just on changing behaviour but is aimed at penetrating deeper into the internal aspects of individuals and is designed to change sentiments. It is based on an internal way of learning rather than an external technique. Its importance lies in helping people to understand, but also to predict and control, these interrelations, almost as 'human engineering' techniques (Ripley, 1989). As Rose (1990: 239) comments:

> Life has become a skilled performance. You can learn to be socially sensitive by recognizing the signs by which others indicate such feelings as anxiety, interest and boredom and by recognizing and adjusting the signs that you yourself give off through eye contact, body language, proximity and the like. You can learn self-regulation, combining an awareness of the messages from others with a monitoring and adjustment of the messages you give off yourself . . . You can learn how to manage social situations . . . You can learn the arts of relationships . . . It is the codification of the arts of existence as social skills.

The increased insight these practices hope to promote is that of allowing individuals to become better managers through facilitating group and team work. But its effects may also be seen in the Self-Awareness Class, part of Delta Airlines Stewardess Training Centre. This is a programme designed to make flight attendants more aware of their own emotional and physical responses to 'irates' (difficult customers) in order to be able to 'cope' with them, through 'anger-desensitization', thereby developing their skills (Hochschild, 1983). As individuals, their role is to become 'managers of emotion', they must suppress anger and any sense of effrontery, no matter how justified.

Outdoor pursuits have developed over the last ten years as a means of training, based on the view that physical and psychological outdoor experiences are the bases for organizations to install team spirit, leadership skills, and self-actualization (Crawford, 1988). On these personal growth programmes individuals scale cliffs, shoot river rapids, and negotiate tricky rope courses all in the name of – male – bonding. It is a programme designed to encourage individuals to examine their lives, values and fears, or to reawaken an internal adventurous self. 'People who lack self-awareness or tend not to question their assumptions may get a beneficial jolt from such a programme' (Broderick, 1989: 86). Participants may find this enjoyable, as with any practice which tests initiative, or introduces individuals to something they have not tried before and find that they like or are able to do. But it is questionable whether such initiative, autonomy or sense of self is required in the constraints of job and organizational hierarchy. It is interesting to note that non-managerial workers who have been on such courses return to work less settled, feeling that their abilities are not being used to the full. There is also resistance to supervision. In short, the courses which had made the individuals more lively, critical and independent, inhibited their adjustment to the routines of work (White and Roberts, 1972).

Mentoring
Part of an increasing tendency in employee development is to move away from centralized training programmes to individually tailored development, and is reflected in the increase in the reported number of mentoring projects and support for their use in management development circles (Kizilos, 1990; Stanley, 1991; Zey, 1988). Their advent stems from criticisms that centrally organized training programmes lead to a passive response to training, the effects of which are not usually long-lasting, nor are they incorporated into the job on return to work (Seymour, 1988). Decentralized learning, on the other hand, based on group learning, self-managed learning, work experience based learning and mentoring, emphasizes experience and responds to individual needs. These decentralized systems also have the advantage of tapping informal or tacit knowledge. They usually follow a programme based on individuals assessing themselves, identifying development and learning needs, and a process of commitment to action plans. For example, participants might examine key events in their lives, evaluate specific methods of self-development, engage in an exercise which focuses on aspirations, and complete questionnaires on development needs (Spero, 1987). It is confession with a view to development and change, and is often accompanied by 'group confessions' as training participants explore their experiences with other trainees (Sweeney, 1988).

Mentoring is a process whereby an older, more experienced member of an organization aids a junior or less experienced colleague in the process of organizational socialization. It is a relationship which involves the imparting of knowledge and guidance to new employees. In this sense it is similar to an apprenticeship system. Mentoring on an informal level has long been a feature of organizational life. Formal mentoring programmes, however, are directed by organizations facilitated through selection, performance appraisal, training and reward mechanisms. Middle and senior managers are to be made aware that it is part of their job to act as mentors (D. Jacoby, 1989). Nevertheless, guides warn against the dangers of 'forced coupling' (Kizilos, 1990).

Claims for the benefits of these programmes are broad: improved job performance, early socialization, clearer managerial succession, preparation of leaders, improved motivation, improved employee loyalty, better exposure to ideas, the promotion of teamwork and shared values, and the fostering of a stable organizational culture (Clutterbuck, 1986; B. Smith, 1990). 'A mentoring programme can add value to a company and give it a competitive advantage' (D. Jacoby, 1989). The advantages for the individual are access to corporate hierarchy and culture; for the organization, a 'deep sensing' apparatus for top management and a means of transmitting corporate culture.

Research indicates a favourable response from protégés in terms of satisfaction, career mobility and opportunity, recognition and higher promotion rates (Fagenson, 1989; Noe, 1988). The beneficial effects are not surprising, the early Hawthorne studies would indicate that recognition has positive benefits. Protégés also report greater influence within, and access to, the hierarchy (Fagenson, 1988). Disadvantages, although rarely mentioned, involve dominance, control, overprotection and the continuation of 'old boy' networks. They may also lead to unrealistically high expectations in protégés who may be insular having failed to develop other relationships, as well as being discouraging for the 'non-selected' (Keele et al., 1987). For women and ethnic minorities there are problems of sufficient numbers in positions to act as role models.

Whilst the intention of such programmes are admirable – that 'an environment should exist in which knowledge is valued and people are encouraged to grow' (Kazemek and Dauner, 1988) – it is important to ask: by what methods are these intentions achieved? To what extent does learning from involve emulation and what is involved in emulation? What is involved in the processes of guiding, counselling and protecting?

As with the confession, the process of mentoring has a long tradition in the West, and again its function has varied. In the Greek (Senecan) model 'the relationship of the disciple with the master was important, but it was instrumental and professional. It was found upon the capacity of the master to lead the disciple to a happy and autonomous life through good advice. The relationship would end when the disciple got access to that life' (Foucault, 1988b: 44). The later Christian model, however, placed the emphasis on obedience and contemplation. 'Here obedience is complete control of behaviour by the master, not a final autonomous state. It is the sacrifice of the self, of the subject's own will. This is the new technology of the self . . . the self must constitute self through obedience' (Foucault, 1988b: 45). As with the confession, the basis of the latter is the renunciation of one's own self and will. These two disparate themes may be identified in the modern day approaches to mentoring. The 'Christian' model, for example, is identifiable in a recommendation to use the SELF method of mentoring:

> Managers can assume responsibility for providing the socialization, education, leadership, and time for fruition (SELF) that is needed by junior employees to *become interwoven into an organization's cultural structure*. The SELF framework illustrates ways senior managers can use mentoring *to help cultivate desired norms and values* in their organization. Participating in the socialization of junior employees permits senior managers *to help frame the inculcation process*. The informal influence that emanates from a mentor relationship has a potential effect on the behaviour predicted in the organization. Leadership by senior managers represents tangible role models that junior managers often emulate. Through serving as mentors, senior managers guarantee that these *role models embody core values that best promote desired organizational culture*. The socialization, education, and leadership linked with mentoring should result in a more wholesome working environment upon fruition. (White, 1990; emphases added)

Here formal mentoring programmes are organized social relationships. They are a directed relationship of 'host, friend, confident and adviser' (Buonocore, 1987). However, these relationships are instrumental rather than reciprocal. The mentor is typically portrayed as the 'giver' in the relationship. 'A good mentor challenges the mentee [sic], forcing reexamination and reprioritising' (Buonocore, 1987: 7). The model underpinning its use is the classic model of (hierarchical) development. Help is only required at certain stages in a career; mentors do not need to express fears or insecurities. In addition, certain aspects of 'self' do not get acknowledged. Thomas (1989), for example, illustrates that despite issues of race and gender being highly salient dimensions of self in the minds of black men and women, and white women participating in mentoring programmes – these issues were never openly addressed. He concludes that the mentoring programme acted as a social defence – 'a system of procedures that detach people from their experiences'. He concludes that there is a need to 'develop a social technology that will help blacks and whites confront their history and the present and create a corporation that truly supports pluralism'.

Instrumentalism in the relationship may sometimes be overtly acknowledged. 'For a mentor to be advantageous to a protégé's career, the protégé must select and cultivate an appropriate mentor, using selection criteria tailored to the individual protégé's career goals' (Bushardt and Allen, 1988). Formal mentoring programmes, as a result, have been labelled 'instrumental mentoring programmes' (Collin, 1988). Instrumentalism may also be a facet of broader relationship patterns which mentoring establishes, for example, 'a manager who is effective as a mentor must be skilled at *getting and using power*, building and *using relationships*, and teaching and coaching others' (Orth et al., 1987; emphases added).

The deliberate attempts to reconstitute self illustrated above may be contrasted with the following which advocates mentoring as a practice for nurses. In tenor and objectives it is more akin to Greek practices:

> Mentorship is a process by which an older, wiser seasoned nurse *guides and nurtures* a younger, less experienced nurse into the health care system. Mentoring tends to promote professional development, career satisfaction and success. Mentors often have an established power base and can use this power *on behalf of the protégé to facilitate expansion* of the neophyte's sphere of influence within the system. Having the support of a mentor and serving as a mentor to others are essential factors in achieving influence. (Kinsey, 1990; emphases added)

The Productive Subject

The previous section concentrated on a range of schemes designed to reconstitute a sense of identity. Its focus is the individual. This section concentrates on schemes which introduce a very specific aspect of identity – that of the individual as a productive subject. These are usually designed to influence individuals on a collective level. These are schemes specifically designed to encourage individuals to constitute themselves as active agents in a productive role. They are manifest in such programmes as quality circles, job enrichment and enlargement, and remuneration systems of profit sharing and performance-related pay, and suggestion schemes. An extension of the productive subject, the entrepreneurial subject, is that of the subject as an owner of production, as may be seen in the introduction of stock option or share ownership plans.

Welfare and Employee Assistance Programmes

The concern with the welfare of the individual as a whole has had a long history in personnel. Early welfare concerns of employers reflected an interest in the good health and suitable habits of employees. Welfare workers or social secretaries visited the families and homes of workers, advising individuals on family and financial matters, and the conduct of their affairs, in a manner which, in effect, constituted the supervision of the health, hygiene and morality of the worker (Niven, 1967; Rose, 1990). Ford's Sociology department was equally concerned with the morals of its employees. Ultimately, however, the link is to the productive subject.

The most recent version of these welfare programmes are employee assistance programmes or EAPs, programmes developed by employers designed to help employees cope with personal problems. For example, issues dealt with relate to alcohol and drug use; personal and family problems (constitute about 40–50 per cent of referrals (Feldman, 1991)); and financial and legal concerns. Again EAPs acknowledge that the worker is not an 'isolated monad' and that family issues directly affect the ability of the employee to do their job. EAPs are geared to maintain the health and the productivity of employees. They are 'an investment in human resources designed to maintain and enhance worker's productive capacities' (Smits et al., 1989: 96). Employee assistance programmes may help with chemical dependency, physical abuse, finance and domestic problems. 'Solutions' are provided in stress-management training or stress counselling, general and financial counselling.

EAPs were established in the late 1960s. In 1972, there were about 300 company-sponsored programmes. Now there are more than 10 000 employee assistance programmes in the US. Between 60 to 80 per cent of Fortune 500 companies are using them, at a cost of $798 million, excluding treatment (Cohen, 1991; Luthans and Waldersee, 1989). Previously covering about 12 per cent of US workers, EAPs now number 36 per cent. IBM has trained more than 50 000 supervisors to be sensitive to employees whose work may be affected by non-work problems. The company also requires its supervisors to participate in one to two day EAP-oriented seminars as part of an annual forty-hour course in people management training (*Personnel*, 1991).[10]

The claimed benefits of such programmes include reductions in absenteeism, lateness, turnover, accidents and in the US, workers' compensation claims. One estimate puts savings at four dollars in health claims and absentee rates for every dollar spent (Feldman, 1991). It is no coincidence, however, that these programmes are fuelled in the US by rising health care insurance and costs, although there are some indications that judicial interpretations on dismissal are also prompting an interest in them (Luthans and Waldersee, 1989).[11]

An offshoot of these programmes are employee wellness programmes, which concentrate on issues such as nutrition, awareness education, as well as exercise. Elaborate programmes include a fitness centre, cholesterol screenings, on-site health fairs, cash incentives for participating in exercise programmes, and incentives to stop smoking. Combined with the EAPs these promote both the physical and mental aspects of workforce health, and it is assumed, organizational productivity.

Although uncommon in the UK, where one of the first was being introduced in 1981 (Megranahan, 1990), there is evidence that an increasing number of companies now use them (Berridge, 1990; Carty, 1990). They are now being recommended in practitioner journals 'for employees who cannot give their full attention to work and are therefore less effective employees', and to 'identify and resolve problems at an early stage before health has been affected or work performance impaired' (Carty, 1990; Steddon 1990: 24). Wellness programmes have been introduced in a region of the Post Office, where employees have been screened to measure blood clotting and cholesterol levels. Those with high levels have been taught relaxation and meditation techniques, and encouraged to participate in sessions on coping with pressure in the work-place (Fewster, 1989).

Quality Circles

Quality circles are often discussed in terms of employee participation, enhanced motivation and commitment, but they actually function to reconstitute the individual as a productive subject. The basis of quality circles, and many of their derivatives such as employee involvement groups, continuous improvement through teamwork, problem-solving teams and taskforces, is that of teams meeting, usually weekly, to develop and implement plans for improving productivity and minimizing waste. Teams, usually of ten to fifteen, may be primarily from the same department and focus on departmental issues, but have to be delegated sufficient authority to be able to complete their tasks. The emphasis is on the team identifying, investigating and solving work-related problems. Presentation of proposed solutions is to a group of managers, whose support is important for the continued viability of the group (Tang et al., 1989). Usually the group meets in company time and there is formal recognition of the group within the company.

Originally developed in the US in the 1920s in Bell Laboratories, the idea was adopted and implemented in Japan, featuring in Japanese industry in the 1960s (Juran, 1991). With the dominance of Japan in international trade, and the growth of Japanese owned subsidiaries in North America and Europe, quality circles with other aspects of 'Japanese management' have been transplanted into non-Japanese firms. In 1985, over 90 per cent of US Fortune 500 firms reported having quality circles (Piczak, 1988).

Although neither attitudes nor quality may significantly improve over time, results indicate cost savings (Adam, 1991). Other studies indicate that although employees may not be more satisfied with their particular job, they are more satisfied with the organization (Verney et al., 1989). The main failings of quality circles stem from lack of management support, the latter being uncomfortable with the change in the purely directive role in which they usually see their jobs (Harrington and Rieker, 1988). There are some indications that quality circles have a life-span of about two years (Griffin, 1988), with many being disbanded due to middle management resistance and lack of management support.

Japan has a far higher percentage of employees participating in quality circles than the West, with more suggestions made per employee, and quality circle task performance often directly related to career development programmes (Wolff, 1987). Their success is related to extensive company-specific knowledge within the group and cross-training. Lack of training for quality circle functioning, but also lack of general training may inhibit their effectiveness in the West. In addition the Japanese use of quality circles is based on management training which heavily emphasizes the achievement of quality, again in the West this has tended not to be the case (Juran, 1987). Also in the West, reasons for introducing these schemes may relate more to employee involvement and QWL schemes, and the attempt to increase communication, than for other reasons. When these expected benefits fail to materialize, enthusiasm dwindles.

Despite claims for increased identification and commitment, and their association in the West with QWL, the predominant motive for their introduction centres around interests of production, for people to do more and better work, and make more decisions with less supervision (Grenier et al., 1991). They recognize that those closest to the work have valuable experience and knowledge to develop solutions to job-related problems. Essentially, quality circles are designed to contribute by promoting low-cost rationalization of production methods, and development of the capability of employees – low-cost minor modifications which have an advantage over major technological innovations (Watanabe, 1991). In this sense, it is related to the Kaizen approach of continual incremental improvement that breaks larger problems into smaller, more manageable ones. Gradual, constant improvement, making use of the resources at hand is the essence of this approach. It is also the process of constituting the individual as a productive subject, as well as being designed to allow individuals to develop their diagnostic skills. Continuous improvements or innovations, conceived and implemented by workers to improve the job, are, as Wood (1989) notes, aimed at making the worker think like an industrial engineer.

Profit-sharing

Another dimension of trying to reconstitute the subject is profit-sharing or gain-sharing, as a means through which individuals identify with the organization, in particular focusing on the means to improve productivity. It is another mechanism which attempts not only to persuade employees to identify themselves as producers, but to constitute themselves as productive subjects and to be concerned with the performance of the company as a whole.

Although profit-sharing schemes have been a feature of employment policies as early as the nineteenth century (Hatton, 1988; Lindop, 1989), there has been a considerable expansion in such schemes in the UK in the 1980s (Blanchflower, 1991; Poole and Jenkins, 1991), when they were promoted by the Conservative government, which claimed that profit-sharing schemes lead to greater wage flexibility (Blanchflower and Oswald 1987). Under these systems, employees receive supplemental income based on the profitability of the organization or selected subunits, either in deferred plans, cash plans, or discretionary arrangements. By connecting pay and profit, they are a tool in 'educating' employees. In some systems, the educative role is emphasized as profit-sharing plans are linked to a percentage of the employees' pay being at risk. In a division of du Pont, USA, for example, if a unit meets its goals the percentage at risk is restored; if the unit exceeds its goals employees are rewarded with up to a 12 per cent increase in pay; if goals are not met 6 per cent of pay is at risk (*Employee Benefit Plan Review*, 1990). Through such schemes, employees are 'educated' in the effort–reward bargain.

There is evidence that firms with profit-sharing schemes and/or share-ownership schemes have lower absenteeism and turnover than other firms in both the US (Wilson and Peel, 1991) and the UK (Wilson et al., 1990). In the UK, whilst there is some evidence of increased productivity (Cable and Wilson, 1989), there is little strong evidence that profit-sharing significantly improves profitability or productivity. However, in this case, average payouts of the schemes were under 5 per cent of an employee's total remuneration (Blanchflower, 1991). Later studies have reported improved job satisfaction and internal communications, though limited improvement in work practices (Poole and Jenkins, 1988). The effect of profit-sharing schemes on their own is difficult to gauge, as their introduction is associated with employee consultation and involvement practices (Poole, 1988).

The disadvantages of such schemes in creating the productive subject involve the time lag between effort and reward, in addition to profit levels being affected by a range of factors over which the organization has little control – interest and exchange rates, for example. Lack of control and deferment of payment in relation to effort result in organizations considering other methods of constituting the productive subject.

Gain-sharing is a US term for compensation packages which are designed to reward employees based on financial performance, productivity and quality measures. It differs from profit-sharing in that the system is based on operational as opposed to financial measures, and is paid out as current compensation. Its aim is to provide an incentive for the workforce to improve organizational performance. Basically it is a system of sharing 'improvement' from cost reductions with employees. Programmes are initiated to generate changes which will reduce costs. Most systems are based on a comparison of input to output, or standard productivity ratios, with the intention of decreasing the ratio by increasing sales or decreasing costs. Improvements, from a measured 'baseline' are calculated in financial terms and distributed to employees on an announced ratio. They therefore depend on cost accounting systems which can calculate the baseline, and measure improvement based on this. Their intention is to generate operating efficiency, employee involvement in decision-making and the generation of ideas, and they are accompanied by suggestion schemes and a committee structure. Examples include the Scanlon Plan (introduced in the US in the 1930s), Rucker plans and Improshare. Scanlon is based on the ratio of total payroll costs to sales value of production, while the Rucker plan calculations are based on the ratio of payroll costs to the production of added value. Usually conducted on a plant-wide basis, they may sometimes have departmental components. Spot gain-sharing, is a variation of gain-sharing, which ties it either to a specific problem or a specific time period, with the bonus tied to the extra effort during the period (DCamp and Ferracone, 1989).

Advantages are claimed in productivity and profitability improvements, quality and cost reduction, as well as in higher participation, lower absenteeism and turnover (Doherty et al., 1989; Gowen, 1990). There are, however, disadvantages in that there is limited control over the size of the bonus, and the objectives of participating groups may conflict over the implications of cost reduction plans (Marchington, 1991). Other problems relate to the complexity of the mathematical formula and calculations of productivity improvement, infrequent pay-outs and insufficient information as to how the scheme operates (Panos, 1990).

The Entrepreneurial Subject – Employee Share Ownership

These are schemes which emerged in the 1980s, associated with the British Conservative government's privatization programme, although there are some examples of employee owned companies which have existed for a long time (Bradley et al., 1990). Attempting to link individual rewards to company performance, a principal purpose of such schemes is to enhance employees' concern for the company's overall performance.[12] Formal ownership is deemed to be linked to psychological ownership, with claims that these programmes enhance motivation and morale, encourage new sets of attitudes and teamwork.[13] They operate on a number of bases but principally allow the purchase of shares, usually at a discounted rate.

In the UK, a joint Stock Exchange Treasury survey of share ownership showed that approximately 2 million employees owned shares in the companies for which they worked (Peel et al., 1991). There are approximately 1950 schemes which distribute shares or share options to employees in general, with 4700 share option schemes aimed principally at executives (*The Economist*, 1991). In the US, estimates vary from 9000 corporations covering 9 million employees (Parks, 1991), to over 11 000 programmes with 12 million workers, approximately 13 per cent of the civilian workforce (Rosen, 1991).

The transformational potential for these schemes, however, has been questioned (Moss, 1991). Employees may not understand the plans in which they participate (Phillips and Crehan, 1989), and ownership is not necessarily translated into active or able concern with the management of the company. Physical ownership does not necessarily turn into social ownership. Some studies show greater commitment to the company after the introduction of share-ownership (Tucker et al., 1989), although this may be in response to share-ownership being introduced with more participative decision-making (Klein, 1987; Rosen and Quarrey, 1987; Taplin, 1988).[14] In other cases share-ownership may result in divisiveness and dissension (Hyman et al., 1989). Some research has indicated that responses to share-ownership schemes are a reflection of how they are viewed generally, rather than their being associated with the organization (Dewe et al., 1988).

Towards a Genealogy

Why and how these practices for constituting the subject are adopted varies again. For example, once the individual is employed in Japan the emphasis of the organization focuses on moulding the productive subject. Control of activity in Japanese systems has concentrated far more on work organization, elaborate on-the-job training (which includes an emphasis on the philosophy and the history of the organization), quality consciousness and quality circles. Part of the production ethic in which the individual is situated includes taking criticism and suggesting improvements. In this, it has been described as reconciling the 'autonomous aspirations of the employee with the collective entrepreneurialism of the collective culture' (Rose, 1990: 117). Life-time employment is also an important dimension of constituting the individual as a productive subject, as is a supplementary payment system based on seniority. Promotion is tied reasonably tightly to seniority, with employees rotated within departments. Bonus systems tie the annual income of workers to the performance of the firm; and informal profit-sharing links employee and organizational interests. In the West only a few of these practices are followed: the most common being the reduction in partitioning through single-status facilities and conditions; control of activity through training and education; and an attempt at reconstituting the subject through quality circles and other quality control methods (Pang and Oliver, 1988).

In the West, this emphasis on the productive subject has been incorporated into human resource management. It carries with it, however, flavours of the earlier human relations. The recognition of the importance of being part of a group has been extended to include the importance of contributing effectively to worthwhile organizational objectives, exercising initiative, creativity and responsibility. The team emphasis has been extended to cover employees making direct production recommendations and suggestions, increased self-direction and self-control. Sharing information, previously recommended as important for satisfying needs of belonging and individual recognition, now becomes important for improving the quality of decision-making, facilitating self-direction and self-control thereby requiring less supervision (Miles, 1965). The subtle shift in emphasis is from the description of the individual as social being to the emphasis on the productive subject.

The legal framework has also influenced the extent to which the productive subject may be established. In the US, for example, quality circles raise the issue of employer domination which would render them unfair labour practices under the National Labour Relations Act (Grenier et al., 1991). In the UK, state encouragement of the productive subject has included the Finance Act of 1978, the 1980 Act establishing save-as-you-earn plans, and tax exemption for profit-sharing schemes for certain employees (Rothwell, 1987). The role of the State in prescribing national standards is also important. Japan, for example, has no national standards relating to quality assurance. Japanese quality control, started after the Second World War, began as quality control by the seller. The priority was on continuous improvement and the marketplace, hence the emphasis on creating and securing customers who will support this (Kume, 1990). Total Quality Commitment therefore was designed to achieve steady business growth. In contrast, the US and Western countries establish quality control standards from the buyer's point of view by specifying production processes, control methods and quality standards. Also, in the US and UK, emphasis on close articulation of skill and competency has been paralleled by the State establishing standards for public education.

Again, the diffusion of practices reflects the nature of professional organizations. One aspect of the 'de-layering' or 'de-massing' which has occurred amongst managerial ranks in US and UK companies in the 1980s and 1990s has been the 'balkanization' of the personnel department. Those who were formerly employed as specialists within the organization now find themselves in the role of management consultants. The need for increased differentiation amongst those specializing in various aspects of human resource management has given rise to ever more specialized techniques and practices.

> Experts on work play a crucial role in linking these distinct concerns into a functioning network. In doing so they come to have a key role, constructing a language and set of techniques simultaneously based upon an esoteric scientific knowledge they possess, realized through detailed technical prescriptions and devices they can construct and operate. (Rose, 1990: 117)

It is interesting to note that it has been the Japanese Union of Scientists and Engineers, for example, which has played the important role in sustaining the use and role of quality circles in Japan (Juran, 1987).

No doubt the financial interest of consultants, the labour market concerns of professional bodies maintaining a basis for accreditation and their skills, and employment circumstances which have led to the 'downsizing' of personnel departments in an age of flexible employment, may explain the promulgation of techniques. Whilst these factors might offer an explanation of the growth of consultant services, they do not explain the variation in techniques offered. The latter reflects the institutional bases which generate knowledge. For example, approaches to job design differ. In the UK, emphasis was placed on the recognition of social and technical systems and the optimization of these, an approach associated with the Tavistock Institute. In the US, the focus was the individual and the single job. Organizational development (OD), in the UK, came to mean planned organizational change, rather than a sensitivity awareness (Hollway, 1991: 113).

The earlier distinction between Taylorism and human relations is most problematic in relation to the role of personnel practices in contributing to the creation of identities. As was argued in Chapter 4, human relations is often depicted as a paradigmatic break. Hollway, for instance, argues 'Human relations moved the understanding of people at work from a psychology interested in measurement and performance to one in which the whole person of the employee, including sentiments and interpersonal relations, had to be addressed in the interests of changes at work' (Hollway, 1991: 21). Human relations 'discovered' the importance of the group for individual behaviour: the relation of the individual to the work-group, the relations between work-group as well as the group's relationship with management (Rose, 1981: 157).

As was argued in Chapter 4 these distinctions privilege the content of knowledge over the process of how it is acquired. Thus we have the basis for the individual as a holistic individual with wants and needs, not an addendum to a machine. Also behind the distinction is the individual/collective split. The individualistic motivation of Taylor's 'economic man' is distinguished from the 'social' or 'collective' man of the human relations school. Certainly the knowledge of the individual expanded in that human relations advocated knowledge of community attachments and union affiliations. When combined with interpersonal skills, job redesign and participative leadership to influence morale, attitudes and feelings, then human relations was designed to align the 'whole' person with the objectives of the organization. Nor is it to deny that the individual was not constructed in a distinct way: as a social animal, with specific needs and affiliations.

The significance of human relations is not its identification of personality, attitudes and needs, etc., which merely became other dimensions for the increased objectivization of the individual under the gaze, but how it encouraged a new dimension of extracting knowledge of, or from, the individual, by recognizing the importance of the confession to access the reasons why someone behaves as they do. This involves the technology of the confession. The distinction is not what differentiates individuals, but how they are constituted. On this basis, it is possible to identify a growth in practices which attempt to constitute the individual as subject, at the same time as there is an increase in objectification. The 'new' industrial relations involves both the individual as subject and object. For example, the New United Motor Manufacturing Inc. (NUMMI) joint venture between GM and Toyota to produce the Chevrolet Nova involves the use of an assessment centre, as well as the team concept. This reflects an increased emphasis on 'knowing' labour, with management being required to invest more time and resources to ensure that they hire individuals who will be amenable to the ethos of the organization, and through appraisal, training and development will contribute to its success.

Notes

1 The important role of individuals' acknowledging and recognizing aspects or dimensions of themselves is recognized in a number of personnel practices. Human relations, for example, stresses the importance of recognizing inherent needs and attitudes which have to be uncovered for the effective basis of work organization. The Foucauldian view of the subject, however, emphasizes the constitutive role of practices in forming an identity. There is no presumption of an alienated individual whose true potential lies repressed, waiting to be unleashed or self-actualized when their true nature is uncovered. This understanding of subject plays on the ambivalence of subject/object in Foucault's work. Subject is understood in the political sense of being in an inferior relation to – to be subject to, tied to someone else through control and dependence. His later work returns to the subject as constituted through a particular concept of subjectivity. This reflects a theme apparent throughout his work: how individuals govern themselves and others by the production of 'truth' and how this comes to effect their being able to act on others (Foucault, 1991a).

2 Prior to its adoption by the Christian church the confession was a well-established practice in Greek civilization. The Greeks as free citizens, possessors of reason and bound by codes of honour, could not be tortured. Their slaves, however, could. Not being bound by a code of honour, ordeal by torture was the only guarantor of truth.

3 An extension of this can be seen in the recommendations on using video interviews. The video-tape interview can provide a more complete picture, enabling interviewers to evaluate interviews in different sequences, thus enabling a more 'accurate' appraisal of interview behaviour (Johnson, 1991). It is part of the emphasis which requires that the dynamics of the process become known and as a result controllable. Computer administered interviews, recommended to overcome the disadvantages of personal interviews in terms of time and first impression, involve the reading of a printout of candidate responses. 'While some applicants tend to be intimidated by the procedure, many are more open and truthful when interacting with the computer' (Rodgers, 1987: 152).

4 It is interesting to see the degree of validity which is given to individuals' self-assessment, especially evaluations of performance. Whilst self-assessment may be valued in selection, and even appraisal interviews, it is rarely acknowledged as being as valid as 'organizational evaluation' (George and Smith, 1990). (This despite indications that in order of preference employees favour their own feedback, feedback from the job itself, the boss, co-workers and then formal organizational assessment.) Whilst self-assessments may be influenced by attribution theory and 'self-esteem' (Farh and Dobbins, 1989), and there are

indications of gender effects with women having a lower assessment of their achievements, there is a range of assumptions here as to what constitutes the correct evaluation or 'truth'. Self-assessment seems to be given greater validity when related to identification of the need for development or change, despite some indications that self-assessment may successfully predict subsequent performance (Farh et al., 1988; Fox and Dinur, 1988; Somers and Birnbaum, 1991).

5 Foucault (1981a: 62) notes, 'The agency of domination does not reside in the one who speaks (for it is he who is constrained), but in the one who listens and says nothing; not in the one who knows and answers, but in the one who questions and is not supposed to know.'

6 The sources used to confirm self-knowledge vary. National Westminster Bank, for example, uses self-report inventories to enable staff members to gain insight into their own preferences and to value others with similar or different preferences, but also uses information from assessment centres, supervisors, peers and subordinates in addition to self-rating questionnaires (Cockerill, 1989).

7 Hollway uses the term subjectification (1991: 95) but defines this as 'convincing the individual who is the object of change that they are choosing it'. Here, reconstituting the subject is meant in the Foucauldian sense, of tying the individual to different models of self-knowledge, which might have this effect.

8 It is a process which locates the 'problem' with the individual, irrespective of the relationship being constrained through hierarchy. Development takes place through a spatially and temporally distinct entity of training. It is not something which occurs everyday in a myriad of different contexts as part of human engagement with the world. It also maintains the enclosure of work/non-work distinctions (thus the statement that one of the advantages of outdoor training is that it facilitates 'learning about oneself both in life and at work' (Crawford, 1988: 20). Rarely is the family, for example, recommended as an important source of learning these interpersonal skills.

9 It is interesting to note that one approach to management development is called the Bonsai approach, a reference to Japanese miniature trees which are trained, through tying the tree whilst it is growing, to twist it into ornamental shapes it would not otherwise assume. This is reminiscent of one of the pictures in Foucault's *Discipline and Punish* of a tree tied to a pole to change or 'correct' its shape. The idea of the Bonsai approach is that it provides a physical focus of what is happening to the individual. The parallel is maintained by those who have taken part in the workshop being given a Bonsai tree to keep at work, a visual reminder of what is happening to the individual. Thus movement across departments or organizations is reflected in the way the individual decides to shape the tree (Gledhill, 1990).

10 This stimulates new knowledge of the individual, who can become known in a different way. Is it surprising that these developments have generated their own measuring scale, the Behaviour Index of Troubled Employees (BITE) (Bayer and Gerstein, 1988), which measures supervisors' attitudes towards the behaviour of 'impaired' employees?

11 Employers are obliged to ensure reasonable accommodation in cases of disability. A legal development having implications for the confidentiality of EAPs is that if information arises in the course of EAP treatment that the individual may be a danger to himself or others, the employer may be obliged to disclose that information (Lehr and Middlebrooks, 1986).

12 Their value as a tax incentive, and in the US as a form of financing, should not be underestimated.

13 Employee board representation or employee ownership are rarely advocated as means of securing the productive subject (Russell, 1988).

14 Research indicates that there is little worker participation in organizations with

employee share-ownership plans (Rooney, 1988), although the extent of this is increased when unions help negotiate them. Despite historical opposition to employee ownership, American unions have become involved in their negotiation, identifying them as a useful political leverage on management. Their involvement is associated with the negotiation of accompanying voting rights (McElrath and Rowan, 1992).

6

Towards an Ethical Subject

HRM is a discourse and technology of power that aims to resolve the gap inherent in the contract of employment between the capacity to work and its exercise and, thereby, organize individual workers into a collective, productive power or force. The techniques of the art of distribution order a workforce. Taxonomies differentiate capacities to act and provide the basis for aligning activity with time and, thereby, lay the basis for control over effort. These same techniques constitute the individual worker as both an object and subject of power and knowledge. Taken one by one, these HRM techniques – enclosure, partitioning, ranking, the timetable, the temporal elaboration of the act, the examination and the confession – appear quite insignificant. In combination, they are very much more than the sum of their parts.[1] This chapter examines this technology of power in its entirety and concludes with a proposal for an alternative politics.

Panopticism and HRM

Foucault refers to the operation of disciplinary power as 'panopticism' (Foucault, 1977). A panopticon is an architectural design which originated from Bentham's model for a prison. This model envisages a supervisor in a central tower observing inmates in buildings encircling the tower. Because of the architecture of power through which it operates, the panopticon is adaptable to a range of contexts and organizations. It is a system economical in material, personnel and time, in the sense that it reduces the number of those who operate it, whilst increasing the number on whom it is exercised. Because it is polyvalent in its applications, Bentham described it as 'a great and new instrument of government' (quoted in Foucault, 1977: 206). The panopticon is a model of organization which is active in a range of different functions. For example, education (the recording of examination marks and grades by central administration), and medical treatment (centralized medical records and administrative evaluation of efficacy of certain types of medical treatment). It also bears strong resemblances to the modern corporation (Fox, 1989). Its utility in production was foreseen by Bentham, who argued that the panopticon 'makes it possible to note the aptitudes of each worker, compare the time he takes to perform a task (and if they are paid by the day, to calculate their wages)' (quoted in Foucault, 1977: 203). He continues, 'in his central tower, the director may spy on all the employees that he has under his orders; he will be able to judge them continuously, alter their behaviour, impose upon them the methods he thinks best' (quoted in Foucault, 1977: 204). The nature of the panopticon also allows for outside inspection. 'Those at the centre may also be judged – inspectors arriving from outside may also be able to judge at a glance how an establishment is functioning' (Foucault, 1977: 204).

Panopticism is an exercise of power based on analysis and distribution. It operates through hierarchy, surveillance, observation and writing. In this sense, power is not located in a person but in practices.[2] It is a process of mapping, providing for managers and administrators the numbers and formulae which represent the internal map of the organization (Cooper, 1992). Panopticism operates through hierarchical observation and normalizing judgement. Visibility from the centre captures the activities of the periphery in reports and registers, which then form the basis of comparative, evaluative judgements. Panopticism entails a dissociation between seeing and being seen. Hierarchical observation provides axial visibility, but lateral invisibility. The crowd is replaced by a collection of separated individuals or units, a multiplicity which may be numbered and supervised, with the individual or unit never sure if it is observed, only that this might be the case.

The seemingly mundane and innocuous techniques of HRM form a panopticon. They categorize and measure tasks, behaviour and interactions. Taxinomia and mathesis simplify and clarify, fixing individuals in conceptual space, articulating activity and effort. Processes of individualization and individuation capture the individual within a form of visibility, a gaze. HRM techniques are microtechnologies for producing a known and calculable subject, enhancing governmentality through constructing the individual as a more manageable and efficient entity. Through systems of patterning or the re-presentation of the world of work, they render organizations calculable arenas. HRM techniques are the means by which activities and individuals are made knowable and governable. It is this construction of knowledge, through rules of classification, ordering and distribution, fixing of scales, rules of procedure, which has created a distinct personnel discourse. Associated with concepts of rationality, measurement, grading – the language and the knowledge of the personnel specialist – personnel practices reinforce the image of technicist knowledge, accuracy, and objectivity, as though they are simple empirical mechanisms to access a predetermined world. They are, however, disciplinary technologies. HRM techniques actively create reality, they do not merely reflect it.

Through a process of inscription or translation, HRM facilitates the operation of action at a distance. By providing 'objectively' measurable characteristics of an organization, personnel practices impose standardized meanings and a calculative order on a social domain. They reduce information about a whole variety of situations to a common and hence comparable form. In offering an ordered account of organizational activities, and by structuring meanings and orienting actions, HRM holds out the promise of control. The re-presentation of an arena as comprising well-structured tasks and clearly measurable outputs gives both 'a rational account of the organization as a whole, to itself, and to controlling . . . bodies' (Meyer, 1983: 235).

The uninterrupted network of writing links the centre with the periphery, allowing the centre to calculate things, people, events, and processes from a distance. The provision of information in a calculable form enables decisions to be made far removed from the context which they reflect, but which they are taken to re-present. It provides the links between the disparate organizations and geographical locations of large organizations. Through such mechanisms a 'centre' may act from a distance on many other points in this web of power. Questionnaires or forms, for example, which translate events into writing, numbers, lists, tables, may be combined with other questionnaires or forms from different locations, to provide the 'overall' picture. Personnel techniques are a form of translation – constructions between an inscription and an event, between an activity and its method of representation (Latour, 1987). To be effective, inscriptions must be mobile (able to move to and from particular locations), stable (recognizable in multiple locations), and combinable (that is offer the possibility of aggregating and tabulating inscriptions, in order to establish new relationships, and calculate norms) (Latour, 1987). Through such mechanisms, remote events may be brought 'to hand' or into vision, whilst at the same time keeping them at a stage removed. The mechanisms of personnel do not provide the basis of social consensus on meaning and interpretation: rather, they are a technology of power which enable those who use it to minimize their contact with that which is re-presented. In this way, personnel information provides the basis of the information panopticon (Townley, 1993a; Zuboff, 1988).

This function of mapping or re-presenting is one of the main reasons that the professional personnel literature continues to emphasize the importance of job descriptions, job analyses, and effective performance evaluations, and so on. This discourse is maintained, even intensified, when faced with evidence to the contrary: job descriptions are often out of date (Mirabile, 1990) and rarely used in hiring decisions (Wood, 1986); performance appraisals meet with limited enthusiasm on the part of those who are obliged to undertake them, or those for whose benefit they are undertaken. This evidence stimulates a technicist response: an appeal for more objective or accurate procedures. These practices are consistently emphasized because they form the basis of an organizational and disciplinary matrix. Their importance lies in their formal qualities of promising control and the ease with which they support action at a distance. They provide the promise of formal rationality through technical knowledge. They also perpetuate technicism. As Cooper (1992: 259) notes, it is 'the substitution of a symbol or technical device for direct human involvement'. Information becomes impersonal, evaluated on technical matter as to whether it accurately represents or captures the 'full picture'. The personal impact or moral and ethical dilemmas which are the consequence of direct human contact are thereby removed or sanitized.

Although measuring systems offer the promise of control this is not to imply that they are inherently effective. There is no implicit determinism or functionalism in their operation – 'these programmes don't take effect in the institutions in an integral manner, they are simplified or some are chosen and not others, and things never work out as planned' (Foucault, 1991b: 10). Though such techniques are intentional, that is, they are usually introduced with very specific purposes, their effects are largely unanticipated, and in all probability not known: 'people know what they do and why they do what they do but they do not know what it is that they do does' (Foucault quoted in Dreyfus and Rabinow, 1983). There are problems with action at a distance in terms of what gets lost and the type of decisions which get made, the loss of tacit or local knowledge, erroneous assumptions, and the irrationality of translations. As Miller and Rose (1990: 10) remark, 'whilst governmentality is eternally optimistic, government is a congenitally failing operation . . . the will to govern needs to be understood less in terms of its success than in terms of the difficulties of operationalising it'. Reports of organizational failures are testament to the difficulties of constructing the perfect information panopticon.

I do not claim that these techniques produce a totally obedient subject. Nor do I mean to suggest that these practices are purely negative, acting only to constrain the individual. Disciplinary power is simultaneously productive and repressive. That is the essence of its appeal. Indeed, the productive nature of these technologies is the principal reason why individuals actively and voluntarily participate in these practices (Knights, 1990). Both the confession and the examination are examples of what Knights and Willmott (1985) refer to as the development of the subjective force of labour. They confirm and sustain a sense of identity through which individuals secure knowledge of themselves, their competence, abilities, etc. All of the procedures which constitute the subject take place with varying degrees of individual engagement and participation. Indeed the reasons for their success lies in the positive benefits they may bring to individuals. There is some evidence, for example, that participation in quality circles can translate into personal benefits in terms of employee development and motivation (Buch and Spangler, 1990). Being given the opportunity and the authority to implement change in production has implications, usually positive, for the individual's concept of self and there are indications that quality circle participation increases a sense of competence (Steel and Lloyd, 1988). Processes which constitute the individual as an object or as a subject have important consequences for a sense of self.

However, although identities are constituted through power/knowledge practices they are also made vulnerable. Objectivizing and constituting the individual as subject atomizes individuals and turns them back on themselves, prompting what has been referred to as the magnification of self-consciousness (Willmott, 1990). The disciplinary effect emerges when the individual becomes tied, through the desire to secure the acknowledgement, recognition and confirmation of self, to practices confirmed by others as desirable. It is the preoccupation with judgements and evaluations of others that the disciplining effect is secured and is self-administered. As Rose (1990: 239) notes, 'as the other side of their promise of autonomy and success [they institute] a constant self doubt, a constant scrutiny and evaluation of how one performs'. As the result of the individualizing strategies, individuals face uncertainty and insecurity in the requirement to meet successful performance. One of the effects of this is the preoccupation with material and status rewards to sustain an institutional and interpersonal confirmation of identity (Knights, 1990).

The actual effect of these practices has to be discovered by detailed empirical observation. An example of such an analysis is provided by Quaid (1993), in her presentation of the implementation of a job evaluation scheme as part of a pay equity project in Manitoba, Canada. Although it is not a Foucauldian analysis, her study illustrates the processes through which the provincial government tried to create a panoptic effect through slotting all the province's employees into a series of statistical charts, with the aim of providing a centralized map of who was employed, at what level, and in what geographical location. By analysing issues such as, who is able to speak and which sites are privileged in the introduction of personnel practices, Quaid shows how the position of the expert is reinforced. She illustrates the techniques, mechanisms or rituals through which individuals' knowledge of their own jobs is downgraded as part of what she identifies as a process of humiliation and degradation. Through various processes, salary administration ceases to be a matter of common sense, but becomes the province of professionals. Her analysis of the structure and timing of job evaluation committees illustrates how the role of consultant was reinforced. Political issues, what Quaid refers to as horsetrading and manipulation in committees, were rendered technical issues, translated into processes of gaining familiarity with guide charts. She indicates how certain statements and areas do not receive visibility, how certain issues remain unuttered, as for example the technical need for a job evaluation or the details of the Hay plan which was used, how details of the job evaluation scheme were not communicated. Part of the power to silence reflected a broader discourse which contains a belief in the greater power and validity of the quantitative over the qualitative, with the former associated with fairness and rationality. Focus on specifics of practices, how aspects of power/knowledge have been constructed and their effects for those at work, also allows for the possibilities of identifying space for political intervention. Her analysis indicates those spaces which would have allowed for concerted political intervention, in issues, for example, of what is brought into visibility and with what effect, that is, what is left out of the map.

Personnel discourse and practices cannot be dismissed as administrative, or data-handling systems, separate from their micropolitical effects. They are not 'only' or 'merely' the applications of techniques which can be dismissed with the derogatory label personnel management or administration, in favour of the more 'important' policy-making concerns of human resource management. They do not constitute knowledge as an aid to power but, in themselves, constitute power/knowledge systems. It is through these that labour is organized into a productive force. Through mechanisms of registration, assessment and classification – areas of study often neglected or dismissed as technical or administrative procedures – it becomes possible to understand how a body of knowledge operates to objectify those on whom it is applied.

This view of personnel has implications for traditional conceptions of HRM, which stress the rights of labour and the importance of the 'human' side of the organization. The discourse of welfare and the human relations school clouds personnel's role in providing a nexus of disciplinary practices aimed at making employees' behaviour and performance predictable and calculable – in a word, 'manageable'. Personnel is better understood as the 'will to knowledge', a disciplinary system of power/knowledge, a 'great web of bureaucracy' which evolves 'endless ways to count and classify people' (Hacking, 1986: 34).

HRM acts in four specific dimensions: it organizes populations; inscribes and controls activity and constitutes the individual as an object and subject of knowledge. Organizing material in this way allows for a range of seemingly disconnected practices to be integrated into a comprehensive whole which is not accessible using conventional classification systems of recruitment, appraisal, remuneration, etc. In this, Foucault provides a *template* for the basis of grounded contemporary, comparative and historical analysis. A genealogical analysis of HRM would trace systems of patterning within organizations, or dominant patterns in different countries, focusing on how populations are partitioned; strategies for maintaining enclosure; the extent to which and how activity and time are articulated; and the technologies through which the individual becomes 'known'. A comparative analysis across these areas would also reveal different patterns, different personnel systems, which result both organizationally and nationally, in the attempt to specify or make known the indeterminacy of contract. This would provide the basis of a topography of employment systems according to the depth of knowledge produced and the areas in which this was concentrated. In doing so, it enables considerations of employment strategies to escape from the simplistic binary divisions – Taylorism/human relations, individualism/collectivism – which have dogged its analysis.

Portraying personnel as the constitution of knowledge and order, a process of representation for the purpose of governance, also illustrates its similarities to the other 'disciplines' of governance. Personnel's links and interface with engineering and accounting in particular are important dimensions of its functioning. Personnel's relationship with accounting is one area ripe for reinterpretation, their association having been blurred through functional analyses which identify accounting's concerns as being with the financial, and personnel's with the behavioural (Townley, 1991). As Knights and Collinson (1987: 471) note, 'it is important to avoid treating psychological and financial discipline as discrete entities'. Like personnel, accounting is a means by which the internal world of the organization is rendered known, visible and potentially manageable. Accounting practices also act as disciplines articulating the analytical space of the organization (Roberts and Scapens, 1985). As a language or a structure of meaning, accounting provides organizational members with a set of categories, an order through which organizations may be enacted (Cooper et al., 1981; Lavoie, 1987; Roberts and Scapens, 1985). It facilitates governance by making a domain visible and mobile (Burchell et al., 1980; Hopwood, 1987). It organizes time, as, for example, accounting periods creating the boundaries of present and future (Loft, 1986; Roberts and Scapens, 1990); it defines events such as what shall and shall not count as significant within an organization (Roberts and Scapens, 1985); and provides organizational segmentation (units of accountability). It allows information to bridge physical distance by making what is physically remote 'visible' to senior managers, and giving the latter a 'presence' at lower levels in the organization, through budgets and targets (Roberts and Scapens, 1985: 451). Accounting information makes individuals and their activities visible. 'It becomes the mirror through which others must view, judge and compare individual and group performance' (Roberts, 1990: 363). Boland and Pondy (1983: 224) note, 'accounting is one of the major formal sets of symbols available to organizational actors for ordering and interpreting their experience'. As a discourse, the categories of accounting impose a coherence on chaotic organizational processes, define what is real, dignify certain questions as important and stop others from being addressed (Boland and Pondy, 1983: 224).

In this way accounting, like personnel, is a technology which affects a strategy of governance and imposes an order on the world. They come together in human asset or human resource accounting (HAA, HRA), perhaps the epitome of the disciplinary practices, given its emphasis on applying financial equivalences to time and activity of individual and organizational procedures. HAA represents an attempt to measure the costs and value of people to the organization. It is a process which operates to inscribe the activities of workers, thereby creating a visibility which ultimately becomes the basis for constructing norms and trends. As Flamholtz (1985: 244) notes, human asset accounting 'represents a type of balance sheet of the potential services that can be rendered by people at a specified time'. It is the detail of activity through time, related to cost – the partitioning of time, space and movement allied to a financial equivalent.

From this perspective, both personnel and accounting constitute systems of recording, classifying, and measuring. They represent the operation of governance through calculative order. They render power invisible by presenting information as an objective fact independent of the interests of those who produce and use it (Roberts, 1991: 359). They express a belief in the 'reality' which is produced, to the effect that this becomes the basis upon which decisions are made.[3] They are participants in enhancing rationalization. They participate in the disciplining of undisciplined domains. Again, how these combine is a matter of detailed empirical investigation. For example, the domination of various professions in managerial hierarchies, engineers in Germany and Japan, and accountants in the UK and US, has implications for the type of disciplinary systems which may be introduced, for instance, the role of cost accounting procedures in supporting gain-sharing schemes in the US (Oakes and Covaleski forthcoming); the symbiosis between the operation of zero-based budgeting (ZBB), planning, programming and budgeting (PPB), and MBO systems (Bromiley and Euske, 1986; Duffy, 1989; Williams et al., 1985); the lack of formal statistical process control in Japan (Williams et al., 1991).

The Ethics of HRM

Critics argue that Foucault's conception of an all pervasive and oppressive disciplinary power is fatalistic, pessimistic and leaves little room for change. I argue to the contrary, believing that Foucault's emphasis on the 'how' of power has significant implications for the politics of work. The remainder of this chapter explores and develops Foucault's understanding of politics and considers its implications for HRM practices.

The basis of criticisms of Foucault is that he fails to construct an adequate theory of 'resistance'. Systems of power/knowledge do not offer a discrete focus against which to resist. In offering no locus of power, neither is there a clear opponent against whom to struggle, a focus or centre.

There is 'no single locus of great Refusal, no soul of revolt, source of all rebellions, or pure law of the revolutionary' (Foucault, 1981a: 95). As Rajchman (1985: 47) notes, 'in short, Foucault seems to be proposing a critical analysis without reformist or revolutionary possibilities for change'.

But these criticisms miss the point of Foucault's conception of power. Power, for Foucault, cannot be understood simply as the overcoming of resistance. He denies that there is 'on the one side, Power . . . and on the other side, the resistance of the unhappy ones who are obligated to bow before power. I believe an analysis of this kind to be completely false, because power is borne out of a plurality of relationships' (Foucault, 1989: 187). There is not a simple division between those discourses which embody power and those which struggle against it. Foucault's relational view of power rejects a preconceived framework which operates in terms of 'repression versus liberation' or 'legitimacy versus illegitimacy' (Fraser, 1989: 27). But a new concept of power also requires a new concept of politics. Just as power is diffused and is immanent in all social relations, thus political action must be diffused and varied. Foucault's concept of power stresses the local and specific. As power does not emanate from a centre, so, for Foucault, the focus of political action is not centralized: 'On the contrary . . . a demanding, prudent, "experimental" attitude is necessary' (Foucault, 1984c: 374). Emancipatory potential, in other words, is not exclusive to any one social position.

Foucault's concept of power focuses on an important dimension of political action: the ability to constitute who we are.[4] Foucault is sceptical of the negative and juridic 'freedoms from', which stem from power as negation or repression, and encourages the more positive 'freedom to'. This is a freedom to reject and to pose other things. From the recognition that there is no 'essential, natural or inevitable way of grouping or classifying people' or things comes the freedom to rebel against ways in which we are already defined, categorized and classified (Rajchman, 1985: 62). Clearly, disciplinary power has real effects which constrain us, but it is possible to resist the ways people have been identified, classified and constituted as individuals: 'at every moment, step by step, one must confront what one is doing . . . what one is' (Foucault, 1984c: 374). Foucault offers a 'politics of revolt', a 'constant "civil disobedience" within our constituted experience' (Rajchman, 1985). He advocates a permanent questioning of the experience in which we find ourselves. Rajchman captures Foucault's philosophical commitment to 'political freedom' well. For Foucault, freedom

> resides in who is willing to do what in concrete situations of power. It is rooted . . . in the unwillingness to comply, the refusal to acquiesce, to fit ourselves in the practice through which we understand and rule ourselves and each other. Such noncompliance in concrete situations of power is not

something we can abstract and institute in a new form of life. It is specific and unpredictable, not universal and grounded. (Rajchman, 1985: 93)

This view of power and politics stresses the importance of active intervention in the processes through which meaning is produced, disseminated and transformed (McNay, 1992). It lays the foundation of a politics which questions 'the mode of existence and the functioning of discourse in the name of political practice' (Foucault, 1991a: 68). Essentially, what Foucault calls for is a process of critique or deconstruction of discourse and practices.[5] What follows is an elaboration of how this alternative conception of politics may be used to critique personnel practices. This is done through allying Foucault's focus on practices with a feminist analysis.[6]

Feminism and Foucault are complementary.[7] Both focus on critique, deliberately set out to challenge and reconstruct the existing organization of knowledge, question fundamental assumptions, categories and methods of disciplines, and challenge existing power/knowledge structures. Both debunk the 'scientific' and its appeals to objectivism by stressing the importance of recognizing who speaks, who is recognized to speak, and how sites of speech are privileged. Both, therefore, challenge the nature of knowledge, the premises upon which it is formulated and granted significance. Both concentrate on the day-to-day practices which inform people's lives and the importance of these 'normal' practices of life for what constitutes political questions. From 'the personal is political', grounds for resistance must be placed within typical or everyday experiences – in this case those constituting the experiences of work.[8]

Feminist critique indicates some of the criteria which might be used to question our practices on an individual and institutional basis. These are: the importance of visibility; the importance of voice; the rejection of technocracy/the integrity of the individual and the value of experience; the importance of difference; the relational nature of knowledge; and the rejection of hierarchical order or privileging. These principles are designed to inform practice, but they are not a specific set of practices to be followed. This distinction is important. In an early work, Legge (1978) suggests that there are two alternatives for the personnel function: conformist or deviant innovation. Conformist innovation corresponds to an intensification of power/knowledge practices. Deviant innovation represents, for Legge, the opportunity for personnel to establish a different set of criteria for the evaluation of organizational success, based on effectiveness rather than efficiency. For Legge, the criteria for evaluation were to be self-actualization and job satisfaction, with the suggested routes for achieving them being organizational development techniques and legislation. Legge's analysis, however, is based on the 'content' of practices, the 'what' rather than the 'how', and as such indicates an implicit essentialism, that is, that certain personnel practices operate in a specific way. It is important to go beyond an analysis in terms of 'what' to one which challenges the effects of practices, the 'how'. The following section shows how these principles may be used to critique personnel practices and how they may also form the basis of an alternative discourse.

The Importance of Visibility

Foucault's denial of the transparency of language in his depiction of power/knowledge stresses the importance of the unrecognized and unacknowledged. In common with feminist critiques, it indicates the privileged site of those who have defined that which is to be recognized or acknowledged, and the important political action involved in the ability to name (Spender, 1980). This in turn highlights the importance of disqualified or subjugated knowledges, forms of knowledge that 'have been disqualified as inadequate to their task, or insufficiently elaborated: naive knowledges, located low down in the hierarchy, beneath the required level of cognition or scientificity' (Foucault, 1980a: 82). There follows a presentation of job analyses as an example of what is involved in rendering visible. Its purpose is to bring to light dimensions of social actions which are often overlooked or ignored. It is the recognition of the normally invisible and the attempt to lay claim to these disqualified or subjugated knowledges.

Job Analyses

The role of visibility is perhaps most relevant with regard to traditional approaches to describing jobs. Visibility involves the recognition that skill is a constructed category very much influenced by the gender and power of those who perform it.[9] As Ferguson (1984: 163) notes, 'women's less visible and prestigious domestic and familial labour is more rooted in the maintenance of processes than in the production of products', and as a result has been devalued. An example of some of the dimensions of work often overlooked in female jobs can be seen in Table 6.1.

An important dimension of invisible or disqualified knowledge is emotional labour, the core component of which involves dealing with other people's feelings (Fineman, 1993; Hochschild, 1983). Emotional labour is defined, by Hochschild (1983: 7), as 'the labour one requires to induce or suppress feeling in order to sustain the outward countenance that produces the proper state of mind in others'. It is the management of feeling to create publicly observable facial and bodily display, which is sold for a wage. Emotional labour involves being responsive to the needs of others; being able to understand and interpret their needs; being able to provide a personal response to these needs; the ability to juggle the delicate balance of each individual and of that individual within a group; and being able to pace the work, taking into account other responsibilities (James, 1989). It involves the co-ordination of mind and feeling and the regulation of

Table 6.1 *Frequently overlooked job content in female jobs*

Fine motor movement skills like rapid finger dexterity
Special body co-ordination or expert use of fingers and hands (e.g. typing, giving
    injections, sign painting)
Scheduling appointments
Co-ordinating meetings
Record keeping
Filing
Writing standard letters
Reading forms
Protecting confidentiality
Working office machines
Cleaning up after others
Sitting for long periods of time
Time stress
Communication stress (dealing with upset people; gathering information from upset or ill
    people; calming upset people)
Stress from distractions
Stress from concentration (e.g. video display terminal)
Stress from exposure to the sick and disabled with no hope of recovery
Stress from multiple role demands (being asked to work quickly and to provide better
    service to several people)
Working with constant noise
Working in an open office setting: with room dividers, without room dividers
Answering questions for the public on the phone or in person
Answering complaints from the public
Responsibility for inmates, patients, or residents of institutions
Degree to which new or unexpected problems on the job arise
Damage to equipment from a mistake

Source: Weiner and Gunderson, 1990

feelings which draws on a sense of self integral to individuality. Hochschild (1983) estimates that roughly one half of working women have jobs which demand emotional labour.

An example of emotional labour which does not fit in with standard ideas of what should occur at the work-place or with the standard idea of work-place skills is James' (1989) study of work carried out in a hospice. This work involves total care, defined as 'social, spiritual, emotional and physical care', and encompasses elements of care which are usually obscured in medical settings. As well as personal attention, warmth, involvement and empathetic understanding, 'care' involves hard practicalities. It is a form of skilled, regulatory labour, as exhausting as physical labour, requiring learned skills, access to which is open to anyone who has the interest or who has the obligation to learn them. In the work-place the employment of emotional labour is widespread in tasks where close personal attention is required, though the value of what is done is often unrecognized.[10] The hidden component of work does not stop it from being vital.

Privileging the apparent and the visible, requiring a standardized language, as activity becomes translated into a taxinomia, reduces the area of knowledge. James (1989) cites the example from a female doctor who reveals an inability to define the skills she uses with patients – skills vital to her work but indescribable within the dominant medical phraseology. She is also reticent to talk about labour because explanations involve reference to 'emotion', intuition, and instinct. By direct reference or association, emotion is used as a contrast with rational. When emotions are thought to be irrational it is hard to associate them with organization, emotional labour therefore contravenes 'scientific' or objective approach and remains undefined, unexplained and usually unrecorded. Yet managing it requires anticipation, planning, timetabling and trouble-shooting as does other 'work', paid and unpaid. It is a form of work which is recognized on those occasions when it goes wrong, not when the outcome is right. The product is invisible, with its value only recognized in negative form in disorder rather than positive form of adjustment.

As Dex (1985) notes, the nature of skill, far from being clear and unambiguously defined, is integrally bound up with the sexual division of labour. Stereotypical images of masculinity and femininity guide, direct and shape perceptions. Emotional labour is seen as 'natural', unskilled women's work, and obscured by the privacy of the domestic domain, the significance of its contribution is ignored. Child care, nursery nurses and social servicing jobs done by women are judged to be generally fairly unskilled. 'In practice what this means is that the skills involved are not recognized as skills, either by employers or society or often women themselves' (James, 1989: 30). Part of women's caring role is that they are deemed to be naturally good at dealing with other people's emotion because they themselves are naturally emotional. The supposed 'naturalness' of women's caring role is central to the significance, value and invisibility of emotional labour and its development through gender identity and work roles. This is especially so where the job draws on skills developed in household management, on the experience in the home, handling emotions and creating an appropriate atmosphere for the task in hand, 'one which capitalizes on the qualities and capabilities a woman had gained by virtue of having lived her life as a woman' (James, 1989: 32).

Part of the significance of a critique is to sustain demands for change. Building the psychosocial elements of nursing work into staffing ratios, for example, is a relatively new concept, but is at least a partial attempt to render visible that which remains largely invisible. (The caring role has traditionally been associated with the biological functioning of the patient.) Its main significance, however, lies in indicating the centrality of the management of feelings within social processes.

An important dimension of visibility is to challenge the public–private divide in the analysis of skills and job content and gendered definitions of work. It is an issue raised by Mant (1977: 1) in his book on the nature of management. He introduces his book with the following:

> the idea for this book came originally from two quite different experiences. One was connected with the experience of getting married and having children. In those days I was styled a 'manager' and my wife, so far as the tax people were concerned was a 'housewife'. I can remember well the blessed relief of leaving my house and its attendant chaos each morning to go off to my oh-so-demand-ing 'management' job. In what sense, I had to ask myself in the end, was my wife not managing and in what sense was my work more difficult or more essentially managerial than hers? At work, I had another woman to make sure I managed properly. This one was paid, indeed positively relied on, to nag me about detail in precisely the way that my wife was (and is) not allowed to. This one wasn't styled a 'manager' either, but the same essential question held good for her; in what sense is the work of a secretary not managerial.

Although the challenge to the public–private debate was not taken up in management literature, following the publication of Mant's book, it has recently been questioned in the discussion of the 'female advantage' in management. This argues that skills developed in the private sphere not only are transferable, but are also an advantage in managing the organi-zations of the future. Examples given of skills developed in managing home and family include the endurance of stress, the ability to manage diverse tasks, intuition and problem solving skills (Helgesen, 1990; Sharma, 1990). Others emphasize the relational aspect of women's engagement with the world (Gilligan, 1982; Keller, 1986), informing organizational interactions based on networks rather than hierarchy. These elements are identified as, firstly, typifying women's ways of managing and, secondly, being superior in that they do this (Coppolino and Seath, 1987). Claims are made that 'the full potential of feminine leadership will only be realized when a large number of women managers begin to assert their true identity and use their special talents' (Sharma, 1990: 17). This literature varies in the extent to which it is based on the recognition of the importance of skills developed in the private sphere, arguing that these should be recognized as important in the public; or whether it sup-ports an argument based on some notions of female essentialism. It is the latter aspect which has drawn some criticisms. Both, however, call for a questioning of what constitutes management and managerial skills, ques-tioning what is traditionally visible in the literature.

The Importance of Voice
A corollary of bringing to light domains of hitherto unrecognized knowl-edge is the importance of voice: claiming the right to name and as such acting to end silence. As was noted in Chapter 5, voice has been

specifically defined in personnel practices. Equally the role for 'alternative voices' has traditionally been considered in formal systems of communication and participation. As a practice, this is informed in Foucauldian terms by a sovereign view of power – the granting of rights based on principles of legitimacy and constraints on power. For Foucault, however, free speech is defined as a concrete practice rather than as an abstract right, the province of the governed rather than the governors. It is an infinite labour. 'It is a form of political obligation on the part of those who are governed to demand "in the name of knowledge" from those who rule' (McNay, 1992: 136). But as Foucault (1989: 308) notes, the function of free speech does not have to take legal form. Here the issue of voice is considered in relation to the personnel practice of subordinate appraisals, taken as an example of those in subordinate positions who have not been allowed to articulate their own experiences. Subordinate appraisal has been identified because it illustrates how seemingly dominant discourses may be countered. The current managerial concern with quality and the customer as sovereign allows for appeals to subordinate appraisal to be made on these grounds – the 'right' of the internal 'customer' to improve 'quality' by having a 'voice' – but illustrates the potential for disruption or challenge to hierarchy which may result from their adoption.

Subordinate Appraisals

Subordinate appraisals or 'non-traditional' performance appraisals are those in which employees evaluate supervisors as part of the latter's performance appraisal process, and/or each other in peer reviews. It is an attempt to formalize more informal assessments of an organization and management. Petrini (1991), for example, argues that an assessment of management lies in employees' quality, quantity and accuracy of work, meeting commitments, attendance, and turnover, and that subordinate appraisals of management would formalize this.

Given that managerial effectiveness is a nebulous phenomenon, the advantage of subordinate appraisals is that they provide a different perspective on how managers' skills are viewed, as well as providing views on how employees think they should be managed (Osborne, 1990). Hierarchy necessarily limits the degree of information those in such positions get, given isolation and power ensure limited communication. Bernardin and Beatty (1987: 64) recommend subordinate appraisals as being able to provide a 'unique and critical perspective on management performance'. In addition, as appraisals are usually collected from several subordinates, multiple assessments provide a more representative view of perceptions than single assessments. Subordinate appraisal is also identified with 'leadership' models of the future, especially in team and service-oriented organizations where the participation of employees is recognized as of increasing importance. As more responsibility moves to lower level employees, the emphasis becomes how well managers help subordinates to achieve better work performance.

Issues in subordinate appraisals involve what topics are to be addressed, reporting format to be used, who administers the process, who is asked to participate and when the information is to be collected. Topics which might be identified include delegation, fostering open communication, development and motivation of others, decision-making ability, supervision of tasks, technical ability, organization and control, and communication, the ability to conduct meetings, being open to employee suggestions. An important aspect is the confidentiality of participants (London et al., 1990). 'Standard' models involve the completion of an anonymous questionnaire, the results of which are then communicated to the manager. 'Deluxe' versions of upward appraisals involve the use of an outside consultant to interview employees and present a condensed summary to the manager. 'Safeguards' for those being appraised include that subordinates are aware of the requirements of the supervisors' jobs, and that they rate only the performance of those they can directly observe (McEvoy, 1988, 1990).

Despite recommendations that they are practical and efficient methods for diagnosing management problems and improving performance, subordinate appraisals are not widely used,[11] although some research indicates an increase in their use, from 10 to 20 per cent in a four year period 1984–88 (Bernardin and Beatty, 1987). Some firms, for example, Johnson and Johnson, General Electric and Xerox, IBM, Libby-Owens-Ford incorporate subordinate appraisals as well as customer satisfaction surveys into an overall corporate performance system to evaluate performance and determine rewards (Nelson-Horchler, 1988). Some organizations, however, stress that subordinate appraisal of management has to be acceptable to the managers being appraised (Petrini, 1991), and that it should be used in conjunction with other evaluations, for example, from peers as well as superiors (Lee, 1990). Some organizations restrict their use to that of development and training (Buhalo, 1991).

Employees criticize their managers for not spending enough time with them, not listening to their concerns, or not taking them seriously when they do (Carew, 1989). Other criticisms are that managers are perceived as being militaristic and territorial (Levinson, 1987). Although appraisals are generally recommended as a process whereby those lower in the organization may be motivated and their performance enhanced, managers' responses to such systems are generally very resistant (Nevels, 1989). About one third exhibit shock and disbelief in response to negative feedback (Nelson-Horchler, 1988), so comfortable have they been with the view that they were aware of subordinates' views. Upward appraisals in an organization with minimum communication generally only serves to feed paranoia (Kiechel, 1989). There is very limited management support of subordinate appraisal as part of an evaluative assessment (McEvoy, 1990), however there is some management support and acceptance of them for developmental purposes.

Whilst subordinate appraisal may be an example of an intensification of the gaze (Townley, 1992),[12] their use may have advantages. It gives a voice to those who do not normally have a formal mechanism for expression of opinions on such views. (Other examples of this include the move away from traditional hierarchical interviewing to the use of peer interviews, the involvement of those who are going to work with the individual being included in the selection process often recommended as the corollary of team work organization (Ott et al., 1990; Redeker and Segal, 1991).) It gives subordinates the opportunity to consider seriously what they would like their relationship with their supervisor to be, thereby at least recognizing or articulating the importance of their own role within the dyad. It provides the opportunity for an examination of the values which sustain social relationships, and the potential for extending discussion and debate as to the criteria to be used in accountability. Experience of subordinate appraisal may also have the advantage of ameliorating some of the effects of hierarchy. Thus future hierarchical appraisals may be modified, especially where the same performance evaluation form that managers use of employees is used (Werther, 1990), and in some cases the interdependence of the relationship between supervisor and subordinate may be re-established.

The Rejection of Technocracy, the Value of Experience and the Integrity of the Individual

The importance of the role of visibility and voice is that it allows for a rediscovery and revalorization of experience. Feminist theory, in particular, has placed great importance on the belief that experiences of everyday life are an appropriate access to knowledge, that there should not be the denial of subjective experience or the dismissal of the ways in which people make sense of their lives. At the basis of this position is a critique of scientific objectivism, based on a subject–object dualism, with its view that truth is identified by autonomous subjects, an abstract knowing subject, a disengaged self (Harding, 1986; Keller, 1985; Longino, 1989). In essence, what is involved is a critique of technicism.[13] The technocratic ethos attempts to reduce political questions into technical considerations: that there is one best way which can only be understood and found by experts, and that parameters of choice are dictated by technical imperatives rather than political ones. It turns the problems of politics into problems of administration, and problems of decision-making into questions of expertise (Heydebrand, 1977). Rather than knowledge providing the potential for a basis of social consensus on meaning and interpretation, it enables those who use it to minimize their contact with that which is represented. It fosters the monopolizing of an area to the exclusion of those most directly concerned with it. As Ferguson (1984) notes, however, to resist meanings or deny or devalue meanings through the creation of an alternative discourse is a political act. 'By claiming to be the nonideological instrument of technical progress, [technocracy] clothes itself in the guise of science and renders itself "ideologically invisible" ' (Ferguson, 1984: 16). What is required is to challenge technocracy as a basis of knowledge.

This would allow space for the importance of non-technicist views of knowledge and create a role for experience. It emphasizes the importance of experientially based self-reflexive knowledge, with the individual and their conscious activities as the source of knowledge. It is a rejection of the objectification, the individual as an object to be known but allows the individual the ability to participate in the constitution and definition of self-hood. It allows for the integrity of the subject by recognizing the importance of the 'other' as an equivalent to the self in terms of status and respect. In recognizing the importance of personalized relationships, it also places ethical relations at the centre of these. An example of this principle in practice may be seen in realistic job previews.

Realistic Job Previews
As the name suggests, realistic job previews give the applicant important and realistic information about the nature of the job. They involve a realistic description of undesirable job aspects, for example, that it may lack variety, is routine or may become boring, whether there is close supervision. This is in contrast to presentations in which the job is described as being challenging, important, having plenty of variety, or the opportunity for social contact. The more accurate examples of work are presented either in film or videos as part of the selection procedure, or in recruitment booklets giving examples of 'typical' incidents. These aspects may also be incorporated into realistic work sample tests. Often the sources for this information are those newly recruited to the organization or from information drawn from those leaving the organization. An important factor in this is timing, with realistic information being more readily assessed at earlier stages in the recruitment process, that is, its constituting a preview, before the applicant has a large investment in the process.

The essence of the process is to deflate unrealistic expectations of potential employees. It is premised on the view that individuals have less regret making a decision if they can anticipate its probable negative consequences. (This type of approach is also filtering into some medical health practices in terms of the amount of information which is disclosed to individuals prior to medical practice, rather than these issues being in the hands of 'experts' who inform the patient of their decision and expect acquiescence.) Examples of the types of jobs for which this has been used include sewing machine operators (Farr et al., 1973); telephone operators (Wanous, 1973, 1980) and life insurance agents (Weitz, 1956). Entry level positions are usually better for this type of procedure but it has also been used in the transfer of personnel to new geographical areas or new assignments.

The advantage for the organization is that it reduces post-entry employee turnover (Meglino and DeNisi, 1987) and can lead to substantial 'employee-replacement cost savings' (Wanous, 1980). Concerns are whether realism hampers the ability of an organization to attract competent applicants. Studies have shown that it does not have a negative impact on this (Wanous, 1989) nor on the acceptance of job offers. Generally, its influence has been in the lowering of inflated expectations, with individuals staying in jobs for a longer period of time. There has, however, been no impact on job performance. This is not to say that criteria such as selection ratios, the pressure of labour markets, especially unemployment do not have an effect on the process.

The significance of RJP lies not in what is said or in the circumstances or intentions which prompted its use, but rather in what it states about the relationship which is to be held with the individual. RJPs are based on a different conception of the subject, in which the organization attempts to treat the individual on an equal footing with itself (Herriot and Fletcher, 1990). It is the recognition that someone has the right to certain types of information, previously considered better to be withheld, and can be trusted to arrive at a judgement based on his or her own self-knowledge and information about a prospective position.[14] The individual is neither an object of knowledge for the organization, to be examined to see if there is the likelihood of a good 'fit'; nor is the individual a 'subject' to be manipulated in order to fit into the organization, but there is an authentic subject who can exercise independent judgement. It is based on a different view of truth, with the latter being 'a dialectic, as process, as the making of truth in time, between people . . . not . . . the revelation of something lost in the past, but as the production of something in the present' (DuBois, 1991: 107). It is the creation of a dialogue. Favourable responses to RJP are a recognition of the degree of honesty with which the relationship is conducted.[15]

The Importance of Difference
The revalorization of experience places an emphasis on the importance of specificity and the problematic of events. It underlines the importance of the relative, contextual and the multiple. Experience requires the recognition of various subject positions and the recognition of the plurality and difference which arises due to social, economic and cultural origin, differences in situations and needs.[16] This highlights the problematic

nature of appeals to universal laws, the depiction of the universal as the natural or the grounded. Difference is thus the attempt to break away from universals and unitary norms. It is the recognition of the varied bases of experience and with this alternative systems of values (Gilligan, 1982). This emphasizes the need to move away from the preservation of identity or its imposition on others and to move towards an exploration of differences. It lays stress on the importance of tolerance and equality in which differences can be expressed and, as McNay (1992: 110) notes, 'encourages us to think of difference as a resource . . . the aim is not to overcome difference in order to achieve a political unity'. Although the primacy of difference has been criticized by some feminists (MacKinnon, 1991), the value of its role may be identified in the developments in the moves toward employment equity.

Employment Equity
The issue of difference is of central importance to employment equity policies.[17] However, there has been debate about what constitutes equality, whether it is, for example, equal opportunity or numerical equality; equal access to higher paid male jobs or equal shares of these jobs; whether equity involves equal rewards for equal effort, as in equality of pay, or the recognition and mitigation of differences in access. Equal opportunity policies influenced by liberal feminism stress equity of opportunity rather than equity of results. Equal opportunity is defined as the chance to achieve the same goals in the absence of specified obstacles or sets of obstacles. Examples include the Equal Pay Act and the Sex Discrimination Act, which provide for equal pay for the same work, and among other things, restrict discrimination in employment on the grounds of sex.

Equality, as expressed in this legislation, has been criticized, for its emphasis on a programme of formal equality rights abstracted from sources and relations of power, and from real inequalities based on gender and race. The application of an equal standard causes problems where a group is not homogeneous, but different and unequal. Also within the notion of equality is a universal or unitary norm, equality is to be 'the same as'. There has been concern that the male is the norm or standard, and that equality implies the acceptance of a male norm, to be judged in terms of male standards, the attempt to mould and evaluate a woman 'as if' she were a man. The issue is raised, for instance, in 'assertiveness training' included as part of some liberal feminist equal opportunities programmes. Whilst this may have advantages as, through a series of structured exercises, participants are allowed to explore stressful situations and present alternative ways of handling them (Sears, 1986), there is a danger that it stifles difference, holding out male standards of behaviour. There is a danger that it reconstitutes the woman 'as if' she were a man.

The same philosophy underpinned the Equal Pay Act, in the UK, as women were paid 'as if' they were men when they were doing the same work.

Presenting equality as the absence of a set of obstacles has also been criticized for being a negative freedom rather than advancing substantive equality, which of necessity must take into consideration equality of prospects and equality of means. Debate has therefore centred increasingly on the importance of difference with a specific emphasis on the significance of pluralities and diversities, rather than unities and universals (Scott, 1988). It is the recognition that managing diversity requires an awareness of individual and cultural characteristics of different groups.

The importance of 'difference' can be seen underpinning the equal pay for work of equal value provisions. The European Commission, under Article 119, introduced an equal pay directive which allowed for work of equal value.[18] In the UK, an amendment to the 1970 Equal Pay Act, passed in 1983, but coming into effect in 1984, allowed an employee to claim equal pay due to like work or work of comparable value.[19] Equal pay for work of equal value, or as it is sometimes referred to comparable worth or pay equity, refers to equal pay for jobs which are dissimilar but considered to be of equal value to the organization. It is a development from the original pay equity claims for equal pay for equal work, granted when male and female jobs are the same or broadly similar. Comparable worth[20] is aimed at redressing biases in the compensation of women. It requires paying men and women equally for jobs which require the same level of skill, effort, responsibility and working conditions.[21] In this, comparable worth challenges conventional definitions of skill. At its basis is the requirement that management and unions examine the values which sustain different pay systems. It is the attempt to incorporate into job evaluations some of the overlooked, hidden or invisible aspects of work, thereby allowing for these factors to be evaluated and compensated adequately. Issues which comparable worth attempts to counter include inadequate or imprecise job evaluation, market pricing based on job titles or occupational categories alone. In UK local authorities, for example, a job evaluation taking into account equal value included responsibility for people resources and supervision, resulting in an increased evaluation for many women's jobs and a decrease in many heavily physical jobs (Lodge, 1987).

The payment of equal wages for jobs which have the same job evaluation score generally requires that one evaluation system is used to measure the relative value of all jobs within the organization. One response to the 1983 Equal Pay (Amendment) Regulations in the UK has been to hasten the spread of job evaluation schemes within UK industries, particularly those which measure the relative value of all jobs within the organization. In order to avoid claims based on equal pay for equal work, these schemes must be analytical and the jobs in question have to have been evaluated on a factor basis (Paddison, 1988). There is a problem, however, as to how sensitive job evaluation systems may be to potential discrimination (Scholl and Cooper, 1991).[22] Certainly, the view before the 1984 amendment was that job evaluation schemes operated to reinforce sex segregation (Collinson, 1987).

Although there has been a lot of work on the social construction of skill (Steinberg, 1990), it is debatable whether job evaluation schemes are sensitive enough to these aspects. Also point–factor rating of a particular job is a direct result of how a job has been designed and the possibilities of bias in this must be recognized. In addition, the potential for bias can occur in the criteria which are established to be measured, and the relative weighting of each measure. In a study seeking to identify what contributed to a relatively unbiased job evaluation scheme, Ghobadian and White (1987) found that positive factors were the scheme's degree of formality, the importance of voice and the extent of employees' participation. Participation of women in evaluation panels and their inclusion as job analysts also reduced the likelihood of bias.[23]

Comparable worth was heralded as introducing widespread changes in how people are paid and how jobs and productivity are seen by managers (Wright, 1987), as well as having a far-reaching impact on the workforce.[24] Its potential lies in its challenge to systems of categorization, as Foucault (1970: 54) notes, 'a thing can be absolute according to one relation yet relative according to others; order can be at once necessary and natural (in relation to thought) and arbitrary (in relation to things) since, according to the way in which we consider it, the same thing may be placed at differing points in our order'. Comparable worth is the recognition that a category of classification is relative, like all other categories, to the criteria one adopts, and attempts to make explicit the gendered nature of the labour market and status hierarchy. Comparable worth/equal pay claims also try to reorganize the dividing practices of organizations with areas of comparison to range outside establishments, and 'pay' to include fringe benefits.

Job evaluation was considered earlier as typifying the introduction and practice of taxinomia, mathesis and a disciplinary matrix to an organization. This is still the case here. The difference, however, lies in the nature of equivalences which have been drawn. Comparable worth represents a different political map of the organization, in which certain skills are recognized as being equal to others. It is important because it represents the recognition of difference. It is not just 'equal to' in the equal pay for like or broadly similar work, which established that women were equal to men, or that they should be paid 'as if' they were men. Comparable worth has within it a recognition that women are different from, but for the purposes of remuneration, their value is the same as that of men. In this sense it challenges the status quo and cultural devaluation of women. It is for this reason that Burns (1991) claims that the comparable worth movement is an effort to change institutions and political definitions. The significance of these developments, however, lies in their potential, the extent to which they are actively supported and fought for in specific contexts. There is no assumption that their existence alone will result in change per se.

The recognition of difference has also broadened interest in areas other than pay discrimination. Employment equity, or affirmative action, is a broader attempt to achieve the recognition of difference and value within an organization through an examination of personnel policies to examine those which, having no basis 'in fact', work towards the systematic discrimination of those who do not belong to the dominant group within the organization. The search for universal norms in personnel practices involves the evaluation of, for example, merit increases and promotional procedures, performance appraisal systems, incentive programmes and their awards. Factors which may work against employment equity include: study leave restrictions, closed promotion procedures and tiering. As employment equity is designed to increase representation of women, the disabled and visible minorities at all levels in employment, it involves a comprehensive planning process whereby an employer identifies and removes discrimination in employment policies and practices and remedies the effects of past discrimination through active recruitment, selection and training of minorities. It also includes the provision of such policies as job sharing schemes, career breaks, maternity leave, access to training, and the re-examination of career ladders with, in some cases, their redesign. Other measures include sexual harassment policies, accessible day care, work-place nurseries, extended maternity leave, flexi-time work scheduling, and work-at-home plans. It also requires 'voice' policies which can identify problems. Awareness training also stresses the importance of difference, through enabling participants to identify sexist and racist attitudes, beliefs and practices. It is usually part of a policy of monitoring, training and institutionalizing an equal opportunities policy (Simmons, 1989). Again, it represents the attempt to achieve recognition of difference and value within the organization. As such it has serious implications for those organizations attempting to build a strong organizational 'culture', often hiding male standards (Stokes, 1988).

The importance of recognizing difference is crucial at all stages in an organization. For instance, the limited representation of women and ethnic groups in corporate leadership (Hardesty and Jacobs, 1986; Morrison and Gilnow, 1990), leads to the inherent danger of racial and gender stereotyping of leadership traits, and sex-biased values influencing recruitment, induction and promotion (Alvesson and Billing, 1992; Mills, 1988). The androcentric nature of leadership research and its single society assumptions has already been commented on (Millman and Kanter, 1975; Morouney, 1991). There is both limited awareness that leadership research favours stereotypically male tasks and that certain constructs such as achievement motivation is based on male behaviour (McHugh et al., 1986). There is also the assumption that certain manners of speaking or acting will elicit the same responses regardless of the sex or race of those involved (Hare-Mustin and Marecek,1988). Nor is there the recognition that different groups have differential access to economic and social resources. All the examples are based on the presumption of the universal and the failure to recognize and valorize difference adequately.

The Relational Nature of Knowledge

The recognition of difference also has implications for how we understand meaning. Rather than meaning being universal it has to be seen as relative, contextual and multiple. Meaning, in other words, derives from context and perhaps, more importantly, only from contrast. A concept or entity is not a unitary thing, but has within it that which is denied or repressed, thus 'hot', for example, only derives its meaning from an implicit contrast with 'cold'. Identities are not in this sense absolute but always relational, 'one can only ever be seen in relation to something else' (Clegg, 1989: 159). The second element of a binary pair gives meaning to the first. In practice, however, there is a failure to recognize this 'other', even though it is this which gives meaning. Terms are presented as independent and autonomous rather than interdependent or relational. Binary divisions are constituted as being separate and opposed, logical contradictions, rather than relationally defined. They become fixed oppositions which deny the extent to which they are dependent upon that which they deny or negate.

This has several implications for the way in which we derive knowledge. Some feminisms, for example, are concerned to challenge the dualisms in the way in which knowledge is posed, in particular the public and the private, which informs many other dichotomies, particularly influential in the way work is perceived, for instance, heavy/light, dirty/clean, dangerous/boring, mobile/sedentary, with the former being privileged and usually associated with the male (Game and Pringle, 1983). Pringle (1988) illustrates how secretary is a gendered category which takes its meaning from another category, the 'boss'. It is, as Pringle notes, a category of employment for which it is difficult to establish a clear job description, in part because of an emphasis placed on what she is rather than what she does. Recognition of the relational nature of meaning is also the basis of feminist critiques of established concepts in management literature, for example, leadership, which necessarily invokes a concept of 'followship' in order to establish meaning.[25]

The relational nature of meaning also creates a world of contested meanings and the fragility of identity. As was stated earlier, traditional interpretations have taken the individual as the self-evident unit with which to begin analysis. Through scientific enquiry this has led to the objectification of the individual, and with this a particularly unidimensional way to understanding individuals in the work context. Feminism critiques this model of separateness, stressing an alternative understanding of social relations. In rejecting the humanistic view of the individual as, in essence, unique, fixed and coherent, Foucault with feminism proposes a subjectivity which is contradictory and precarious, always in a process of becoming (Weedon, 1991).[26] It recognizes that identity is constructed and is open-ended, contrary and an amalgam of different subject positions. This also has implications for methodologies for understanding personnel practices, advocating a feminist based research methodology (H. Roberts, 1990). Rather than begin analysis with the individual, it may be more constructive to view the individual as constituted through relations with others. An example of this is Pye's (1988) work on the study of management competencies.

Management Competencies

In her analysis of the literature on management competencies, Pye (1988) criticizes traditional approaches which attempt to isolate, enumerate and preferably measure these dimensions, principally for the prospects of control that such an approach offers. This, she argues, derives from an additive and static model of competencies, based on a 'sum of parts' or an assembly model of managing. In this type of analysis particular types of situations are thought to require the exercise of particular 'tools'. This list building approach to competencies assumes that components can be separately isolated and described. Pye (1988) contrasts this with a constitutive and relational concept of competence where the latter are constructed in social contexts and develop through social relationships. As Pye notes, competence is a social construct based very much on the observer who attributes competence to particular behaviour. 'In this sense, competence is not something to be "possessed", rather it is something "given" by other people in their evaluation of the actions of others in a particular situation at a particular time' (Pye, 1988: 63). The importance, therefore, of what constitutes competence depends on the context in which judgements are being made and given the dynamic nature of social interaction this must inevitably be continually changing. Pye stresses the importance of dimensions of context and timing: 'Any definition of effectiveness must also be relational: dependent on time, context and evaluating audience. In essence, there can be no absolute conception of managerial competence or effectiveness' (Pye, 1988: 63). This means that the ability to access managerial competence is strictly limited to personal experience, and the concomitant difficulties of translating this into static language or lists. Rejecting the absolute or ultimate criteria in favour of the importance of contextual or relational dimension to evaluations of competence and performance, calls for a rethinking and reconstructing of the way in which we conceptualize managerial competence. It cannot be perceived as an absolute quality or isolated into component parts for definition and measurement. 'Both competence and effectiveness are active terms: they are known through action and performance' (Pye, 1988: 64).

The Rejection of Hierarchical Order or Privileging

The relational view of meaning has wider implications than influencing how things are known. A relational view of the world, rather than one based on an atomistic individualism, is the recognition of interdependence and connectedness. It basically posits a change in thinking from one that automatically analyses in terms of hierarchy. From the recognition of the relational comes the critique of meaning based on the privileging of one half of a binary pair, a hierarchical relationship which is posed of one term being dominant over the other. It requires a rejection of a philosophy that has systematically and repeatedly construed the world in hierarchical terms, and an emphasis on connectedness and relatedness, the importance of reciprocity, mutuality and vulnerability. This principle of reciprocity, the importance of the other in a non-hierarchical relation, is one which may inform analyses of all social relationships, being a feature of every interaction. It is not a utopian argument for relationships to be symmetrical. Foucault, for example, recognized the probability of the inevitability of asymmetries of power in relationships, given the nature of power. It is, however, the recognition of the importance of not abusing this power relationship – to conduct oneself in one's relations with others on the principle of non-domination. He writes:

> relations of power are not something bad in themselves, from which one must free oneself. I don't believe there can be a society without relations of power, if you understand them as means by which individuals try to conduct, to determine the behaviour of others . . . The problem is . . . to give oneself the rules of law, the techniques of management and also the ethics . . . the practices of self, which would allow these games of power to be played with a minimum of domination. (Foucault, 1991c : 18)

It is a principle which seeks to eliminate oppressive and dominant behaviour, and opposes institutionalized dominance and subordination, and the rejection of horizontally graded authority relations entailing top–down supervision and control.

Alternatives to hierarchy again have traditionally been in terms of the juridical subject, based on a view of power located in a centralized source and thus requiring constraints. This prompts an appeal to formal rights on behalf of those in subordinate positions. The practice of personnel may in many respects be identified as the clarification of rights of employees who are judged to require greater clarity and precision in work. It is an appeal for clarity, however, on behalf of individuals who manage to operate in everyday social contexts where clarity is largely absent. Not only are there nuances which have to be recognized and managed in order to facilitate social engagement, lack of clarity is an important dimension of social functioning. The principal reason for the need for greater clarity, although this is not confronted, lies in the fact that social engagement at work largely takes place within a hierarchy. When individuals are in positions of power it is necessarily in the interests of those in subordinate positions to require increased clarity in the criteria used in decisions that affect them at work. The question remains as to whether the answer lies in greater clarity and through this an assumed protection, or in the dismantling of hierarchy.

Non-hierarchical Social Relations
Alternatives to hierarchy are notoriously difficult to envisage because the vast majority of experience, certainly institutionalized experience in work, family, schools and hospitals, takes place within hierarchical relationships. The rather restricted range of organizations which are presented in the studies of work also reduce our ability to visualize difference. Because hierarchy is the norm, alternatives to its practice are hard to visualize. Non-hierarchical social relations are something which in principle may potentially inform all social relationships. The importance of mutuality, for example, has influenced views on the nature of the teaching (Foucault, 1984c) and parental relationship, which stresses both parties equally learning and giving; a bigger/more knowledgeable person helping a smaller/less knowledgeable person, both absorbing elements of the other perspective. It is also a theme which can be identified in new politics which wishes to see change in public service institutions. Themes of the importance of quality, the new customer-oriented approach, are an attempt to renegotiate the relationship between supplier/producer and consumer, to revalorize the position of the customer, the other. Their effect in practice has largely been to reverse hierarchy, not to remove it, maintaining hierarchical ordering in the myth that the consumer is sovereign, and in doing so, not surprisingly, prompts opposition to these practices.

There has, however, been some work on non-hierarchical organizations (Wine and Ristock, 1991). The basis of such organizations is that hierarchical patterns of authority are not essential for the achievement of important goals. Rather than follow traditional organizational concerns that hierarchy should run more smoothly, the premiss of such organizations is to deny its necessity. This is not to say that organizations dispense with expertise, but that the latter is linked to a different form of power. Expertise is shared for the benefit of all, whereas power becomes the 'ability to act with others to do things that could not be done by individuals alone' (Ferguson, 1984: 206). Authority is based on displayed skill and knowledge, but with each used according to their strengths, not educational background. It is ability and expertise not rank or position which is important. Differentiation and division of labour is minimal with the goal of demystifying expertise, with an emphasis on the maximization of skills of membership. There is the recognition that it is not possible to obliterate power differentials, given differences in personal power and skills, but that differences are recognized and valued.

In an ideal arrangement, responsibility, knowledge and accountability would be shared by all, with a collective rather than individual ownership of outcomes. Organizational practices which reflect this philosophy include rotation of leadership roles and the sharing of service roles, consensus decision-making, commitment to decentralization, concern for accessibility, and an egalitarianism reflected in flat pay scales. There is a rejection of formal leadership roles and voting. By rejecting the latter no-one is forced by a majority into a decision (Ferguson, 1984; Iannello, 1992; Martin, 1990). This depiction of organizations has traditionally been criticized for insufficient attention to efficiency. Iannello (1992) describes a process of modified consensus as a method of decision-making and form of organization which encapsulates this, and responds to concerns with efficiency. There is a reversal of traditional organizational practices in that there is outward (not downward) delegation of routine decisions (the latter are differentiated by organizational members), to those with skill and knowledge. Critical decisions, however, those dealing with the overall path and goals of the organization, are reserved for the entire membership and matters are discussed until a decision acceptable to everyone is reached.[27] There is a rejection of permanent placement of people in roles not only because it prevents others from learning but also because it guards against specialization which fosters hierarchy. Contrary to traditional organizational theory, consensual non-hierarchical decision-making was found to lead to a clarity of goals, not as traditional organizational theory would have it, the clarity of goals determining a decision-making structure. In such organizations rules are minimal, based on the substantive ethics of the situation. Control is achieved through respect of principles. Consideration is for personal, not professional, identities.

The preponderant image in the description of alternative organizational forms is the web. From Hartsock (1974) is the recognition that 'to lead is to be at the centre of a group rather than in front of others'. Gilligan (1982: 62) notes how the images of hierarchy and web inform different modes of assertion and response:

> the wish to be alone at the top and the consequent fear that others will get too close; and the wish to be at the centre of connection and the consequent fear of

being too far out on the edge. These disparate fears of being stranded and being caught give rise to different portrayals of achievement and affiliation, leading to different modes of action and different ways of assessing the consequences of choice.

Leadership in such scenarios is not the power handed to someone but that which emerges as a product of capabilities and skills of individuals and operates in a way constructive to all members of the group.

It is important to realize that such organizations do not offer 'blueprints'. They are very much open-ended, ongoing social processes struggling with alternative ways of accommodating authority and leadership. The fragility of these practices reinforces the importance of guiding principles which should inform actors, and the importance of continuous vigilance of all participants in social relations. These indicate that non-hierarchical relationships lie within the realm of participative ongoing experience, rather than being readily reducible to a set of specific practices. An overriding criterion which might identify whether non-hierarchical work relations are achieved or not is captured by a respondent in Iannello's (1992: 70) study, who says that in essence the distinguishing feature of such organizations is 'the right to say "I can't do something" and not to have to feel guilty about it'.

Politics as Ethics

The criteria I have used to critique personnel raise one central question: how might we conduct ourselves in our relations with others? This is an ethical question. To raise it is to place ethical considerations at the heart of political action. This is the strength of Foucauldian politics.

A criticism raised earlier is that Foucault does not offer a 'focused' political agenda.[28] There is no general scheme of transformation, no attempt to predetermine what this change will be, in this sense, no predetermined or idealized 'alternative'. In this failure to provide 'sure truths, rational grounds or prescriptive policies' (Rajchman, 1985: 5), Foucault apparently undermines the basis of a political or ethical position for social change. These criticisms, however, stem from Foucault's denial of expectations. As he comments: 'The questions I am trying to ask are not determined by a pre-established political outlook and do not tend toward the realization of some definite political project . . . This is doubtless what people mean when they reproach me for not presenting an overall theory' (Foucault, 1984b: 375). His failure to address concerns in conventional terms, however, does not imply that they are not addressed at all in his work: they are addressed differently.

Foucault's work does contain a 'political' message. In his later work, in which he addresses issues of identity, liberty and an ethical way of living, he attempts to engage with an alternative political 'agenda'. The locus of Foucault's politics is grounded in *how one conducts oneself*: one's daily practices *vis-à-vis* oneself and others.[29] Drawing upon the theme of governmentality, it is a schema for the ethical interrogation of experience. Foucault refers to this as 'care of the self'. It addresses 'the kind of relationship you ought to have with yourself, *rapport à soi*, which I call ethics, and which determines how the individual is supposed to constitute himself as a moral subject of his own actions' (Foucault, 1984a: 352).[30] Put simply, it is self-critique, the ability to reflect on the import of one's actions, stipulating the criteria through which one wants to live and judge practices.[31]

In this sense, politics merges with ethics. He says, 'what interests me is much more morals than politics or, in any case, *politics as an ethics*' (Foucault, 1984b: 375; emphasis added) and regrets that the question of an ethical subject does not have much of a place in contemporary political thought (Foucault, 1991c: 14). The essence of a political programme, for Foucault, is an ethical way of being a self. 'Ethos was the deportment and the way to behave. It was the subject's mode of being and a certain way of acting visible to others' (Foucault, 1991c: 6). It is an attempt to get at a form of becoming a subject that would furnish the source of an effective resistance to a specific and widespread type of power (Foucault, 1988a: 251). It is for these reasons that Foucault characterizes the concern of his final work as 'politics as an ethic' (Foucault, 1984b: 375).

Foucault's concern with a politics or an ethics of the self was derived from his work on Greek ethics.[32] For Foucault, the importance of the *practice* of ethics provides important insights for a modern politics. Greek ethics were based not on a code 'which determines which acts are permitted or forbidden' but on ethics 'which determine the positive or negative value of the different possible behaviours' (Foucault, 1984a: 352). Morality is thus not 'a set of imposed rules and prohibitions' (codes) but the 'real behaviour of individuals in relation to the rules and values that are recommended to them' (ethics) (McNay, 1992: 52). At the basis of the distinction between codes and ethics is the recognition that large-scale systems of belief are untenable, and that there must be a more localized basis of morality. Hence, the stress is not on abstract codes but on real practices and questions. Ethics are not to be seen in transcendental terms but as *practical* critique, part of 'concrete processes of ordering one's day-to-day existence' (McNay, 1992: 52). Ethics are critical self-awareness. Politics as ethics pose the following questions. How should practices be exercised? What should inform them? What is desirable? What are the criteria for governmentality? How do individuals govern themselves and govern others? Answers to these questions, however, do not form a code. For Foucault, ethics are not a dogmatic and totalizing discourse: 'ethics can be a very strong structure of existence, without any relation with the juridical per se, with an authoritarian system, with a disciplinary structure' (Foucault, 1984a: 348). Ethics are not tied to a social or legal institutional system. They are not 'rooted . . . in autonomy or the capacity to determine actions according to rules all must rationally accept' (Rajchman, 1985: 93).[33]

An obvious danger is that this ethics of the self might retreat into 'a form of unregulated introversion' (McNay, 1992: 8). Foucault denies that he advocates an endless examination of an inner self.[34] However, to guard against this danger, his political project which focuses on practices (how do we behave with what effects?) must be allied with feminism's emphasis on the principles which guide conduct or practices of the self in relation to others.[35] Both Foucault and feminism stress the importance of non-exploitative social relations, recognize the importance of the inter-subjective dimension of social relations, regard the Self as constituted in relation to the Other, sustained through a continuous redefinition of the boundaries between Self and Other.[36] This view of social relations and the principles it sustains – voice, visibility, integrity, difference and non-hierarchical relations – form the basis of a political ethics. These principles stress the importance of an ethics based on reflexivity, reciprocity and respect for the specificity of the Other. They work to reduce the social production of distance (Bauman, 1989).

This political and ethical basis to Foucault's work can provide the basis of a new politics. Foucault talks about political action based on a new concept of rights. A corollary of his concept of disciplinary power is the recognition of the limitation of the rights devolved from State bodies, important though these may be. To be effective, rights must be understood through and claimed from experience. Politics, for Foucault, is not a matter of winning abstract rights from the State, but of creating a subject who claims the practical right to voice, integrity and visibility. This might, in fact, constitute a negative appreciation of rights; for example, the right *not* to be treated or engaged with in a particular way. This concept of rights places the question of one's relationship with others – everyday social practices – at the heart of political concerns (Bauman, 1989). It emphasizes the importance of a practical ethics: how one relates to the Other (internal or external). It poses, as the basis of an ethical existence, the question: how does one act?

Notes

1 It is for these reasons that Foucault describes the disciplines as 'an ensemble of minute technical inventions that made it possible to increase the useful size of multiplicities by decreasing the inconveniences of a power which must control them' (Foucault, 1977: 220). For Foucault, it was these methods of administering the accumulation of men, rather than the technological inventions of the period, which allowed for the accumulation of capital, industrialization and the development of capitalism.

2 Foucault describes the panopticon as a mechanism which automizes and individualizes power. Automizes in the sense that it operates independently of the person who is located in the central tower (be they madman or schoolboy, as Foucault notes), and independently of what motivates him or her; and individualizes in that the unit of observation becomes the individual.

3 There are, of course, differences between the maps which accounting creates and other maps through which the organization is rendered visible. Accounting, for example, 'has been institutionalized as the most important, authoritative and telling means whereby activity is made visible' (Roberts, 1991: 359).

4 Freedom in this sense requires a much more complex politics. Acts of liberation are not sufficient to establish practices of liberty: 'I do not think that there is anything that is functionally – by its very nature – absolutely liberating. Liberty is a practice . . . The liberty of men is never assured by the institutions and laws that are intended to guarantee them. That is why almost all of these laws and institutions are quite capable of being turned around. Not because they are ambiguous, but simply because "liberty" is what must be exercised...It can never be inherent in the structure of things to guarantee the exercise of freedom' (Foucault, 1989: 264–5). His work thus points to the antinomy between real and nominal freedoms, and the rejection of freedom as formal instituted liberty. Liberty or freedom has to be understood in more basic terms than the guarantee of civil or social rights. Response has to be broadened to deal with disciplinary power which requires an alternative system of rights.

5 Deconstruction undermines the hierarchical opposition on which a concept rests. Feminism argues that the dichotomization of thought underlies a lot of Western thinking, not only public/private, but culture/nature, reason/emotion, rational/intuitive, independence/dependence, strong/weak, reflecting the exclusion of women from spheres of citizenship and employment. These dichotomies value the former identified with the male, at the expense of the latter identified with the female. The criteria which form the basis of the following critique of HRM are derived from an analysis of who and what is absent from that which forms part of our knowledge.

6 There are many feminisms – liberal feminism, radical feminism, cultural feminism, socialist feminism, post-modern feminism, eco-feminism. They diverge in the centrality accorded the critique of patriarchy *vis-à-vis* other structures of domination, their views on the relative autonomy of the political sphere, their definitions of equality, and the political programmes they advocate. It is not the intention here to go into their differences, but to suggest that there are sufficiently common themes from which to extract from them a shared view of the world which may inform a set of practices and with which to judge actions. For the sake of brevity distinctions will only be made between Marxist and radical feminism. Radical feminists are critical of the privileging of the labour/capital distinction, as well as the dualism of the ideology/material base in Marxist analyses, arguing that these marginalize women, given the emphasis on economic determination and privileging the site of production, and the reduction of women's concerns to an ideological effect. Radical feminists seek to rectify the position whereby gender is secondary to class. Radical feminism emphasizes the material effects of discourse (discourse as an amalgam of material practices and forms of knowledge), formulating analyses around discursive practices rather than the material/ideology distinction and denying the primacy afforded to the economic realm.

7 They share many common themes: particularly self, identity, power and ethics. Foucault's stress on historically specific discursive relations and social practices, and the concomitant rejection of essentialism, has been particularly pertinent to feminist analyses (Diamond and Quinby, 1988; Hekman, 1992; Nicholson, 1990). For example, Foucault's identification of the body as a site of power has been the basis of feminist critiques of biological determinism and essentialism. It is, however, Foucault's analysis of power, its

rejection of power as being possessed, flowing from a centralized source, and its primarily repressive exercise, which resonates most with feminist theorizing. The non- or anti-statist analyses; the significance of an ascending analysis of the microphysics or capilliary action of power; the centrality of practices, and power as relational, are all themes which feminism embraces. Equally, removing analyses of power from the arena of production and the problematizing of other areas have also been welcomed by feminists. As a result, there has been a diversification and renegotiation of 'politics', with the recognition of the politicization of the personal domain, and the need to analyse the politics of personal relations and everyday life (Smith, 1974). Personal relationships are no longer outside power, the 'private' domain of liberal politics.

8 Of course, there are some problems with the direct equation of Foucault's work with feminism, in particular the problems of essentialism in some feminist writing – an essential, and celebrated, 'feminine' or female. Also problematic is the centrality of gender in the analysis of patriarchy and feminism's political programme based on a 'metanarrative' of emancipation. Implicit with a feminist politics is the idea of progression and personal emancipation, prompting concern amongst some feminists of immanent relativism and the possibilities for an emancipatory politics in Foucault's work. There are, however, sufficient similarities between the themes to support a Foucauldian feminist analysis even if its full justification cannot be attempted here for reasons of space.

9 The focus here is primarily on the effects of gender influencing definitions of skill, but would apply equally well to race and age. Friedan (1993), for example, illustrates how youth becomes the defining comparator, thus, quickness of thought and speed in decision-making become prized over a more deliberative approach. The emphasis on the present defines skills developed over a period of time as obsolete. Depth of experience and the wisdom of elders are too readily dismissed. I am grateful to Karen Legge for drawing my attention to the importance of ageism.

10 The emphasis on visibility stems from the importance of job analysis in job evaluation systems, for instance. Bringing these issues to light, however, would not necessarily result in their inclusion in conventional practices such as job evaluation. This would depend on the criteria which have been identified as compensable factors, although it might indicate some dimensions of these compensable factors in operation which had previously been neglected. Its emphasis is to make management develop a more incisive method of analysing job functions.

11 The relatively limited use of subordinate appraisals to identify managerial talent is surprising given that research indicates that subordinate assessment of managers is more accurate than assessment centre predictions of 'success', in a two to four year time span. Over seven years they also accurately predict successful managers, more so than supervisor ratings (McEvoy and Beatty, 1989).

12 Whilst subordinate appraisal may be recommended as a means whereby those in positions of power may find out their strengths and weaknesses, in some cases this might become quite formalized as, for example, when recommended by consultants in specialist practitioner journals. For example, the recommendation to use a Management Practices Survey or MPS (Asherman and Asherman, 1990). This is a diagnostic instrument which enables managers to determine how their practices affect the performance, motivation and career satisfaction of those reporting to them. It is a questionnaire containing forty-eight items which assess practices on six dimensions of management effectiveness. Each level of management is assessed. The composite results of the anonymous responses are then sent to the respective managers. Others include software packages designed to discover perceptions of leadership skills and behaviour (Edwards, 1990). Such techniques are antithetical to any emancipatory agenda, merely serving to objectivize both management and subordinates.

13 As Ferguson notes technicism involves a reliance on a limited and prescribed set of processes: 'rationality (a linear, rule-governed, instrumental order), artificiality (distance from and opposition to nature), automatism (efficiency and control as self-justifying virtues), and universalism (no distinction between techniques and the use to which they are put) (Ferguson, 1984: 16).

14 The importance of this approach to knowledge can also be identified in non-juridical responses to the issue of sexual harassment, which recognize the validity of the individual's definition of what constitutes harassment rather than try to codify actions, and introduce a formulaic response on these issues.

15 It may, of course, be argued that in the context of high unemployment, negative information is downplayed, or that the individual loses the right or ability to complain. I am grateful to Karen Legge for bringing my attention to these points. I do not argue that RJP removes the inequality of the employment exchange, but that it has the potential to ameliorate it. How it operates in practice would depend on the context and the extent to which it is complemented with other policies designed to give voice to the other.

16 An important aspect of this debate is the criticism of black and third world feminists of the ethnocentric nature of feminist writings. These criticisms stress the importance of different experiences in relation to racialism, colonialism, etc., with the result that gender interacts with race, ethnicity, etc. to produce a different range of experiences. This has the advantage of encouraging 'a politics that is designed to avoid dogmatism in our categories and politics, as well as the silencing of difference to which such dogmatism can lead' (Sawicki, 1991: 45).

17 Employment equity, a Canadian term, is used rather than equal opportunity because it avoids the liberal associations of the latter. It is in this sense stronger, focusing on outcomes, rather than the liberal assumption that providing people with equal opportunity will significantly redress discrimination in access to jobs and power. It is distinguished from affirmative action, sometimes referred to as positive or reverse discrimination, which in the US is associated with the use of quotas to address previous racial and gender imbalances.

18 In the US, equal pay for equal work without regard to sex has been part of federal policy since the 1963 Equal Pay Act, where employers have had to equalize wages paid to male and female employees who hold jobs which demand equal skill, effort, and responsibility and are performed under equal working conditions. In a landmark case involving the state of Washington and female prison guards, the Supreme Court ruled that action could be brought for sex-based salary discrimination under Title VII of the Civil Rights Act. This opened up the possibility of litigating comparable worth under Title VII (Cohen and Cohen, 1987), as applicants did not have to satisfy the equal work standards of the Equal Pay Act (Wisniewski, 1982).

19 Equal value legislation is complaint-driven, filed individually. Once at an industrial tribunal an independent expert may decide if the jobs in question are of equal value, using whatever method they view appropriate (Arthurs, 1988). Where the two jobs have been evaluated under a job evaluation scheme as unequal, there is no basis for a case unless the evaluation system itself discriminates on the grounds of sex.

20 I am using this US reference because it is a shorter version of the more usual UK reference to equal pay for work of equal value. Pay equity does not sufficiently distinguish between equal pay for like or similar work, and equal pay for work of equal value.

21 Whereas in the US specification of evaluation factors was determined by the 1963 Equal Pay Act and involves skill, effort, responsibility and working conditions. Equal pay regulations in the UK do not give clear guidance as to what equal value means.

22 Or even the sensitivity of those 'interpreting' results, as for example, one study of a PAQ job analysis of a homemaker, where the job profile found most similar was that of a

police patrolman. The commentary merely recorded that because the activities of homemakers and patrol officers 'are obviously not alike', then the analysis serves to reinforce the importance of the type of job descriptor selected in job classification.

23 Another problem is the relative importance of 'market factors' and the introduction of merit pay in the administration of job evaluation. As noted earlier they are mechanisms which politically arrange a population. They present a system of paying for the position not the person. Although salary grades may be based on point factor job evaluations, employers may deviate from this for market factors. With increasing flexibility, especially as jobs become defined around business necessity and individual capabilities, the person comes to define the position, the prospects for comparability become more difficult to sustain. The argument is emerging that a single, point-factor job evaluation system using an a priori approach, although important from a pay equity perspective, does not serve organizational objectives. Advocates argue that a policy-capturing approach may be superior (Tompkins et al., 1990).

24 It is perhaps the political implications of comparable worth claims, as well as their financial costs, which have limited its adoption (Graham and Hyde, 1991). In the US there is no comparable worth provision except the Equal Pay Act 1963.

25 The implications of this are paramount for men given their positions of dominance, having implications for new forms of masculinity, and concepts such as leadership (Hearn, 1989).

26 This emphasizes the importance of consciousness-raising as an important dimension of political action. Not as a process of telling us who we are 'but rather to free us from certain ways of understanding ourselves' (Sawicki, 1991: 44). Consciousness-raising is premised on a view of our relationship to ourselves and 'reality'. It also presupposes that the meaning of experience is not fixed.

27 Native Canadian decision-making runs on this basis.

28 There is, for example, no political programme in the form of sovereignty constituted from subjects on issues such as legitimacy, consent and rights, emphasizing questions about who should 'hold' power, and the constraints on power (Sawicki, 1991). Foucault's critique of sovereign power also effects his views of 'rights'. The view of power as domination leads to a juridical view of the subject: a powerful centre, in other words, requires the liberal response of the establishment of certain rights in order to ensure against the abuse of power. Foucault's critique points to the inadequacies of a response solely along these lines.

29 The rejection of an essentialist human nature refocuses attention from an 'uncovering' of this essential humanism, however, to the act of creation. It is not an ethics in which freedom lies in discovery or authenticity. There is no 'authentic' self-relation to which we must conform, in the Sartrean sense of a free self with the uncovering or removing of repression – this would hint of essentialism. Authentic is in the sense of created or crafted with a degree of choice, not uncovered. It is a process of constructing.

30 It involves determination of ethical substance (the way the individual chooses the prime material of moral conduct (aspects of behaviour, part of self)), mode of subjection (how does the individual establish his or her relation to a rule of conduct), forms of elaboration of ethical work (what specific transformation of oneself is invited by ethical commitment), and a telos (at what mode of being does the ethical subject aim) (Bernauer, 1990: 176).

31 His view of ethics was also inevitably influenced by his homosexuality. See 'Friendship as a Way of Life' (Foucault, 1989), where he talks of homosexuality raising the issues of ways of life. 'To be gay . . . is . . . to try to define and develop ways of life' (Foucault, 1989: 207). Creating the self was a practice identified by one biographer as leading to Foucault's death, as he experimented with different types of experiences ultimately

leading to his death from Aids (J. Miller, 1993).

32 Their relevance, however, has to be seen in contrast to early Christian ethical practices. As was noted in Chapter 5, Christian ethics of the confession are based on the notion of the truth lying buried within the individual; it requires a process of objectivization of the self in order to decipher the real. Christian ethics was based on a code of self-renunciation and self-mastery (so that the False One could not ensnare the soul) and was intimately tied to an institutional base. Greek ethics, on the other hand, allowed far more autonomy to the individual who is free to arrive at his or her own relationship with the rules. It is not conformity to a law, rather an ethics elaborated from within not imposed from without. It is important to note that Foucault does *not* advocate the adoption of the content of Greek ethics, merely the means through which an emphasis on ethics was achieved. Foucault is quite explicit on this, on content he says 'the Greek ethics of pleasure is linked to a virile society, to dissymetry, exclusion of the other, an obsession with penetration, and a kind of threat of being dispossessed with your own energy, and so on. All that is quite disgusting!' (Foucault,1984a; 346).

33 The questions raised are: 'Not "What can I know" but rather, How have my questions been produced? How has the path of my knowing been determined? Not "What ought I to do?" but rather How have I been situated to experience the real? . . . Not "What may I hope for?" but rather What are the struggles in which I am engaged? How have the parameters for my aspirations been defined?' (Bernauer, 1990: 18–19). What we have to train ourselves for is a new way of thinking, but this requires the rejection of dogmatic theory, learning to live without. This requires the invention of new modes of thought and action (Rajchman, 1985: 124).

34 Foucault is clear that there is a difference between Greek ethics of the self and modern culture of the self. He says, 'In the Californian cult of the self, one is supposed to discover one's true self, to separate it from that which might obscure or alienate it, to decipher its truth thanks to psychological or psychoanalytical science, which is supposed to be able to tell you what your true self is . . . I do not identify this ancient culture of the self with what you might call the Californian cult of the self, I think they are diametrically opposed' (Foucault, 1984a: 362).

35 Many commentators identify a political/normative position in his work (Bernauer, 1990; Fraser, 1989; Habermas, 1992; McNay, 1992; Rajchman, 1985). As McNay (1992: 141) notes, 'At an unarticulated level Foucault clearly makes value judgements about what constitutes progressive political behaviour and what constitutes an abuse of power or domination of truth, yet he fails to make these assumptions explicit.'

36 There have been criticisms of Foucault's presentation of ethics with its stress on the autonomy of the individual, and the primacy of this as an ethical focus, particularly the statement that 'One must not have the care for other precede the care for the self' (Foucault, 1991c: 7). This has been criticized by some feminists because of its denial of the self-in-relation to others and the ethics of care. These debates reflect a difference in focus. Foucault's stress on the importance of the ethics of the self, and the autonomy of the individual in relation to an ethical code, must be placed in the context of his analysis of Greek practices in comparison with later Christian mores on ethics. In the latter care of the self became subservient to care of others. This dominance of others, particularly the Other, God, provides the basis for Foucault's rejection of this as an ethical framework because it denies a role for individual responsibility. Foucault argues that care of the self implies a relationship with others. Care of self is 'the place one occupies among others' (1991c: 9).

References

Abercrombie, Nicholas (1991) 'The Privilege of the Producer', pp. 171–85 in Russel Keat and Nicholas Abercrombie (eds), *Enterprise Culture*. London: Routledge.

Adachi, Kazuhiko (1989) 'Problems and Prospects of Management Development of Female Employees in Japan', *Journal of Management Development*, 8(4): 32–40.

Adam, Everett E., Jr (1991) 'Quality Circle Performance', *Journal of Management*, 17(1): 25–39.

Aho, Kaye L. (1989) 'Understanding the New Job-Analysis Technology', *Personnel*, 66(1): 38–40.

Alcoff, Linda and Elizabeth Potter (eds) (1993) *Feminist Epistemologies*. New York: Routledge.

Allen, Keith R. (1990) 'Compensation in Context: Adapting to the Needs of the Nineties', *Benefits and Compensation International*, 20(5): 19–24.

Alvesson, Mats and Yvonne Due Billing (1992) 'Gender and Organization: Towards a Differentiated Understanding', *Organization Studies*, 13(1): 73–103.

Anderson, Neil R. (1990) 'Repertory Grid Technique in Employee Selection', *Personnel Review*, 19(3): 9–15.

Anderson, Neil and Vivian Shackleton (1988) 'The Chosen Few', *Management Today*, 133–8.

Anderson, Neil and Vivian Shackleton (1990) 'Staff Selection Decision Making into the 1990s', *Management Decision*, 28(1): 5–8.

Anstey, E. (1971a) 'The Civil Service Administrative Class: Extended Interview Selection Procedure', *Occupational Psychology*, 45: 199–208.

Anstey, E. (1971b) 'The Civil Service Administrative Class: A Follow-Up of Post-War Entrants', *Occupational Psychology*, 45, 27–43.

Anthony, P.D. (1977) *The Ideology of Work*. London: Tavistock.

Arac, Jonathan (ed.) (1988) *After Foucault: Humanistic Knowledge, Postmodern Challenges*. New Brunswick: Rutgers University Press.

Arkin, Anat (1991) 'Turning Managers into Assessors', *Personnel Management*, 23(11): 49–51.

Armstrong, Peter (1987) 'The Abandonment of Productive Intervention in Management Teaching Syllabi: An Historical Analysis'. Warwick Papers in Industrial Relations, No. 15. School of Industrial and Business Studies, University of Warwick, Coventry.

Arthurs, Alan (1988) 'Job Evaluation: The Impact of Equal Value', *Equal Opportunities International*, 7(6): 3–5.

Arvey, Richard D. (1986) 'Sex Bias in Job Evaluation Procedures', *Personnel Psychology*, 39(2): 315–35.

Arvey, R.D. and M.E. Begalla (1975) 'Analyzing the Homemaker Job Using the Position Analysis Questionnaire (PAQ)', *Journal of Applied Psychology*, 60(4): 513–17.

Ash, R.A. and E.L. Levine (1980) 'A Framework for Evaluating Job Analysis Methods', *Personnel*, 57(6): 53–9.

Ash, R.A. and E.L. Levine (1985) 'Job Applicant Training and Work Experience Evaluation: An Empirical Comparison of a Few Methods', *Journal of Applied Psychology*, 70(3): 572–6.

Asherman, I. and S. Asherman (1990) 'Management on the Line', *Journal of Personal Selling and Sales Management*, 10(3): 73–6.

Atkinson, J. (1984) 'Manpower Strategies for Flexible Organisations', *Personnel Management*, August: 28–31.

Baldamus, W. (1961) *Efficiency and Effort: An Analysis of Industrial Administration*. London: Tavistock.

Baron, A. (1992) 'The Masculinization of Production: The Gendering of Work and Skill in US Newspaper Printing', in D. Helly and S. Reverby (eds) , *Gendered Domains: Rethinking Public and Private in Women's History*. Ithaca: Cornell University Press.

Baron, J. (1986) 'War and Peace: The Evolution of Modern Personnel Administration in US Industry', *American Journal of Sociology*, 92: 350–83.

Baron, J. and W. Bielby. (1986) 'The Proliferation of Job Titles in Organisations', *Administrative Science Quarterly*, 31: 561–86.

Baron, J., A. Davis-Blake and W. Bielby (1986) 'The Structure of Opportunity: How Promotion Ladders Vary Within and Among Organisations', *Administrative Science Quarterly*, 31: 248–73.

Barrett, Gerald V. and Mary C. Kernan (1987) 'Performance Appraisal and Terminations: A Review of Court Decisions since Brito V Zia with Implications for Personnel Practices', *Personnel Psychology*, 40(3): 489–503.

Batstone, E. (1984) *Working Order: Workplace Industrial Relations over Two Decades*. Oxford: Basil Blackwell.

Bauman, Zygmunt (1989) *Modernity and the Holocaust*. Cambridge: Polity Press.

Bayer, Gregory, and Lawrence Gerstein (1988) 'Supervisory Attitudes toward Impaired Workers: A Factor Analytic Study of the Behavioural Index of Troubled Employees (BITE)', *Journal of Applied Behavioural Science*, 24(4): 413–22.

Beckert, John and Kate Walsh (1991) 'Development Plans Replace Performance Reviews at Harvey Hotels', *Cornell Hotel and Restaurant Administration Quarterly*, 32(4): 72–80.

Beechey, V. and T. Perkins (1987) *A Matter of Hours: Part-time Employment in Coventry*. Cambridge: Polity Press.

Beer, M., B. Spector, P.R. Lawrence, D.Q. Mills and R.E. Walton (1984) *Managing Human Assets*. New York: Free Press.

Benhabib, Seyla and Drucilla Cornell (eds) (1987) *Feminism as Critique: On the Politics of Gender*. Minneapolis: University of Minnesota Press.

Benson, Philip G. and Jeffrey S. Hornsby (1988) 'The Politics of Pay: The Use of Influence Tactics in Job Evaluation Committees', *Group and Organization Studies*, 13(2): 208–24.

Benson, Philip G. and Jeffrey S. Hornsby (1991) 'Job Evaluation Committees as Small Groups: Implications of Group Dynamics for Fairness in Pay', *International Journal of Public Administration*, 14(5): 845–69.

Berger, L. (1986) 'Using the Computer to Support Job Evaluation Decision-Making', *Journal of Compensation and Benefits*, 2(1): 15–19.

Bernardin, H. John and Richard W. Beatty (1987) 'Can Subordinate Appraisals Enhance Managerial Productivity?', *Sloan Management Review*, 28(4): 63–73.

Bernauer, James W. (1990) *Michel Foucault's Force of Flight: Toward an Ethics for Thought*. New Jersey: Humanities Press.

Bernauer, James and David Rasmussen (eds) (1991) *The Final Foucault* . Cambridge, MA: MIT Press.

Berridge, John (1990) 'The EAP and Employee Counselling', *Employee Relations*, 12(1): S4.

Berry, John K. (1990) 'Linking Management Development to Business Strategies', *Training and Development Journal*, 44(8): 20–2.

Blackham, R.B. and D. Smith (1989) 'Decision-Making in a Management Assessment Centre', *Journal of the Operational Research Society*, 40(11): 953–60.

Blanchflower, David G. (1991) 'The Economic Effects of Profit Sharing in Great Britain', *International Journal of Manpower*, 12(1): 3–9.

Blanchflower, David G. and Andrew J. Oswald (1987) 'Profit Sharing – Can it Work?', *Oxford Economic Papers*, 39(1): 1–19.

Blocklyn, Paul (1988) 'Preemployment Testing', *Personnel*, 65(2): 66–8.

Blyton, Paul and Peter Turnbull (eds) (1992) *Reassessing Human Resource Management*. London: Sage.

Blyton, P. et al. (1989) *Time, Work and Organization*. London: Routledge.

Boak, George (1991) 'Three Dimensions of Personal Development', *Industrial and Commercial Training*, 23(5): 21–4.

Boelter, Dwain and Hannah Olsen (1991) 'Technology Makes Selection More Efficient and Accurate', *Personnel*, 68(10): 15.

Boland, Richard J. (1987) Discussion of 'Accounting and the Construction of the Governable Person', *Accounting, Organisations and Society* 12(5), 267–72.

Boland, R. and L. Pondy (1983) 'Accounting in Organisations: A Union of Natural and Rational Pespectives', *Accounting, Organisations and Society*, 8(2/3): 223–34.

Bordman, S. and G. Melnick (1990) 'Keep Productivity Ratings Timely', *Personnel Journal*, 69: 50–1.

Botterill, Meaghan (1990) 'Changing Corporate Culture', *Management Services*, 34(6): 14–18.

Bowen, David E., Gerald E. Ledford Jr and Barry R. Nathan (1991) 'Hiring for the Organization, Not the Job', *Academy of Management Executive*, 5(4): 35–51.

Boyatzis, R. (1982) *The Competent Manager*. New York: Wiley.

Bradley, Keith, Saul Estrin and Simon Taylor (1990) 'Employee Ownership and Company Performance', *Industrial Relations*, 29(3): 385–402.

Briskin, Linda (1991) 'A New Approach to Evaluating Feminist Strategy', pp. 24–40 in Jeri Dawn Wine and Janice L. Ristock (eds), *Women and Social Change: Feminist Activism in Canada*. Toronto: James Lorimer.

Broderick, Richard (1989) 'Learning the Ropes', *Training*, 26(10): 78–86.

Bromiley, Philip and K.J. Euske (1986) 'The Use of Rational Systems in Bounded Rationality Organizations: A Dilemma for Financial Managers', *Financial Accountability and Management*, 2(4): 311–20.

Buch, Kimberly and Raymond Spangler (1990) 'The Effects of Quality Circles on Performance and Promotions', *Human Relations*, 43(6): 573–82.

Buckley, M. Ronald, and Robert W. Eder (1988) 'B.M. Springbett and the Notion of the "Snap Decision" in the Interview', *Journal of Management*, 14(1): 59–67.

Buhalo, Irene H. (1991) 'You Sign My Report Card – I'll Sign Yours', *Personnel*, 68(5): 23.

Bunning, C.R. (1992) 'The Reflective Practitioner: A Case Study', *Journal of Management Development*, 11(1): 25–38.

Buonocore, A. (1987) 'Reducing Turnover in New Hires', *Management Solutions*, 32(6): 5–10.

Burack, Elmer H. and Nicholas J. Mathys (1987) *Human Resource Planning: A Pragmatic Approach to Manpower Staffing and Development* (2nd edn). Lake Forest, IL: Brace–Park Press.

Burawoy, M. (1979) *Manufacturing Consent*. Chicago: University of Chicago Press.

Burchell, G., C. Gordon, and P. Miller (1991) *The Foucault Effect: Studies in Governmentality*. London: Harvester Wheatsheaf.

Burchell, S., C. Clubb, A.G. Hopwood and J. Hughes (1980) 'The Roles of Accounting in Organizations and Society', *Accounting, Organisations and Society*, 5–27.

Burgoyne, John (1988) 'Management Development for the Individual and the Organisation', *Personnel Management* , 20(6): 40–4.

Burgoyne, John and Calvin Germain (1984) 'Self–Development and Career Planning: An Exercise in Mutual Benefit', *Personnel Management* (April): 21–3.

Burgoyne, John and Roger Stuart (1991) 'Teaching and Learning Methods in Management Development', *Personnel Review*, 20(3): 27–33.

Burns, Nancy Elizabeth (1991) 'Institutions and Social Movements: The Case of Comparable Worth', *International Journal of Public Administration*, 14(5): 773–98.

Burrell, G. (1988) 'Modernism, Post-Modernism and Organisational Analysis 2: The Contribution of Michel Foucault', *Organisation Studies*, 221–35.

Burrell, G. (1992) 'Back to the Future: Time and Organization', pp. 165–83 in Michael Reed and Michael Hughes (eds), *Rethinking Organization: New Directions in Organization Theory and Analysis*. London: Sage.

Bushardt, S. and B. Allen (1988) 'Role Ambiguity in the Male/Female Protégé Relationship', *Equal Opportunities International*, 7(2): 5–8.

Bycio, Peter, Kenneth Alvares and June Hahn (1987) 'Situational Specificity in Assessment Center Ratings: A Confirmatory Factor Analysis', *Journal of Applied Psychology*, 72(3): 463–74.

Cable, John and Nicholas Wilson (1989) 'Profit-Sharing and Productivity: An Analysis of UK Engineering Firms', *Economic Journal*, 99(396): 366–75.

Calas, M. and L. Smircich (1990) 'Thrusting toward More of the Same with the Porter-McKibben Report', *Academy of Management Review*, 9: 698–705.

Calas, M. and L. Smircich (1991) 'Voicing Seduction to Silence Leadership', *Organisation Studies*, 12(4): 567–602.

Calas, M and L. Smircich (1992) 'Using the "F" Word: Feminist Theories and the Social Consequences of Organizational Research', pp. 222–34 in Albert J. Mills and Peta Tancred (eds), *Gendering Organizational Analysis*. Newbury Park, CA: Sage.

Cameron, Keith (1985) 'Applying Standard Reward Systems', *Benefits International*, 14(7): i–v.

Campion, Michael A., Elliot D. Pursell and Barbara K. Brown (1988) 'Structured Interviewing: Raising the Psychometric Properties of the Employment Interview', *Personnel Psychology*, 41(1): 25–42.

Carew, Jack (1989) 'When Salespeople Evaluate their Managers', *Sales and Marketing Management*, 141(4): 24–7.

Carley, Michael (1988) 'Beyond Performance Measurement in a Professional Public Service', *Public Money and Management* (Winter): 23–7.

Carty, Peter (1990) 'Workplace Solutions to Private Problems', *Accountancy*, 106(1168): 98–9.

Catt, Jon (1986) *Northern Hiring Fairs*. Chorley, Lancashire: Countryside Publications.

Chua, W., T. Lowe and T. Puxty (1989) *Critical Perspectives in Management Control*. Basingstoke: Macmillan.

Cixous, H. (1992) Address to Convocation, University of Alberta, Edmonton, June 1992 (translated by L. Penrod).

Clark, P. (1990) 'Chronological Codes and Organisational Analysis', in J. Hassard and E.D. Pym (eds), *The Theory and Philosophy of Organizations*. London: Routledge.

Clegg, H.A. (1971) *How to Run an Incomes Policy*. London: Heinemann.

Clegg, S. (1989) *Frameworks of Power*. London: Sage.

Clement, Ronald W. (1987) 'Performance Appraisal: Nonverbal Influences on the Rating Process', *Review of Public Personnel Administration*, 7(2): 14–27.

Clutterbuck, D. (1986) 'Mentoring', *Industrial and Commercial Training*, 18(6): 13–14.

Cockburn, C. (1983) *Brothers: Male Dominance and Technological Change*. London: Pluto Press.

Cockerill, Tony (1989) 'The Kind of Competence for Rapid Change', *Personnel Management*, 21(9): 52–6.

Cohen, Murray E. and Cynthia Fryer Cohen (1987) 'Comparable Worth and Compensation: Complexities and Controversies in the United States', *Equal Opportunities International*, 6(2): 7–10.

Cohen, Patricia Cline (1982) *A Calculating People: The Spread of Numeracy in Early America*. Chicago: University of Chicago Press.

Cohen, Paula (1991) 'Does Your EAP Measure Up?', *Personnel*, 68(2): 9.

Collin, Audrey (1988) 'Mentoring', *Industrial and Commercial Training*, 20(2): 23–7.

Collin, Audrey (1989) 'Managers' Competence: Rhetoric, Reality and Research', *Personnel Review*, 18(6): 20–5.

Collinson, David L. (1987) 'A Question of Equal Opportunities – A Survey of Staff in a Large Insurance Company', *Personnel Review*, 16(1): 19–29.

Collinson, David L. (1992) *Managing the Shop Floor: Subjectivity, Masculinity and Workplace Culture*. New York: Walter de Gruyter.

Collinson, David L., David Knights and Margaret Collinson (1990) *Managing to Discriminate*. London: Routledge.

Cook, John C. (1992) 'Preparing for Statistical Battles under the Civil Rights Act', *HR Focus*, 69(5): 12–13.

Cooper, D. J., D. Hayes and F. Wolf (1981) 'Accounting in Organized Anarchies: Understanding and Designing Accounting Systems in Ambiguous Situations', *Accounting, Organisations and Society*, 175–91.

Cooper, Robert (1992) 'Formal Organization as Representation: Remote Control, Displacement and Abbreviation', pp. 254–72, in Michael Reed and Michael Hughes (eds), *Rethinking Organization: New Directions in Organization Theory and Analysis*. London: Sage.

Coppolino, Yolanda and Carol B. Seath (1987) 'Women Managers: Fitting the Mould or Moulding the Fit?', *Equal Opportunities International*, 6(3): 4–10.

Cornelius, Edwin T. III, Theodore J. Carron and Marianne N. Collins (1979) 'Job Analysis Models and Job Classification', *Personnel Psychology*, 32(4): 693–708.

Cosentino, Chuck, John Allen and Richard Wellins (1990) 'Choosing the Right People', *HRMagazine*, 35(3): 66–70.

Craggs, Andy (1990) 'Job Evaluation and Human Resource Management in France', *Benefits and Compensation International*, 19(8): 9–12.

Crandall, N. (1989) 'Computerising Job Evaluation for Greater Efficiency and Effectiveness', *Topics in Total Compensation*, 3(3): 241–50.

Crane, Janet G. (1990) 'MBO Magic', *Association Management*, 42(9): 61–4.

Craver, Gary (1977) 'Survey of Job Evaluation Practices in State and County Governments', *Public Personnel Management*, 6(2): 121–31.

Crawford, Norman (1988) 'Outdoor Management Development: A Practical Evaluation', *Journal of European Industrial Training*, 12(8): 17–20.

Cross, Kevin F. and Richard L. Lynch (1988) 'The "SMART" Way to Define and Sustain Success', *National Productivity Review*, 8(1): 23–33.

Cuddy, Robert W. (1987) 'Performance Appraisal: A Better Way', *Bottomline*, 4(10): 17–22.

Cullen, D. (1992) 'Sex and Gender on the Path to Feminism and Self-actualisation', pp. 22–32 in B. Townley (ed), *Proceedings of the Administrative Sciences Association of Canada (ASAC), Women in Management Division*. Quebec: ASAC.

Cumming, Charles M. (1987) 'New Directions in Salary Administration', *Personnel*, 64(1): 68–9.

Davidhizar, Ruth (1990) 'The Best Approach is Doing "Nothing" ', *Nursing Management*, 21(3): 42–4.

Day, David V. and Stanley B. Silverman (1989) 'Personality and Job Performance: Evidence of Incremental Validity', *Personnel Psychology*, 42(1): 25–36.

Day, Mike (1988) 'Managerial Competence and the Charter Initiative', *Personnel Management* (August): 30–4.

DCamp, Kathryn A. and Robin A. Ferracone (1989) 'Spot Gain Sharing Provides High-Impact Incentives', *Personnel Journal*, 68(9): 84–8.

De Michiel, Y. (1983) 'The Subjected Body', *Australian Journal of Law and Society*, 1: 5–44.

Dewe, Philip, Stephen Dunn and Ray Richardson. (1988) 'Employee Share Option Schemes, Why Workers are Attracted to Them', *British Journal of Industrial Relations*, 26(1): 1–20.

Dex, Shirley (1985) *The Sexual Division of Work*. New York: Harvester Wheatsheaf.

Diamond, Irene and Lee Quinby (eds) (1988) *Feminism and Foucault: Reflections on Resistance*. Boston: Northeastern University Press.

Dinwiddy, John (1989) *Bentham*. Oxford: Oxford University Press.

Doeringer, P.B. and M.J. Piore (1971) *Internal Labor Markets and Manpower Analysis*. Lexington, MA: Heath.

Doherty, Elizabeth M., Walter R. Nord and Jerry L. McAdams (1989) 'Gainsharing and Organization Development: A Productive Synergy', *Journal of Applied Behavioural Science*, 25(3): 209–29.

Drakeley, Russell J., Peter Herriot and Alan Jones (1988) 'Biographical Data, Training Success and Turnover', *Journal of Occupational Psychology*, 61(2): 145–52.

Drazin, Robert and Ellen R. Auster (1987) 'Wage Differences between Men and Women: Performance Appraisal Ratings vs. Salary Allocation as the Locus of Bias', *Human Resource Management*, 26(2): 157–68.

Drennan, David and Susan Walker (1987) 'What Does the Team Think?', *Director*, 41(4): 99–100.

Dreyfus, H. and P. Rabinow (1983) *Michel Foucault, Beyond Structuralism and Hermeneutics*. Brighton: Harvester.

Drucker, P. (1961) *The Practice of Management*. London: Mercury Books.

Drucker, P.F. (1964) *Managing for Results.* : New York: Harper and Row.

DuBois, Page (1991) *Torture and Truth*. New York: Routledge.

Dufetel, Laurent. (1991) 'Job Evaluation: Still at the Frontier', *Compensation and Benefits Review*, 23(4): 53–67.

Duffy, Michael F. (1989) 'ZBB, MBO, PPB and their Effectiveness within the Planning/Marketing Process', *Strategic Management Journal*, 10(2): 163–73.

Dulewicz, Victor (1989) 'Assessment Centres as the Route to Competence (Part 6)', *Personnel Management* , 21(11): 56–9.

Dulewicz, Victor (1991) 'Improving Assessment Centres', *Personnel Management* , 23(4): 50–5.

The Economist (1991) 'Unseen Apples and Small Carrots', *The Economist*, 319(7702): 75.

Edwards, Mark R. (1990) 'Turning the Appraisals Tables', *Information Strategy: The Executive's Journal*, 6(4): 31–4.

Edwards, R. (1979) *Contested Terrain: The Transformation of the Workplace in the Twentieth Century*. New York: Basic Books.

Ekholm, D. and U. Subba-Rao (1989) 'How to Develop a Mathematical Model for Position Evaluation', *Topics in Total Compensation*, 3(3): 251–8.

Elshtain, Jean B. (1981) *Public Man/Private Woman: Women in Social and Political Thought*. Princeton: Princeton University Press.

Emerson, Sandra M. (1991) 'Job Evaluation: A Barrier to Excellence?', *Compensation and Benefits Review*, 23(1): 39–51.

Employee Benefit Plan Review (1990) 'New Directions in Cash Profit Sharing', 44(7): 26–7.

England, John D. and David A. Pierson (1990) 'Salary Ranges and Merit Matrices: The Time Targeting Approach', *Compensation and Benefits Review*, 22(4): 36–46.

England, Robert E. and William M. Parle (1987) 'Nonmanagerial Performance Appraisal Practices in Large American Cities', *Public Administration Review*, 47(6): 498–504.

Epperson, Lawrence L. (1975) 'The Dynamics of Factor Comparison/Point Evaluation', *Public Personnel Management*, 4(1): 38–48.

Erban, Penny (1989) 'How They Manage Performance in Windsor', *Personnel Management*, 21(2): 42–5.

Eribon, D. (1991) *Michel Foucault*. Cambridge, MA: Harvard University Press.

Evarts, Harry F. (1988) 'The Competency Programme of the American Management Association', *Journal of Management Development*, 7(6): 48–56.

Eyres, Patricia S. (1989) 'Legally Defensible Performance Appraisal Systems', *Personnel Journal*, 68(7): 58–62.

Fagenson, E. (1988) 'The Power of a Mentor: Protégés' and Nonprotégés' Perceptions of their Own Power in Organisations', *Group and Organisation Studies*, 13(2): 182–94.

Fagenson, E. (1989) 'The Mentor Advantage: Perceived Career/Job Experiences of Protégés Versus Non-Protégés', *Journal of Organisational Behaviour*, 10 (4): 309–20.

Farh, Jiing-Lih and Gregory H. Dobbins (1989) 'Effects of Self-Esteem on Leniency Bias in Self-Reports of Performance: A Structural Equation Model Analysis', *Personnel Psychology*, 42(4): 835–50.

Farh, Jiing-Lih, James D. Werbel and Arthur G. Bedeian (1988) 'An Empirical Investigation of Self-Appraisal-Based Performance Evaluation', *Personnel Psychology*, 41(1): 141–56.

Farr, J.L., B.S. O'Leary and C.J. Bartlett (1973) 'Effect of a Work Sample Test upon Self-selection and Turnover of Job Applicants', *Journal of Applied Psychology*, 58: 283–5.

Feldman, Stuart (1991) 'Today's EAPs Make the Grade', *Personnel*, 68(2): 3.

Feltham, Rob (1988) 'Assessment Centre Decision Making: Judgemental vs. Mechanical', *Journal of Occupational Psychology* , 61(3): 237–41.

Ferguson, Kathy E. (1984) *The Feminist Case against Bureaucracy*. Philadelphia: Temple University Press.

Ferguson, L.W. (1963) *The Heritage of Industrial Psychology*. Hartford, USA.

Feuer, Dale (1987) 'Employee Attitude Surveys: How to "Hand-Off" the Results', *Training*, 24(9): 50–8.

Fewster, Carol (1989) 'Stress', *Industrial Society*, 29–31.

Finch, J. (1983) *Married to the Job: Wives Incorporation in Men's Work*. London: Allen and Unwin.

Fine, S. and W. Wiley (1971) *An Introduction to Functional Job Analysis*, Washington, DC: W.E. Upjohn Institute for Employment Research.

Fineman, Stephen (ed.) (1993) *Emotion in Organizations* . London: Sage.

Finkelstein, J. and C. Hatch (1987) 'Job Evaluation: New Technology, New Role for HR Managers', *Personnel*, 64(1): 5–10.

Flamholtz, E. (1985) *Human Resource Accounting* (2nd edn). San Francisco: Jossey Bass.

Flanagan, J. (1954) 'The Critical Incident Technique', *Psychological Bulletin*, 51: 327–58.

Fleishman, E.A. (1975) 'Toward a Taxonomy of Human Performance', *American Psychologist*, 30: 1127–49.

Fleishman, Edwin A. (1988) 'Some New Frontiers in Personnel Selection Research', *Personnel Psychology*, 41(4): 679–701.

Fleishman, E.A. and M.K. Quaintance (1984) *Taxonomies of Human Performance: The Description of Human Tasks*. New York: Academic Press.

Fonow, Mary Margaret and Judith A. Cook (eds) (1991) *Beyond Methodology: Feminist Scholarship as Lived Research*. Bloomington: Indiana University Press.

Forbes, R.J. and E.M. Anaya (1980) 'Appraiser and Appraised', *Management Today*, 33–4, 39.

Foucault, M. (1970) *The Order of Things: An Archaeology of the Human Sciences*. London: Tavistock.

Foucault, M. (1972) *The Archaeology of Knowledge*. London: Routledge.

Foucault, M. (1973a) *Madness and Civilization*. London: Tavistock.

Foucault, M. (1973b) *The Birth of the Clinic*. London: Tavistock.

Foucault, M. (ed.) (1975) *I, Pierre Rivière, having Slaughtered my Mother, my Sister, and my Brother: A Case of Parricide in the 19th Century* (translated by Frank Jellinek). Lincoln: University of Nebraska Press.

Foucault, M. (1977) *Discipline and Punish: The Birth of the Prison*. London: Allen Lane.

Foucault, M. (1979) 'Governmentality', *Ideology and Consciousness*, 6: 5–21.

Foucault, M. (1980a) *Power/Knowledge: Selected Interviews and Other Writings 1972–1977*. New York: Pantheon.

Foucault, M. (1980b) *Herculine Barbin: Being the Recently Discovered Memoirs of a Nineteenth Century French Hermaphrodite*. New York: Pantheon.

Foucault, M. (1981a) *The History of Sexuality*. Volume 1: *The Will to Knowledge*. London: Penguin.

Foucault, M. (1981b) 'Questions of Method', *Ideology and Consciousness*, 8: 3–14.

Foucault, M. (1982) *This is Not a Pipe* (translated and edited by James Harkness). Berkeley: University of California Press.

Foucault, M. (1983) 'The Subject and Power', pp. 208–26 in H.L. Dreyfus, and P. Rabinow (eds), *Michel Foucault: Beyond Structuralism and Hermeneutics* (2nd edn). Chicago: University of Chicago Press.

Foucault, M. (1984a) 'On the Genealogy of Ethics: An Interview of Work in Progress', pp. 340–72 in Paul Rabinow (ed.), *The Foucault Reader*. London: Penguin.

Foucault, M. (1984b) 'Politics and Ethics: An Interview', pp. 373–80 in Paul Rabinow (ed.), *The Foucault Reader*. London: Penguin.

Foucault, M. (1984c) 'Polemics, Politics and Problematizations: An Interview', pp. 381–90 in Paul Rabinow (ed.), *The Foucault Reader*. London: Penguin.

Foucault, M. (1988a) *The History of Sexuality*. Volume 2: *The Uses of Pleasure*. London: Penguin.

Foucault, M. (1988b) 'Technologies of the Self', pp. 16–49 in L. Martin, H. Gutman and P.H. Hutton (eds), *Technologies of the Self*. London: Tavistock.

Foucault, M. (1989) *Foucault Live (Interviews, 1966–84)* (translated by John Johnston and edited by Sylvere Lotringer). New York: Semiotext(e).

Foucault, M. (1990) *The History of Sexuality*. Volume 3: *The Care of the Self*. London: Penguin.

Foucault, M. (1991a) 'Politics and the Study of Discourse', pp. 53–72 in G. Burchell, C. Gordon and P. Miller (eds), *The Foucault Effect: Studies in Governmentality*. London: Harvester Wheatsheaf.

Foucault, M. (1991b) 'Questions of Method', pp. 73–86 in G. Burchell, C. Gordon, and P.

Miller (eds), *The Foucault Effect: Studies in Governmentality*. London: Harvester Wheatsheaf.

Foucault, M. (1991c) 'The Ethic of Care for the Self as a Practice of Freedom', in J. Bernauer and D. Rasmussen (eds), *The Final Foucault*. Cambridge, MA: MIT Press.

Fowler, Alan (1988) 'New Directions in Performance Pay', *Personnel Management*, 20(11): 30–4.

Fowler, Alan (1990) 'Performance Management: The MBO of the 90s?', *Personnel Management*, 22 (7): 47–51.

Fox, S. (1989) 'The Panopticon: From Bentham's Obssession to the Revolution in Management Learning', *Human Relations*, 42: 717–39.

Fox, Shaul and Yossi Dinur (1988) 'Validity of Self-Assessment: A Field Evaluation', *Personnel Psychology*, 41(3): 581–92.

Fraser, Nancy (1989) *Unruly Practices: Power, Discourse, and Gender in Contemporary Social Theory*. Minneapolis: University of Minnesota Press.

Freedman, Marcia (1976) *Labor Markets: Segments and Shelters*. New York: Allanhead, Osman/Universal Books.

French, Wendell L. and John A. Drexler, Jr (1984) 'A Team Approach to MBO: History and Conditions for Success', *Leadership and Organization Development*, 5(5): 22–6.

French, Wendell L. and John A. Drexler, Jr (1987) 'Management by Objectives: A Team Approach', *Management Decision*, 25(6): 41–4.

Friedan, Betty (1993) *The Fountain of Age*. New York: Simon and Schuster.

Friedman, A. (1977) *Industry and Labour*. London: Macmillan.

Gabris, Gerald T. and Kenneth Mitchell (1988) 'The Impact of Merit Raise Scores on Employee Attitudes: The Mathew Effect of Performance Appraisal', *Public Personnel Management*, 17(4): 369–86.

Gael, S. (1988) *The Job Analysis Handbook for Business, Industry and Government*. New York: Wiley.

Galagan, Patricia A. (1991) 'Training Delivers Results to Federal Express', *Training and Development*, 45(12): 26–33.

Gallup, George (1988) 'Employee Research: From Nice to Know to Need to Know', *Personnel Journal*, 67(8): 42–3.

Game, R. and A. Pringle (1983) *Gender at Work* . London: Allen and Unwin.

Garland, D. (1987) 'Foucault's Discipline and Punish: An Exposition and Critique', *American Bar Foundation Research Journal*, 4: 847–80.

Gatewood, Robert, George C. Thornton III and Harry W. Hennessey Jr (1990) 'Reliability of Exercise Ratings in the Leaderless Group Discussion', *Journal of Occupational Psychology*, 63(4): 331–42.

George, David I. and Mike C. Smith (1990) 'An Empirical Comparison of Self-Assessment and Organizational Assessment in Personnel Selection', *Public Personnel Management*, 19(2): 175–90.

Georges, James C. (1988) 'Why Soft-Skills Training Doesn't Take', *Training*, 25(4): 42–7.

Ghobadian, Abby (1990) 'Job Evaluation: Trade Union and Staff Association Representatives' Perspectives', *Employee Relations*, 12(4): 3–9.

Ghobadian, Abby and Michael White (1987) 'Factors Contributing to the Implementation of Unbiased Job Evaluation Schemes', *Personnel Review*, 16(5): 21–5.

Ghobadian, Abby and Michael White (1988) 'Personnel Policies, Structural Characteristics, and Equity in Job-Evaluated Payment Systems', *Personnel Review*, 17(5): 29–32.

Gilligan, C. (1982) *In a Different Voice*. Cambridge, MA: Harvard University Press.

Girard, Richard (1988) 'Is There a Need for Performance Appraisals?', *Personnel Journal*, 67(8): 89–90.

Glaze, Tony (1989) 'Cadbury's Dictionary of Competence', *Personnel Management*, 21(7): 44–8.

Gledhill, Michael (1990) 'The Art of Bonsai in Management Development', *Industrial and Commercial Training*, 22(2): 21–6.

Goddard, Robert W. (1989) 'Is Your Appraisal System Headed for Court?', *Personnel Journal*, 68(1): 114–18.

Goffman, E. (1961) *Asylums: Essays on the Social Situation of Mental Patients and Other Inmates*. Garden City, NY: Anchor Books.

Goodnough, Angelique (1990) 'Performance Evaluation as a Management Tool', *Journal of Property Management*, 55(3): 18–20.

Gordon, David M., Richard Edwards and Michael Reich (1984) *Segmented Work, Divided Workers: The Historical Transformation of Labor in the United States*. Cambridge: Cambridge University Press (first published 1982).

Gowen, Charles R. III (1990) 'Gainsharing Programs: An Overview of History and Research', *Journal of Organizational Behaviour Management*, 11(2): 77–99.

Graham, Michael and Albert C. Hyde (1991) 'Comparable Worth in the United States: Legal and Administrative Developments in the 1980s', *International Journal of Public Administration*, 14(5): 799–821.

Green, Hugh (1987) 'Matching People to Jobs: An Expert System Approach', *Personnel Management*, 19(9): 42–5.

Grenier, Guillermo, Raymond L. Holger, Curt Tausky and Anthony F. Chelte (1991) 'Labor Law and Managerial Ideology: Employee Participation as a Social Control System; Employee Involvement: A Comment on Grenier and Holger', *Work and Occupations*, 18(3): 313–42.

Griffin, Ricky W. (1988) 'Consequences of Quality Circles in an Industrial Setting: A Longitudinal Assessment', *Academy of Management Journal*, 31(2): 338–58.

Griffiths, Dorothy (1981) 'Job Evaluation, Technical Expertise and Dual Ladders in Research and Development', *Personnel Review*, 10(4): 14–17.

Gutting, Gary (1990) *Michel Foucault's Archaeology of Scientific Reason*. Cambridge: Cambridge University Press.

Habermas, Jürgen (1992) *The Philosophical Discourse of Modernity: Twelve Lectures* (translated by F. Lawrence). Cambridge, MA: MIT Press.

Hacking, I. (1986) 'The Archaelogy of Foucault', pp. 27–40 in D. C. Hoy (ed.), *Foucault: A Critical Reader*. Oxford: Basil Blackwell.

Hacking, I. (1990) *The Taming of Chance*. Cambridge: Cambridge University Press.

Hackman, J.R. and G.R. Oldham (1975) 'Development of a Job Diaganostic Survey', *Journal of Applied Psychology*, 60(2): 159–70.

Hackman, J.R. and G.R. Oldham (1980) *Work Redesign*. Reading, MA: Addison Wesley.

Hahn, David C. and Robert L. Dipboye (1988) 'Effects of Training and Information in the Accuracy and Reliability of Job Evaluation', *Journal of Applied Psychology*, 73(2): 146–53.

Hakim, C. (1979) *Occupational Segregation: A Comparative Study of the Degree and Pattern of the Differentiation between Men and Women's Work in Britain*. Department of Employment (Research Paper No. 9).

Half, Robert (1988) 'How to Conduct a Successful Interview', *Practical Accountant*, 21(9): 96–102.

Hall, Laura and Derek Torrington (1986) ' "Why Not Use the Computer?" The Use and Lack of Use of Computers in Personnel', *Personnel Review*, 15(1): 3–7.

Hamlin, Bob and Jim Stewart (1990) 'Approaches to Management Development in the UK', *Leadership and Organization Development Journal* , 11(5): 27–32.

Hardesty, Sarah and Nehama Jacobs (1986) *Success and Betrayal: The Crisis of Women in Corporate America*. New York: Simon and Schuster.

Harding, Sandra (1986) *The Science Question in Feminism*. Ithaca, NY: Cornell University Press.

Harding, Sandra (1990) 'Feminism, Science, and the Anti-Enlightenment Critiques', pp. 83–106 in Linda J. Nicholson (ed.), *Feminism/Postmodernism*. New York: Routledge.

Hare-Mustin, Rachel T. and Jeanne Marecek (1988) 'The Meaning of Difference: Gender Theory, Postmodernism, and Psychology', *American Psychologist*, 43(6): 455–64.

Harper, Stephen C. (1988) 'Becoming an Objective-Minded Manager', *Management World*, 17(3): 25–6.

Harrington, H. James and Wayne S. Rieker (1988) 'The End of Slavery: Quality Control Circles', *Journal for Quality and Participation*, 11(1): 16–20.

Hartsock, Nancy (1974) 'Political Change: Two Perspectives on Power', *Quest: A Feminist Quarterly*, 1(Summer).

Hartsock, Nancy (1990) 'Foucault on Power: A Theory for Women?', pp. 157–75 in Linda J. Nicholson (ed.), *Feminism/Postmodernism*. New York: Routledge.

Harvey, R. (1986) 'Quantitative Approaches to Job Classification: A Review and Critique', *Personnel Psychology*, 39(2): 267–89.

Hatton, T.J. (1988) 'Profit Sharing in British Industry, 1865–1913', *International Journal of Industrial Organization*, 6(1): 69–90.

Hayes, Lynn O'Rourke (1991) 'In Search of the Perfect Employee', *Restaurant Hospitality*, 75(10): 68.

Hearn, Jeff (1989) 'Leading Questions for Men: Men's Leadership, Feminist Challenges, and Men's Responses', *Equal Opportunities International*, 8(1): 3–11.

Hekman, Susan J. (1992) *Gender and Knowledge: Elements of a Postmodern Feminism*. Cambridge: Polity Press.

Helgesen, S. (1990) *The Female Advantage: Women's Ways of Leadership*, New York: Doubleday Currency.

Henriques, J., W. Hollway, C. Urwin, C. Venn and V. Walkerdine (1984) *Changing the Subject*. London: Methuen.

Herriot, Peter and Clive Fletcher (1990) ' "Candidate-Friendly" Selection for the 1990s: Comments', *Personnel Management*, 22(2): 32–5.

Heydebrand, W. (1977) 'Organizational Contradictions in Public Bureaucracies: Towards a Marxian Theory of Organizations', *Sociological Quarterly*, 18: 83–107.

Hochschild, A. (1983) *The Managed Heart: Commercialization of Human Feeling*. Berkeley: University of California.

Hollway, W. (1984) 'Fitting Work: A Psychological Assessment of Organisations', pp. 26–59 in J. Henriques, W. Hollway, C. Urwin, C. Venn, and V. Walkerdine (eds), *Changing the Subject*. London: Metheun.

Hollway, W. (1991) *Work Psychology and Organizational Behaviour*. London: Sage.

Hopwood, Anthony (1987) 'The Archaeology of Accounting Systems', *Accounting, Organisations and Society*, 12(3): 207–34.

Hopwood, Anthony (1989) 'Accounting and the Pursuit of Social Interests', pp. 141–57 in W. Chua, T. Lowe and T. Puxty (eds), *Critical Perspectives in Management Control*. Basingstoke: Macmillan.

Hoskin, K. W. and R. H. Macve (1986) 'Accounting and the Examination: Genealogy of Disciplinary Power', *Accounting, Organisations and Society*, 105–36.

Hosni, Djehane A. (1990) 'Women in the Japanese Labour Market', *Equal Opportunities International*, 9(6): 11–14.

Huettner, Charles H. (1988) 'Job Task Systems Management of Government Organizations', *Public Adminstration Review*, 48(4): 783–9.

Hunt, John W. (1990) 'Management Development for the Year 2000', *Journal of Management Development*, 9(3): 4–13.

Huntley, Stephen (1991) 'Management Development', *Industrial and Commercial Training*, 23(2): 20–5.

Hyman, J., H. Ramsay, J. Leopold, L. Baddon and L. C. Hunter (1989) 'The Impact of Employee Share Ownership', *Employee Relations*, 11(4): 9–16.

Iannello, Kathleen P. (1992) *Decisions without Hierarchy: Feminist Interventions in Organization Theory and Practice*. New York: Routledge.

Iles, Paul, Ivan Robertson and Usharani Rout (1989) 'Assessment-Based Development Centres', *Journal of Managerial Psychology*, 4(3): 11–16.

Jackson, Laurence (1991) 'Management Development Programmes', *Industrial and Commercial Training*, 23(4): 9–16.

Jacobs, Robin (1989) 'Getting the Measure of Management Competence', *Personnel Management*, 21(6): 32–7.

Jacoby, D. (1989) 'Rewards Make the Mentor', *Personnel*, 66(12): 10–14.

Jacoby, Sanford (1985) *Employing Bureaucracy: Managers, Unions and the Transformation of Work in American Industry 1900–1945*. New York: Columbia University Press.

Jacoby, Sanford M. (1988) 'Employee Attitude Surveys in Historical Perspective', *Industrial Relations*, 27(1): 74–93.

Jacques, Elliot (1979) 'Taking Time Seriously in Evaluating Jobs', *Harvard Business Review*, 57(5): 124–32.

James, N. (1989) 'Emotional Labour: Skill and Work in the Social Regulation of Feeling', *Sociological Review*, 37(1): 15–42.

Jeanneret, P.R. (1980) 'Equitable Job Evaluation and Classification with the Position Analysis Questionnaire', *Compensation Review*, 12(1): 32–42.

Jenkins, D. and Lawler, E. (1981) 'Impact of Employee Participation in Pay Plan Development', *Organizational Behavior and Human Performance*, 28: 111–28.

John, Andrew (1991) 'Employment Fluctuations in a Share Economy', *Oxford Economic Papers*, 43(1): 75–84.

Johnson, Charles E., Robert Wood and S.F. Blinkhorn (1988) 'Spuriouser and Spuriouser: The Use of Ipsative Personality Tests', *Journal of Occupational Psychology*, 61(2): 153–62.

Johnson, Kerry L. (1987) 'How to Interview for the Truth', *Managers Magazine*, 62(10): 28–9.

Johnson, Mark A. (1991) 'Lights, Camera, Interview', *HRMagazine*, 36(4): 66–8.

Johnson, P. (1992) 'The Cloistering of Medieval Nuns: Release or Repression, Reality or Fantasy?', pp. 27–39 in D. Helly and S. Reverby (eds), *Gendered Domains: Rethinking Public and Private in Women's History*. Ithaca, NY: Cornell University Press.

Jones, Michael B., Carol A. Braddick and Paul M. Shafer (1991) 'Will Broadbands Replace Traditional Salary Structures?', *Journal of Compensation and Benefits*, 7(3): 30–5.

Jones, Peter A. (1990) 'A Profile for Management Development and Training', *Journal of European Industrial Training*, 14(3): 7–12.

Juran, J.M. (1987) 'QC Circles in the West', *Quality Progress*, 20(9): 60–1.

Juran, J.M. (1991) 'The Evolution of Japanese Leadership in Quality', *Journal of Quality and Participation*, 14(4): 72–7.

Kahler, Taibi (1987) 'Assessment and Intervention', *Canadian Manager*, 12(1): 22, 28.

Kane, Jeffrey S. and Kimberly A. Freeman (1986) 'MBO and Performance Appraisal: A Mixture that's Not a Solution, Part 1', *Personnel*, 63(12): 26–36.

Kane, Jeffrey and Kimberly Freeman (1987) 'MBO and Performance Appraisal: A Mixture that's Not a Solution, Part 2', *Personnel*, 64(2): 26–32.

Kanin-Lovers, J. (1987) 'Selecting a Computer-Aided Job Evaluation System', *Journal of Compensation and Benefits*, 3(2): 104–7.

Kanter, R. (1977) *Men and Women of the Corporation*. New York: Basic Books.

Kazemek, E. and J. Dauner (1988) 'Improving your Department by Developing Staff', *Healthcare Financial Management*, 42(8): 112–13.

Keele, R., K. Buckner and S. Bushnell (1987) 'Formal Mentoring Programmes are No Panacea', *Management Review*, 76(2): 67–8.

Keller, C. (1986) *From a Broken Web: Separation, Sexism, and Self*. Boston: Beacon Press.

Keller, E.F. (1985) *Reflections on Gender and Sciences*. New Haven: Yale University Press.

Kenney, J., E. Donnelly and M. Reid (1981) *Manpower Training and Development* (2nd edn). London: Institute of Personnel Management.

Kerr, Clark (1963) *The Uses of the University*. Cambridge, MA: Harvard University Press.

Kerr, Clark (1977) *Labor Markets and Wage Determination: The Balkanization of Labor Markets and Other Essays*. Berkeley: University of California Press.

Kiechel, Walter III (1989) 'When Subordinates Evaluate the Boss', *Fortune*, 119(13): 201–2.

Kinicki, Angelo J., Peter W. Hom, Chris A. Lockwood and Rodger W. Griffeth (1990) 'Interviewer Predictions of Applicant Qualifications and Interviewer Validity: Aggregate and Individual Analyses', *Journal of Applied Psychology*, 75(5): 477–86.

Kinnie, Nick and David Lowe (1990) 'Performance-Related Pay on the Shopfloor', *Personnel Management*, 22(11): 45–9.

Kinsey, D. (1990) 'Mentorship and Influence in Nursing', *Nursing Management*, 21(5): 45–6.

Kizilos, P. (1990) 'Take My Mentor, Please!', *Training*, 27(4), 49–55.

Kizilos, Peter (1991) 'Fixing Fatal Flaws', *Training*, 28(9): 66–70.

Klein, Katherine J. (1987) 'Employee Stock Ownership and Employee Attitudes: A Test of Three Models', *Journal of Applied Psychology*, 72(2): 319–32.

Klimoski, Richard and Mary Brickner (1987) 'Why Do Assessment Centers Work? The Puzzle of Assessment Center Validity', *Personnel Psychology*, 40(2): 243–60.

Klinger, D. (1988) 'Comparable Worth and Public Personnel Values', *Review of Public Personnel Administration*, 9(1): 45–60.

Knights, D. (1990) 'Subjectivity, Power and the Labour Process', in D. Knights, and H. Willmott (eds), *Labour Process Theory*. London: Macmillan.

Knights, D. and D.L. Collinson (1987) 'Disciplining the Shop Floor: A Comparison of the Disciplinary Effects of Managerial and Financial Accounting', *Accounting, Organisations and Society*, 12(5): 457–77.

Knights, D. and H. Willmott (1985) 'Power and Identity in Theory and Practice', *Sociological Review*, 33: 22–46.

Knights, D. and H. Willmott (eds) (1986) *Managing the Labour Process*, Aldershot: Gower.

Kochan, Thomas A. and Peter Capelli (1984) 'The Transformation of the Industrial Relations and Personnel Function', in Paul Osterman (ed.), *Internal Labor Markets*. Cambridge: MIT Press.

Kochan, T., H.C. Katz and R.B. McKersie (1986) *The Transformation of American Industrial Relations*. New York: Basic Books.

Kotter, John P. (1982) *The General Managers*. New York: Free Press; London: Collier Macmillan.

Kowal, Dennis M. (1990) 'Emphasize Integrity Assessment in Interviews', *Personnel Journal*, 69(6): 66–71.

Krajci, Thomas J. (1990) 'Pay that Rewards Knowledge', *HRMagazine*, 35(6): 58–60.

Kritzman, Lawrence (ed.) (1988) *Michel Foucault: Politics, Philosophy, Culture.* New York: Routledge (first published 1988).

Kume, Hitoshi (1990) 'Quality Management: Japan and the West', *Quality*, 29(5): 16–20.

Latour, B. (1987) *Science in Action.* Cambridge, MA: Harvard University Press.

Lavoie, D. (1987) 'The Accounting of Interpretations and the Interpretation of Accounts: The Communicative Function of "the Language of Business" ', *Accounting, Organisations and Society*, 12(6): 579–604.

Lawler, Edward E. III (1986) 'What's Wrong with Point-Factor Job Evaluation', *Compensation and Benefits Review*, 18(2): 20–8.

Lawrence, C.H. (1989) *Medieval Monasticism: Forms of Religious Life in Western Europe in the Middle Ages.* London: Longman (first published 1984).

Ledford, Gerald E. Jr and Gary Bergel (1991) 'Skill-Based Pay Case Number 1: General Mills', *Compensation and Benefits Review*, 23(2): 24–38.

Lee, Chris (1990) 'Talking Back to the Boss', *Training*, 27(4): 29–35.

Lee, Chris (1991) 'What's Your Style?', *Training*, 28(5): 27–33.

Legge, Karen (1978) *Power, Innovation, and Problem-Solving in Personnel Management.* London: McGraw-Hill.

Legge, Karen (1986) 'Women in Personnel Management', in A. Spencer and D. Podmore (eds), *A Man's World.* London: Tavistock.

Legge, Karen (1989) 'Human Resource Management: A Critical Analysis', pp. 19–40 in John Storey (ed.), *New Perspectives on Human Resource Management.* London: Routledge.

Lehr, Richard I. and David J. Middlebrooks (1986) 'Legal Implications of Employee Assistance Programs', *Employee Relations Law Journal*, 12(2): 262–74.

Levasseur, Robert E. (1991) 'People Skills: Self-Awareness – A Critical Skill for MS/OR Professionals', *Interfaces*, 21(1): 130–3.

Levine, E.L., Nell Bennett and Ronald A. Ash (1979) 'Evaluation and Use of Four Job Analysis Methods for Personnel Selection', *Public Personnel Management*, 8(3): 146–51.

Levine, E.L., R.A. Ash and N. Bennett (1980) 'Exploratory Comparative Study of Four Job Analysis Methods', *Journal of Applied Psychology*, 65(5): 524–35.

Levine, Edward L., Ronald A. Ash, Hardy Hall and Frank Sistrunk (1983) 'Evaluation of Job Analysis Methods by Experienced Job Analysts', *Academy of Management Journal*, 26(2): 339–48.

Levinson, Harry (1987) 'How They Rate the Boss', *Across the Board*, 24(6): 53–7.

Lincoln, James R., Hanada Mitsuyo and Kerry McBride (1986) 'Organizational Structures in Japanese and US Manufacturing', *Administrative Sciences Quarterly*, 31(September): 338–64.

Lindop, Esmond (1989) 'The Turbulent Birth of British Profit-Sharing', *Personnel Management*, 21(1): 44–7.

Littler, Craig R. and Graeme Salaman (1985) 'The Design of Jobs', pp. 85–104 in Craig R. Littler (ed.), *The Experience of Work.* Aldershot: Gower.

Lodge, Derek (1987) 'Working Equality into Manual Job Evaluation', *Personnel Management*, 19(9): 27–31.

Loft, A. (1986) 'Towards a Critical Understanding of Accounting: The Case of Cost Accounting in the UK, 1914–1925', *Accounting, Organisations and Society*, 137–70.

London, Manuel Wohlers, J. Arthur and Philip Gallagher (1990) 'A Feedback Approach to Management Development', *Journal of Management Development*, 9(6): 17–31.

Long, P. (1984) 'Would you Put Your Daughter into Personnel Management?', *Personnel Management*, (April).

Longenecker, Clinton O. and Dennis A. Gioia (1991) 'SMR Forum: Ten Myths of Managing Directors', *Sloan Management Review*, 33(1): 81–90.

Longino, Helen (1989) 'Feminist Critiques of Rationality: Critiques of Science or Philosophy of Science?', *Women's Studies International Forum*, 12(2): 261–9.

Lopez, Felix M., Gerald A. Kesselman and Felix E. Lopez (1981) 'An Empirical Test of a Trait-Oriented Job Analysis Technique', *Personnel Psychology*, 34(3): 479–502.

Lowry, Phillip E. (1988) 'The Assessment Center: Pooling Scores or Arithmetic Decision Rule?', *Public Personnel Management*, 17(1): 63–71.

Lukes, Steven (1974) *Power: A Radical View*. London: Macmillan.

Lupton, T. (1978) *Industrial Behaviour and Personnel Management*. London: Institute of Personnel Management.

Luthans, Fred and Robert Waldersee (1989) 'What do We really Know about EAPs?', *Human Resource Management*, 28(3): 385–401.

McBriarty, Mark A. (1988) 'Performance Appraisal: Some Unintended Consequences', *Public Personnel Management*, 17(4): 421–34.

McConnell, Charles R. (1991) 'In Search of Objective Measurement in Performance Appraisal', *Health Care Supervisor*, 10(2): 69–77.

McCormick, E.J., P.R. Jeanneret and R.C. Mecham (1972) 'A Study of Job Characteristics and Job Dimensions as Based on the Position Analysis Questionnaire (PAQ)', *Journal of Applied Psychology*, 56(4): 347–68.

McDaniel, Michael A. (1989) 'Biographical Constructs for Predicting Employee Suitability', *Journal of Applied Psychology*, 74(6): 964–70.

McElrath, Roger G. and Richard L. Rowan (1992) 'The American Labor Movement and Employee Ownership: Objections to and Uses of Employee Stock Ownership Plans', *Journal of Labor Research*, 13(1): 99–119.

McEvoy, Glenn M. (1988) 'Evaluating the Boss', *Personnel Administrator*, 33(9): 115–20.

McEvoy, Glenn M. (1990) 'Public Sector Managers' Reactions to Appraisals by Subordinates', *Public Personnel Management*, 19(2): 201–12.

McEvoy, Glenn M. and Richard W. Beatty (1989) 'Assessment Centers and Subordinate Appraisals of Managers: A Seven-Year Examination of Predictive Validity', *Personnel Psychology*, 42(1): 37–52.

McGinty, Robert L. and John Hanke (1989) 'Compensation Management in Practice – Merit Pay Plans: Are they Truly Tied to Performance?', *Compensation and Benefits Review*, 21(5): 12–16.

McGregor, D. (1972) 'An Uneasy Look at Performance Appraisal', *Harvard Business Review*, (September/October): 133–8.

Machin, J. and T. Lowe (eds) (1983) *New Perspectives in Management Control*. New York: St. Martins Press.

McHugh, Maureen C., Randi Daimon Koeske and Irene Hanson Frieze (1986) 'Issues to Consider in Considering Nonsexist Psychological Research: A Guide for Researchers', *American Psychologist*, 41(8): 879–90.

MacIntyre, Alasdair (1984) *After Virtue: A Study in Moral Theory*. Notre Dame, IN: University of Notre Dame Press (first published 1981).

Mackay, S.C. (1988) 'A Pilot Study: A Short Biographical Questionnaire to be Used in the Assessment of Senior Executives'. Unpublished Master's Thesis, Hatfield Polytechnic.

MacKinnon, Catharine A. (1991) *Toward a Feminist Theory of the State*. Cambridge, MA: Harvard Univesity Press (first published in 1989).

McNally, Joyce and Sylvia Shimmin (1984) 'Job Evaluation and Equal Pay for Work of Equal Value', *Personnel Review*, 13(1): 27–31.

McNally, Joyce and Sylvia Shimmin (1988) 'Job Evaluation: Equal Work – Equal Pay?', *Management Decision*, 26(5): 22–7.

McNay, Lois (1992) *Foucault and Feminism: Power, Gender and the Self*. Cambridge: Polity Press.

McShane, Steven L. (1990) 'Two Tests of Direct Gender Bias in Job Evaluation Ratings', *Journal of Occupational Psychology*, 63(2): 129–40.

Madigan, Robert M. (1985) 'Comparable Worth Judgements: A Measurement Properties Analysis', *Journal of Applied Psychology*, 70(1): 137–47.

Madigan, R. and F. Hills (1988) 'Job Evaluation and Pay Equity', *Public Personnel Management*, 17(3): 323–30.

Madigan, Robert M. and David J. Hoover (1986) 'Effects of Alternative Job Evaluation Methods on Decisions Involving Pay Equity', *Academy of Management Journal*, 29(1): 84–100.

Maguire, Michael (1986) 'Recruitment as a Means of Control', pp. 58–74 in K. Purcell, S. Wood, A. Waton and S. Allen (eds), *The Changing Experience of Work: Restructuring and Recession*. London: Macmillan.

Mandell, Barbara and Susan Kohler-Gray (1990) 'Management Development that Values Diversity', *Personnel*, 67(3): 41–7.

Mant, A. (1977) *The Rise and Fall of the British Manager*. London: Macmillan.

Marchington, Mick (1991) 'Plant-Wide Pay Systems', *Employee Relations*, 13(3): S1–S2.

Marglin, Stephen (1974) 'What do Bosses Do? The Origins and Functions of Hierarchy in Capitalist Production', *Review of Radical Political Economics*, 6: 60–112.

Marsden, Richard (1993) 'Marx, Realism and Foucault: An Enquiry into the Problem of Industrial Relations Theory'. Unpublished PhD Thesis, University of Warwick.

Martin, L., G. Huck and P. Hutton (1988) *Technologies of the Self*. London: Tavistock Publications.

Martin, Patricia Yancey (1990) 'Rethinking Feminist Organizations', *Gender and Society*, 4(2).

Martin, Phyllis (1989) 'Hire Smart, Hire Right', *Working Woman*, 14(3): 71–6.

Marx, Jonathan (1988) 'Organizational Recruitment as a Two-Stage Process: A Comparative Analysis of Detroit and Yokohama', *Work and Occupations*, 15(3), 276–93.

Mayfield, E. (1964) 'The Selection Interview – A Re-evaluation of Published Research', *Personnel Psychology*, 17: 239–60.

Meglino, Bruce M. and Angelo S. DeNisi (1987) 'Realistic Job Previews: Some Thoughts on their More Effective Use in Managing the Flow of Human Resources', *Human Resource Planning*, 10(3): 157–67.

Megranahan, Mike (1990) 'The Organisational Value of Employee Assistance', *Journal of Managerial Psychology*, 5(2): 3–8.

Melossi, Dario and Massimo Pavarini (1981) *The Prison and the Factory: Origins of the Penitentiary System*. London: Macmillan.

Mendelson, J., K. Barnes and G. Horn (1989) 'The Guiding Light to Corporate Culture', *Personnel Administrator*, 34(7): 70–2.

Meng, G. Jonathan (1991) 'Definitive Job Descriptions are Key to ADA Compliance', *Employment Relations Today*, 18(3): 285–9.

Mercer, Michael W. and John J. Seres (1987) 'Using Scorable Interview "Tests" in Hiring', *Personnel*, 64(6): 57–60.

Meyer, H.H., E. Kay and J.R.P. French, Jr (1965) 'Split Roles in Performance Appraisal', *Harvard Business Review*, 43(January/February): 123–9.

Meyer, J. (1983) 'On the Celebration of Rationality: Some Comments on Boland and Pondy', *Accounting, Organisations and Society*, 8(2/3), 235–40.

Meyer, J. (1986) 'Social Environments and Organisational Accounting', *Accounting, Organisations and Society*, 11(4/5), 345–56.

Mies, Maria (1990) 'Women's Studies: Science, Violence and Responsibility', *Women's Studies International Forum*, 13(4): 433–41.

Miles, Raymond E. (1965) 'Human Relations or Human Resources?', *Harvard Business Review* (July/August): 148–63.

Milkovich, G., W. Glueck, R. Barth and S. McShane (1988) *Canadian Personnel/Human Resource Management: A Diagnostic Approach*. Plano, TX: Business Publications.

Miller, J. (1993) *The Passion of Michel Foucault*. New York: Simon and Schuster.

Miller, P. (1990) 'On the Interrelations between Accounting and the State', *Accounting, Organisations and Society*, 315–40.

Miller, P. (1991) 'A Strategic Look at Management Development', *Personnel Management*, 23(8): 45–7.

Miller, P. and T. O'Leary (1987) 'Accounting and the Construction of the Governable Person', *Accounting, Organisations and Society*, 235–65.

Miller, P. and N. Rose (1990) 'Governing Economic Life', *Economy and Society* (February): 1–31.

Millman, Marcia and Rosabeth Moss Kanter (1975) *Another Voice: Feminist Perspectives on Social Life and Social Science*. Garden City, NY: Anchor/Doubleday.

Mills, Albert J. (1988) 'Organization, Gender and Culture', *Organization Studies*, 9(3): 351–69.

Millward, N. and M. Stevens (1986) *British Workplace IR 1980–1984*. Aldershot: Gower.

Millward, Neil, Mark Stevens, David Smart and W.R. Hawes (1992) *Workplace Industrial Relations in Transition: The Ed/ESRC/PSI/ACAS Surveys*. Aldershot: Dartmouth.

Miner, John B. (1988) 'The Development and Application of the Rated Ranking Technique in Performance Appraisal', *Journal of Occupational Psychology*, 61(4): 291–305.

Mintzberg, H. (1973) *The Nature of Managerial Work*. New York: Harper and Row.

Mirabile, Richard J. (1990) 'The Power of Job Analysis', *Training*, 27(4): 70–4.

Mitchell, Daniel J.B. (1987) 'The Share Economy and Industrial Relations', *Industrial Relations*, 26(1): 1–17.

Mitchell, J. (1988) 'History of Job Analysis in Military Organizations', pp. 30–6 in S. Gael (ed.), *The Job Analysis Handbook for Business, Industry, and Government*, Volume 1. New York: Wiley.

Mitchell, John F. (1989) 'Management Development: A Top-Down Optimal Approach', *Journal of European Industrial Training*, 13(8): 14–17.

Morouney, Kim (1991) 'The Social Construction of Leading: Formulating a Critique of the Methodology of Leadership', *Women in Management*, Administrative Sciences Association of Canada (ASAC), 12 (Part II): 21–30.

Morris, Meaghan and Paul Patton (eds) (1979) *Michel Foucault: Power, Truth, Strategy*. Sydney: Federal Publications.

Morrison, Ann M. and Mary Ann von Glinow (1990) 'Women and Minorities in Management', *American Psychologist*, 45(2): 200–8.

Morrow, Paula C. (1990) 'Physical Attractiveness and Selection Decision Making', *Journal of Management*, 16(1): 45–60.

Moss, Geoffrey (1991) 'Employee Ownership in the USA: A Four-Frame Perspective', *Economic and Industrial Democracy*, 12(2): 187–202.

Mount, Michael K. and Rebecca A. Ellis (1987) 'Investigation of Bias in Job Evaluation Ratings of Comparable Worth Study Participants', *Personnel Psychology*, 40(1): 85–96.

Moxon, G.R. (1943) *The Functions of a Personnel Department*. London: Institute of Personnel Management.

Muczyk, Jan P. and Myron Gable (1987) 'Managing Sales Performance through a Comprehensive Performance Appraisal System', *Journal of Personal Selling and Sales Management*, 7(1): 41–52.

Mumford, Michael D., Joseph L. Weeks and Francis D. Harding (1987) 'Measuring Occupational Difficulty: A Construct Validation against Training Criteria', *Journal of Applied Psychology*, 72(4): 578–87.

Murlis, Helen and David Fitt (1991) 'Job Evaluation in a Changing World', *Personnel Management* , 23(5): 39–43.

Murlis, Helen and Derek Pritchard (1991) 'The Computerised Way to Evaluate Jobs (Part 1)', *Personnel Management*, 23(4): 48–53.

Nelson-Horchler, Joan (1988) 'Performance Appraisals', *Industry Week*, 237(6): 61–3.

Nevels, Paul (1989) 'Why Employees are being Asked to Rate their Supervisors', *Supervisory Management*, 34(12): 5–11.

Nicholson, Linda J. (ed.) (1990) *Feminism/Postmodernism*. New York: Routledge.

Niven, M.M. (1967) *Personnel Management, 1913–1963*. London: Institute of Personnel Management.

Nobile, Robert J. (1991) 'The Law of Performance Appraisals', *Personnel*, 68(1): 7.

Noe, R. (1988) 'An Investigation of the Determinants of Successful Assigned Mentoring Relationships', *Personnel Psychology*, 41: 457–79.

Northcott, C.H. (1960) *Personnel Management: Principles and Practice* (4th edn). London: Pitman.

Oakes, Leslie and Mark Covaleski (forthcoming) 'The Implications of Accounting Based Incentives for Labour Management Relations', *Accounting, Organisations and Society*.

Oakley, Ann (1987) 'Interviewing Women: A Contradiction in Terms', pp. 30–61 in H. Roberts (ed.), *Doing Feminist Research*. London: Routledge.

Odiorne, G. (1988) 'Ethics for the Nineties', *Manage*, 40(1): 8–14, 33.

Odiorne, George S. (1991) 'Chaos in Management', *Manage*, 43(1): 4–7.

Offe, Claus (1976) *Industry and Inequality: The Achievement Principle in Work and Social Status* (translated by James Wickham). London: Edward Arnold.

O'Neal, Sandra (1990) 'CAJE: Computer-Aided Job Evaluation for the 1990s', *Compensation and Benefits Review*, 22(6): 14–19.

O'Rourke, N. and H. Doyel (1986) 'Achieving Equity in Classification and Compensation of Secretarial Positions', *Journal of Compensation and Benefits*, 2(2): 80–5.

Orth, C., H. Wilkinson and R. Benfari (1987) 'The Manager's Role as Coach and Mentor', *Organizational Dynamics*, 15(4): 66–74.

Osborne, J.E. (1990) 'Upward Evaluations: What Happens when Staffers Evaluate Supervisors', *Supervisory*, 35(3): 1–2.

Osterman, P. (ed.) (1984) *Internal Labor Markets*. Cambridge, MA: MIT Press.

Ott, Mary Jane, Sharon Esker, Catherine Caserza and Sally Anderson (1990) 'Peer Interviews: Sharing the Hiring Process', *Nursing Management*, 21(11): 32–3.

Overman, Stephanie (1990) 'Different World Brings Challenge', *HRMagazine*, 35(6): 52–5.

Ozanne, R. (1967) *A Century of Labour-Management Relations at McCormick and International Harvester*. Madison: University of Wisconsin Press.

Paddison, Lorraine (1988) 'The Equal Value Amendment: A Flawed Law for Irrational Systems', *Personnel Management*, 20(10): 54–8.

Pang, Ken Khi and Nick Oliver (1988) 'Personnel Strategy in Eleven Japanese Manufacturing Companies in the UK', *Personnel Review*, 17(3): 16–21.

Panos, John E. (1990) 'Manage Group Incentive Systems', *Personnel Journal*, 69(10): 104, 106.

Parish, J.A. and A.J. Drucker (1957) 'Personnel Research for Officer Candidate School, USA, Tago Personnel Research Blank', Technical Research Report, No. 117.

Parks, John P. (1991) 'The Art and Science of an ESOP', *Benefits Quarterly*, 7(2): 23–32.

Paterson, T. (1981) *Pay: For Making Decisions*. Vancouver: Tantalus Publications.

Patten, Thomas H. , Jr. (1977) 'Job Evaluation and Job Enlargement: A Collision Course?', *Human Resource Management*, 16(4): 2–8.

Peel, Mike, Maurice Pendlebury and Roger Groves (1991) 'Wider Share Ownership and Employee Reporting', *Management Accounting*, 69(5): 38–40.

Penner, Maurice (1983) 'How Job-Based Classification Systems Promote Organizational Ineffectiveness', *Public Personnel Management*, 12(3): 268–76.

Perry, James L. and Beth Ann Petrakis (1988) 'Can Pay for Performance Succeed in Government?', *Public Personnel Management*, 17(4): 359–67.

Perry, James L., Beth Ann Petrakis and Theodore K. Miller (1989) 'Federal Merit Pay, Round II: An Analysis of the Performance Management and Recognition System', *Public Administration Review*, 49(1): 29–37.

Personnel (1991) 'Companies Train Supervisors to be EAP Savvy', 68(2): 5.

Petersen, Donald J. and Douglas Massengill (1989) 'The Negligent Hiring Doctrine – A Growing Dilemma for Employers', *Employee Relations Law Journal*, 15(3): 419–32.

Peterson, Janice (1990) 'The Challenge of Comparable Worth: An Institutionalist View', *Journal of Economic Issues*, 24(2): 605–12.

Petrini, Catherine M. (1991) 'Upside-Down Performance Appraisals', *Training and Development*, 45(7): 15–22.

Phillips, Kenneth F. and Herbert F. Crehan (1989) 'Employee Stock Ownership: Who Cares?', *Compensation and Benefits Management*, 6(1): 81–3.

Philp, M. (1985) 'Michel Foucault', pp. 65–82 in Q. Skinner (ed.), *The Return of the Grand Theory in the Human Sciences*. Cambridge: Cambridge University Press.

Piczak, Michael W. (1988) 'Quality Circles Come Home', *Quality Progress*, 21(12): 37–9.

Pierce, Leslie P. (1992) 'Beyond Harem Walls: Ottoman Royal Women and the Exercise of Power', pp. 40–55 in Dorothy O. Helly and Susan M. Reverby (eds), *Gendered Domains: Rethinking Public and Private in Women's History*. Ithaca, NY: Cornell University Press.

Pizzorno, Alessandro (1992) 'Foucault and the Liberal View of the Individual', pp. 204–14 in Timothy J. Armstrong (trans.), *Michel Foucault: Philosopher* . New York: Routledge.

Pollert, A. (1987) ' "The Flexible Firm": A Model in Search of Reality (Or a Policy in Search of a Practice)?', Warwick Papers in Industrial Relations, No. 19.

Poole, Michael (1988) 'Factors Affecting the Development of Employee Financial Participation in Contemporary Britain: Evidence from a National Survey', *British Journal of Industrial Relations*, 26(1): 21–36.

Poole, Michael and Glenville Jenkins (1988) 'How Employees Respond to Profit Sharing', *Personnel Management*, 20(7): 30–4.

Poole, Michael and Glenville Jenkins (1991) 'The Impact of Profit-Sharing and Employee Shareholding Schemes', *Journal of General Management*, 16(3): 52–72.

Prideaux, S. and James E. Ford (1988) 'Management Development: Competencies, Teams, Learning Contracts and Work Experience Based Learning', *Journal of Management Development*, 7(3): 13–21.

Primoff, E. and S. Fine (1988) 'A History of Job Analysis', pp. 14–29 in S. Gael (ed.), *The Job Analysis Handbook for Business, Industry, and Government*. Volume 1. New York: Wiley.

Pringle, R. (1988) *Secretaries' Talk: Sexuality, Power and Work*. London: Verso.

Pye, A. (1988) 'Management Competence in the Public Sector', *Public Money and Management*, (Winter): 62–7.

Pym, D. (1973) 'The Politics and Ritual of Appraisals', *Occupational Psychology*, 47: 221–4.

Quaid, Maeve (1993) 'Job Evaluation as Institutional Myth', *Journal of Management Studies*, 30(2): 239–60.

Quick, Thomas L. (1990) 'Using the "Three Rs" to Achieve your Goals', *Sales and Marketing Management*, 142(11): 170–1.

Rabinow, Paul (ed.) (1984) *The Foucault Reader*. London: Penguin.

Rajchman, John (1985) *Michel Foucault: The Freedom of Philosophy*. New York: Columbia University Press.

Rathie, Mildred (1990) 'Importance of Procedure Manuals', *Supervision*, 51(11): 14–16.

Read, Walter H. (1991) 'Gathering Opinion On-Line', *HRMagazine*, 36(1): 51, 53.

Reddin, Bill (1989) 'Expressing Effectiveness in Terms of Outputs', *Personnel Management*, 21(10): 86–91.

Redeker, James R. and Jonathan A. Segal (1991) 'When Peter Piper Picks his Peers', *Human Resources Professional*, 3(3): 44–6.

Richter, Andrew S. (1989) 'Compensation: Putting some Sanity Back in Salaries', *Business Month*, 133(6): 89–90.

Ripley, David E. (1989) 'Trends in Management Development', *Personnel Administrator*, 34(5): 93–6.

Ristock, Janice L. (1991) 'The Struggles and Contradictions in our Quest for a "Uniquely Feminist Structure" ', pp. 41–55 in Jeri Dawn Wine and Janice L. Ristock (eds), *Women and Social Change: Feminist Activism in Canada*. Toronto: James Lorimer.

Roberts, H. (ed.) (1990) *Doing Feminist Research*. London: Routledge (first published in 1981).

Roberts, J. (1984) 'The Moral Character of Management Practice', *Journal of Management Studies*, 21: 287–302.

Roberts, J. (1991) 'The Possibilities of Accountability', *Accounting, Organisations and Society*, 16(4): 355–68.

Roberts, J. and R.W. Scapens (1985) 'Accounting Systems and Systems of Accountability – Understanding Accounting Practices in their Organisational Contexts', *Accounting, Organisations and Society* , 443–56.

Roberts, J. and R.W. Scapens (1990) 'Accounting as Discipline', in D.J. Cooper and Trevor M. Hopper (eds), *Critical Accounts*. London: Macmillan.

Roberts, Michael (1988) ' "Wating Upon Chance": English Hiring Fairs and their Meanings from the 14th to the 20th Century', *Journal of Historical Sociology*, 1(2), 119–60.

Robertson, Ivan T. and Sylvia Downs (1979) 'Learning and the Prediction of Performance: Development of Trainability Testing in the United Kingdom', *Journal of Applied Psychology*, 64: 42–50.

Robertson, Ivan T. and Sylvia Downs (1989) 'Work-Sample Tests of Trainability: A Meta Analysis', *Journal of Applied Psychology*, 74(3): 402–10.

Robertson, Ivan T., Lynda Gratton and David Sharpley (1987) 'The Psychometric Properties and Design of Managerial Assessment Centres: Dimensions into Exercises Won't Go', *Journal of Occupational Psychology* , 60(3): 187–95.

Robertson, Ivan T., Lynda Gratton and Usharani Rout (1990) 'The Validity of Situational Interviews for Administrative Jobs', *Journal of Organizational Behaviour*, 11(1): 69–76.

Robertson, Ivan T., Paul A. Iles, Lynda Gratton and David Sharpley (1991) 'The Impact of Personnel Selection and Assessment Methods on Candidates', *Human Relations*, 44(9): 963–82.

Rodger, Alec (1983) 'Using Interviews in Personnel Selection', pp. 161–77 in Bernard Ungerson (ed.), *Recruitment Handbook*. Aldershot: Gower (first published in 1970).

Rodgers, Douglas D. (1987) 'Computer-Aided Interviewing Overcomes First Impressions', *Personnel Journal*, 66(4): 148–52.

Rollins, Thomas (1991) 'How an Appraisal System Helps CEOs Perform', *Journal of Compensation and Benefits*, 7(2): 22–7.

Rooney, Patrick Michael (1988) 'Worker Participation in Employee-Owned Firms', *Journal of Economic Issues*, 22(2): 451–8.

Rose, M. (1981) *Industrial Behaviour: Theoretical Developments Since Taylor*. Harmondsworth: Penguin (first published 1975).

Rose, N. (1988) 'Calculable Minds and Manageable Individuals', *History of the Human Sciences*, 179–200.

Rose, N. (1990) *Governing the Soul: The Shaping of the Private Self*. London: Routledge.

Rosen, Corey (1991) 'The Options Option: A New Approach to Employee Ownership', *Management Review*, 80(12): 30–3.

Rosen, Corey and Michael Quarrey (1987) 'How Well is Employee Ownership Working?', *Harvard Business Review*, 65(5): 126–32.

Rothstein, Hannah R., Frank W. Erwin, C. Paul Sparks, Frank L. Schmidt and William A. Owens (1990) 'Biographical Data in Employment Selection: Can Validities Be Made Generalizable?', *Journal of Applied Psychology*, 75(2): 175–84.

Rothwell, Sheila (1987) 'Human Resources Management', *Journal of General Management*, 12(4): 90–8.

Rowe, K.H. (1964) 'An Appraisal of Appraisals', *Journal of Management Studies*, 1(1): 1–24.

Russell, C. (1990) 'Selecting Top Corporate Leaders: An Example of Biographical Information', *Journal of Management*, 16(1): 73–86.

Russell, Raymond (1988) 'Forms and Extent of Employee Participation in the Contemporary United States', *Work and Occupations*, 15(4): 374–95.

Rust, J. and S. Golombok (1989) *Modern Psychometrics: The Science of Psychological Assessment*. London: Routledge.

Sackett, Paul R., Laura R. Burris and Christine Callahan (1989) 'Integrity Testing for Personnel Selection: An Update', *Personnel Psychology*, 42(3): 491–529.

Sackett, P., C. DuBois and A. Noe (1991) 'Tokenism in Performance Evaluation: The Effects of Work Group Representation on Male–Female and White–Black Differences in Performance Ratings', *Journal of Applied Psychology*, 76(2): 263–7.

Salaman, G., S. Cameron, H. Hamblin, P. Iles, C. Mabey and K. Thompson (eds) (1992) *Human Resource Strategies*. London: Sage.

Sauer, Robert L. (1989) 'A New Approach to Salary Structures', *Compensation and Benefits Review*, 21(5): 57–63.

Sawicki, Jana (1991) *Disciplining Foucault: Feminism, Power and the Body*. New York: Routledge.

Sayer, D. (1987) *The Violence of Abstraction*, Oxford: Blackwell.

Scheele, R., R. Peters, K. Irwin and J. Cranor (1988) 'An Experimental Study of Reliability in Evaluating Benchmark Descriptions using the Oliver System', *Review of Public Personnel Administration*, 9(1): 61–9.

Schiebinger, Linda (1992) 'Maria Winkelmann at the Berlin Academy: The Clash between Craft Traditions and Professional Science', pp. 56–70 in Dorothy O. Helly and Susan M. Reverby (eds), *Gendered Domains: Rethinking Public and Private in Women's History*. Ithaca, NY: Cornell University Press.

Scholl, Richard W. and Elizabeth Cooper (1991) 'The Use of Job Evaluation to Eliminate Gender Based Pay Differentials', *Public Personnel Management*, 20(1): 1–18.

Schor, Robert H. (1981) 'Administration by Contract', *Bureaucrat*, 10(4): 22–6.

Scott, J. (1988) 'Deconstructing Equality-versus-Difference: Or, The Uses of Post-structuralist Theory for Feminism', *Feminist Studies*, 14(1): 33–48.

Sears, Maureen (1986) 'Potential for Change: An Examination of Assertiveness Training with Severely Socially Disadvantaged Women', *Equal Opportunities International*, 5(3/4): 36–8.

Seymour, D. (1988) 'Staff Development by Negotiated Learning Contract', *Industrial and Commercial Training*, 20(6): 24–7.

Seyna, Eugene J. (1986) 'MBO: The Fad that Changed Management', *Long Range Planning*, 19(6): 116–23.

Shackleton, Viv and Sue Newell (1991) 'Management Selection: A Comparative Survey of Methods used in Top British and French Companies', *Journal of Occupational Psychology*, 64(1): 23–36.

Sharma, Sarla (1990) 'Psychology of Women in Management: A Distinct Feminine Leadership', *Equal Opportunities International*, 9(2): 13–18.

Sheibar, Paul (1989) 'The Seven Deadly Sins of Employee Attitude Surveys', *Personnel*, 66(6): 66–71.

Sheridan, Alan (1990) *Michel Foucault: The Will to Truth*. London: Routledge.

Shumway, David R. (1989) *Michel Foucault*. Charlottesville: University Press of Virginia.

Silverman, D. (1985) *Qualitative Methodology and Sociology*. Aldershot: Gower.

Simmons, Michael (1989) 'Making Equal Opportunities Training Effective', *Journal of European Industrial Training*, 13(8): 19–24.

Sisson, K. (ed.) (1989) *Personnel Management in Britain*. Oxford: Blackwell.

Smart, B. (1985) *Michel Foucault*. London: Routledge.

Smith, B. (1990) 'Mutual Mentoring on Projects – A Proposal to Combine the Advantages of Several Established Management Development Methods', *Journal of Management Development*, 9(1): 51–7.

Smith, Carlla S., Christopher Reilly and Karen Midkiff (1989) 'Evaluation of Three Circadian Rhythm Questionnaires with Suggestions for an Improved Measure of Morningness', *Journal of Applied Psychology*, 74(5): 728–38.

Smith, Dorothy (1974) 'Women's Perspective as a Radical Critique of Sociology', *Sociological Inquiry*, 44(1): 7–13.

Smith, Dorothy (1987) *The Everyday World as Problematic: A Feminist Sociology*. Milton Keynes: Open University Press.

Smith, Dorothy (1990) *The Conceptual Practices of Power: A Feminist Sociology of Knowledge*. Toronto: University of Toronto Press.

Smith, D. and B. Blackham (1988) 'The Measurement of Managerial Abilities in an Assessment Centre', *Personnel Review*, 17(4): 15–21.

Smith, Jack E. and Sharon Merchant (1990) 'Using Competency Exams for Evaluating Training', *Training and Development Journal*, 44(8): 65–71.

Smith, Michael L. (1990) 'Finding the Right Employee: Peeling the Onion', *Supervisory Management*, 35(5): 11–12.

Smith, Mike (1980) 'An Analysis of Three Managerial Jobs Using Repertory Grids', *Journal of Management Studies*, 17(2): 205–13.

Smith, Mike and Ivan T. Robertson (1989) *Advances in Selection and Assessment*. Chichester: John Wiley.

Smits, Stanley J., Larry A. Pace and William J. Perryman (1989) 'Employee Assistance: EAPs are Big Business', *Personnel Journal*, 68(6): 96–106.

Sobol, Marion Gross and Charles J. Ellard (1988) 'Measures of Employment Discrimination: A Statistical Alternative to the Four-Fifths Rule', *Industrial Relations Law Journal* , 10(3): 381–99.

Somers, Mark John and Dee Birnbaum (1991) 'Assessing Self-Appraisal of Job Performance as an Evaluation Device: Are the Results a Function of Method or Methodology?', *Human Relations*, 44(10): 1081–91.

Spencer, Steve (1990) 'Devolving Job Evaluation', *Personnel Management*, 22(1): 48–50.

Spender, Dale (1980) *Man Made Language*. London: Routledge and Kegan Paul.

Spero, Marlene (1987) 'Self-Development for Women Managers in the Retail Industry', *Industrial and Commercial Training*, 19(5): 9–12.

Stanley, L. (1991) 'Mentoring: What Works? What Doesn't?', *Across the Board*, 28(4): 55–6.

Starkey, Ken (1989) 'Time and Professionalism: Disputes concerning the Nature of Contract', *British Journal of Industrial Relations*, 27(3): 375–95.

Steddon, Peter (1990) 'Protecting the Bottom Line', *Industrial Management and Data Systems*, 90(7): 24–8.

Steel, Robert P. and Russell F. Lloyd (1988) 'Cognitive, Affective, and Behavioural Outcomes of Participation in Quality Circles: Conceptual and Empirical Findings', *Journal of Applied Behavioural Science*, 24(1): 1–17.

Stein, Bernard (1991) 'Management by Quality Objectives', *Quality Progress*, 24(7): 78–80.

Steinberg, Ronnie J. (1990) 'Social Construction of Skill: Gender, Power, and Comparable Worth', *Work and Occupations*, 17(4): 449–82.

Stewart, R. (1967) *Managers and their Jobs*, Maidenhead: McGraw-Hill.

Stohr-Gillmore, Mary K., Michael W. Stohr-Gillmore and Nannette Kistler (1990) 'Improving Selection Outcomes with the Use of Situational Interviews: Empirical Evidence from a Study of Correctional Officers for New Generation Jails', *Review of Public Personnel Administration*, 10(2): 1–18.

Stokes, Jean (1988) 'Assumptions, Distortions, and Myths: Factors which Misguide Organisational Solutions Toward Equal Opportunity', *Equal Opportunities International*, 7(2): 1–4.

Sunseri, Albert J. and David B. Kosteva (1991) 'Psychological Testing Enters the Job Market', *Healthcare Financial Management*, 45(10): 120.

Swan, William S. (1990) 'The Art of the Interview', *Working Woman*, 15(5): 96–7.

Sweeney, J. (1988) 'The Individual Approach', *Industrial Society* (June): 26–7.

Taber, Tom D. and Theodore D. Peters (1991) 'Assessing the Completeness of a Job Analysis Procedure', *Journal of Organizational Behaviour*, 12(7): 581–93.

Talson, Peter (1987) 'Supervisor's Guide to Interviewing', *Supervision*, 49(7): 6–8.

Tang, Thomas Li-Ping, Peggy Smith Tollison and Harold D. Whiteside (1989) 'Quality Circle Productivity as related to Upper-Management Attendance, Circle Initiation, and Collar Color', *Journal of Management*, 15(1): 101–13.

Taplin, Polly T. (1988) 'Sharing Information with Employee-Owners Improves Firms' Productivity, Profitability', *Employee Benefit Plan Review*, 43(2): 46–7.

Taylor, C. (1986) 'Foucault on Freedom and Truth', pp. 69–102 in D. C. Hoy (ed.), *Foucault: A Critical Reader* . Oxford: Basil Blackwell.

Thomas, D. (1989) 'Mentoring and Irrationality: the Role of Racial Taboos', *Human Resource Management*, 28(2): 279–90.

Thomason, George F. (1981) *A Textbook of Personnel Management* (4th edn). London: IPM.

Thompson, E.P. (1974) 'Time, Work-Discipline and Industrial Capitalism', in M.W. Flinn and T.C. Smout (eds), *Essays in Social History*. Oxford: Clarendon Press.

Tjosvold, Dean, I. Robert Andrews and John T. Struthers (1991) 'Power and Independence in Work Groups – Views of Managers and Employees', *Group and Organization Studies*, 16(3): 285–99.

Tompkins, Jonathan, Joyce Brown and John H. McEwen (1990) 'Designing a Comparable Worth Based Job Evaluation System: Failure of an *a priori* Approach', *Public Personnel Management*, 19(1): 31–42.

Torrington, D. and L. Hall (1987) *Personnel Management: A New Approach,* London: Prentice-Hall.

Townley, B. (1989a) 'Selection and Appraisal: Reconstituting "Social Relations"?', pp. 92–108 in J. Storey (ed.), *New Perspectives in Human Resource Management.* London: Routledge.

Townley, B. (1989b) 'Employee Communication Programmes', pp. 329–55 in Keith Sisson (ed.), *Personnel Management in Britain.* Oxford: Basil Blackwell.

Townley, B. (1990) 'A Discriminating Approach to Appraisal', *Personnel Management,* (December): 34–7.

Townley, B. (1991) 'Managing by Numbers: Personnel Management and the Creation of a Mathesis', *Third Interdisciplinary Perspectives on Accounting Proceedings*, 4. University of Manchester, 8–10 July.

Townley, B. (1992) 'In the Eye of the Gaze: The Constitutive Role of Performance Appraisal', in P. Barrar and C. Cooper (eds), *Managing Organizations in 1992.* London: Routledge.

Townley, B. (1993a) 'Performance Appraisal and the Emergence of Management', *Journal of Management Studies*, 30(2): 221–38.

Townley, B. (1993b) 'Foucault, Power/Knowledge, and its Relevance for Human Resource Management', *Academy of Management Review,* 18(3): 518–45.

Townsend, Christina and Michael Freshwater (1978) 'Manpower Mobility and the Grouping of Skills', *Personnel Management*, 10(6): 36–9.

Trow, Timothy J. (1990) 'The Secret to a Good Hire: Profiling', *Sales and Marketing Management*, 142(6): 44–55.

Tucker, James, Steven L. Nock and David J. Toscano (1989) 'Employee Ownership and Perceptions of Work: The Effect of an Employee Stock Ownership Plan', *Work and Occupations*, 16(1): 26–42.

Turner, S. (1983) 'Studying Organisation through Levi Strauss' Structuralism', in G. Morgan (ed.), *Beyond Method.* Beverly Hills, CA: Sage.

Verney, Thomas, Robert Ackelsberg and Stephen J. Holoviak (1989) 'Participation and Worker Satisfaction', *Journal for Quality and Participation*, 74–7.

Vickers, Jill (1991) 'Bending the Iron Law of Oligarchy', pp. 56–74 in Jeri Dawn Wine and Janice L. Ristock (eds), *Women and Social Change: Feminist Activism in Canada.* Toronto: James Lorimer.

Vilere, Maurice F. and Sandra J. Hartman (1991) 'Tapping the Benefits of Knowing Where You are Going: Insights on Goal-Setting Theory', *Leadership and Organization Development Journal*, 12(4): i–iii.

Vroom, V.H. (1964) *Work and Motivation.* New York: Wiley.

Wagel, William H. (1988) 'A Software Link between Performance Appraisals and Merit Increases', *Personnel*, 65(3): 10, 12–14.

Walby, S. (1986) *Patriarchy at Work.* Cambridge: Polity Press.

Wanous, J.P. (1973) 'Effects of a Realistic Job Preview on Job Acceptance, Job Attitudes, and Job Survival', *Journal of Applied Psychology*, 58: 327–32.

Wanous, J.P. (1980) *Organizational Entry: Recruitment, Selection, and Socialization Newcomers.* Reading, MA: Addison-Wesley.

Wanous, J.P. (1989) 'Installing a Realistic Job Preview: Ten Tough Choices', *Personnel Psychology*, 42(1): 117–34.

Warmke, Dennis L. (1988) 'Development and Implementation of First-Line Supervisor Selection System', *Journal of Managerial Psychology*, 3(2): 19–22.

Watanabe, Susumu (1991) 'The Japanese Quality Control Circle: Why It Works', *International Labour Review*, 130(1): 57–80.

Weedon, Chris (1991) *Feminist Practice and Poststructuralist Theory*. Oxford: Basil Blackwell.

Weekley, Jeff A. and Joseph A. Gier (1987) 'Reliability and Validity of the Situational Interview for a Sales Position', *Journal of Applied Psychology*, 72(3): 484–7.

Weiner, Nan and Morley Gunderson (1990) *Pay Equity: Issues, Options and Experiences*. Toronto: Butterworths.

Weitz, J. (1956) 'Job Expectancy and Survival', *Journal of Applied Psychology*, 40: 245–7.

Werther, William B., Jr (1990) 'Memo to the Boss: We Can Help You', *HRMagazine*, 35(4): 112, 110.

White, G.E and K. Roberts (1972) 'A Question of Character', *Personnel Management*, 4(4).

White, H. (1990) 'The Self Method of Mentoring', *Bureaucrat*, 19(1): 45–8.

Whitley, Richard (1986) 'The Transformation of Business Finance into Financial Economics: The Roles of Academic Expansion and Changes in US Capital Markets', *Accounting, Organisations and Society*, 11(2): 171–92.

Wickens, Peter (1988) *The Road to Nissan – Flexibility Quality Teamwork*. London: Macmillan.

Wilkinson, F. (ed.) (1981) *The Dynamics of Labour Market Segmentation*. London: Academic Press.

Wilkinson, Roderick (1987) 'Management by Objectives is Simply Management', *American Salesman*, 32(9): 3–6.

Wille, Edgar (1990) 'Should Management Development just be for Managers?', *Personnel Management*, 22(8): 34–7.

Williams, John J., James D. Newton and Eric A. Morgan (1985) 'The Integration of Zero-Base Budgeting with Management-by-Objectives: An Empirical Inquiry', *Accounting, Organisations and Society*, 10(4): 457–76.

Williams, K., I. Mitsui and C. Haslam (1991) 'How Far from Japan? A Case Study of Japanese Press Shop Practice and Management Calculation', *Critical Perspectives in Accounting*, 2(2): 145–69.

Williamson, O. (1975) *Markets and Hierarchies*. New York: Free Press.

Willis, Quentin (1989) 'Managerial Research and Management Development', *Management Decision*, 27(4): 30–6.

Willmott, H. (1990) 'Subjectivity and the Dialectics of Praxis: Opening Up the Core of the Labour Process Debate', pp. 336–78 in D. Knights and H. Willmott (eds), *Labour Process Theory*. Basingstoke: Macmillan.

Wilson, Nicholas and Michael J. Peel (1991) 'The Impact on Absenteeism and Quits of Profit-Sharing and Other Forms of Employee Participation', *Industrial and Labor Relations Review*, 44(3): 454–68.

Wilson, Nicholas, John R. Cable and Michael J. Peel (1990) 'Quit Rates and the Impact of Participation, Profit-Sharing and Unionization: Empirical Evidence from UK Engineering Firms', *British Journal of Industrial Relations*, 28(2): 197–213.

Wine, Jeri Dawn and Janice L. Ristock (eds) (1991) *Women and Social Change: Feminist Activism in Canada*. Toronto: James Lorimer.

Wisniewski, Stanley C. (1982) 'Achieving Equal Pay for Comparable Worth through Arbitration', *Employee Relations Law Journal*, 8(2): 236–55.

Witz, Anne (1986) 'Patriarchy and the Labour Market: Occupational Control Strategies and the Medical Division of Labour', pp. 14–35 in David Knights and Hugh Willmott (eds), *Gender and the Labour Process*. Aldershot: Gower.

Wolff, Paul J. (1987) 'Western Problems – Eastern Solutions: Mixed Promise of Quality Circles', *Journal of Managerial Psychology*, 2(2): 3–8.

Wood, Stephen (1986) 'Recruitment Systems and the Recession', *British Journal of Industrial Relations* , 23(3): 103–20.

Wood, Stephen (1989) 'The Japanese Management Model – Tacit Skills in Shop Floor Participation', *Work and Occupations*, 16(4): 446–60.

Woodruffe, Charles (1991) 'Competent by Any Other Name', *Personnel Management*, 23(9): 30–3.

Woods, Kenneth (1976) 'Job Evaluation – More than Just a Management Technique', *Personnel Management*, 8(11): 27–9, 39.

Wright, Patrick M. and Kenneth N. Wexley (1985) 'How to Choose the Kind of Job Analysis you really Need', *Personnel*, 62(5): 51–5.

Wright, Phillip C. (1987) 'Equal Pay for Work of Equal Value and How to Achieve it: A Practical Approach', *Equal Opportunities International*, 6(2): 23–38.

Wright, P., P. Lichtenfels and E. Pursell (1989) 'The Structured Interview: Additional Studies and a Meta-Analysis', *Journal of Occupational Psychology*, 62(3): 191–9.

Zey, M. (1988) 'A Mentor for All Reasons', *Personnel Journal*, 67(1): 46–51.

Zuboff, S. (1988) *In the Age of the Smart Machine: The Future of Work and Power*. London: Heinemann; New York: Basic Books.

Index